PSI
"Empowering or Ema
via
Open Banking
for
DevOps(Sec)

Copyright©Alasdair Gilchrist 2017

Chapter 1 –Payment Services

Introduction and background

The revised EU Directive on Payment Services (or PSD2) is a reformed legislative measure that has been adopted by the European Union in response to changing technology and industry innovation. The EU directive aims to increase data openness, competition across all banking boundaries, as well as to integrate payment services across national borders. Being an EU directive it must be in part implemented in all of the EU member states no later than 13 January 2018.

In order to place the directive into context the current Payment Services Directive was adopted in 2007 and as a result implemented into the UK law book through the Payment Services Regulations 2009. Consequently, the Directive created a regulatory framework for payment services in the EU which aimed to create a well functioning, integrated and competitive single market, as well as providing the legal basis for the Single Euro Payments Area (SEPA).

However the current directives have been inconsistently applied throughout the EU and as a result the EU policy makers believe they have not stimulated sufficient innovation and competition. Similarly, there have been concerns regards the effectiveness of security measures, privacy and fraud associated with digital payments. Therefore, the PSD2 seeks to promote digital innovation and change based on a firm structure of strong customer authentication. However to really appreciate the extent of the PSD2 legislation we need to consider it against the current status of the Payment Service environment worldwide.

The Current Status of the Payments Industry

Within the realms of financial services a payment system is a set of processes and technologies that transfer monetary value from one entity or person to another. Payments are typically made in exchange for the provision of goods, services, or to satisfy a legal obligation. Payments can cross borders and hence can be made in a variety of currencies using several methods such as cash, cheques, electronic payments and credit/debit cards. The essence of a payment system is that it uses cash-substitutes, such as cheques or electronic messages, to create the debits and credits that transfer value. The value that is being transferred is typically stored in the depository accounts at banks or other types of financial institutions. The banks, in turn, are interconnected through a network of payment systems that they use to process payments on behalf of their customers or depositors. Banks operating in multiple countries connect to payment systems in each of the countries where they operate either directly or through a correspondent bank. Significantly for the settlement process and for the discussion of less conventional payment systems, banks in many countries typically maintain accounts with their central bank and participate in the central bank's payment systems. In the Eurozone for example the authorities have taken it a step further by creating SEPA, the Single European Payments Area, under the authority of the European Central Bank (ECB). SEPA was created to provide standardized payments processing and costs among all the various countries within the Eurozone. Most US banks are members of a number of different payment systems such as NYCE (New York Cash Exchange, a subsidiary of FIS), CHIPS (Clearing House Interbank Payment Systems) and Fedwire (US Federal Reserve Bank network). Non-US banks are connected into similar national systems such as CNAPS (China), BOJNET (Japan) and SPEI (Mexico).

The Four Corners Payment Model

In the simplest case involving the traditional banking system, payments involve four participants:

1. The payer: Makes the payment and has its bank account debited for the value of the transaction.
2. The payer's financial institution: Processes the transaction on the payer's behalf.
3. The payee's financial institution: Processes the transaction on behalf of the payee and generally holds the value in an account.
4. The payee: Receives value of the payment by credit to their account.

This is illustrated in the "four corners payment model" diagram shown below.

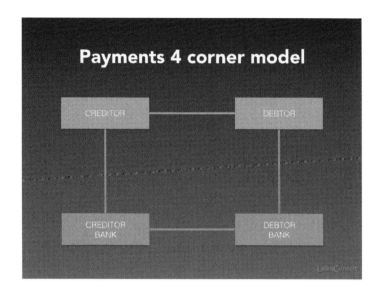

In the simple case illustrated here the two banks may choose to transfer payment instructions and funds directly with each other. It is also possible for the banks to use various intermediaries to help facilitate the transaction. What the diagram does not show is the interconnection hub network which resides in the middle and interconnects all participating parties.

In the real world the network includes central banks such as the Fed (US Federal Reserve), ECB (European Central Bank) and The Bank of England and clearinghouses such as CHIPS. There are also information transmission mechanisms such as SWIFT (Society for Worldwide Interbank Financial Tele-communications) and payment systems such as Fedwire and BOJNet which also include information transmission systems.

Other players such as payroll processors, financial systems providers and card systems such as Visa and MasterCard that are outside of the four corners model also participate in the payment process network. The foundations of the payment networks are built upon decades of development and cooperation between local and international financial institutions hence it is robust, resilient and highly regulated. Non-traditional payment systems such as Bitcoin bypass the banking system almost entirely by fulfilling the role of financial institution, currency and network themselves, so for how evade any regulation.

The operation of the payment system is often slow and cumbersome, which leads many to believe there must be a better way using the available technology. To see why the processes are so convoluted and prone to excessive delays and sometimes even errors we need to examine how payments, transactions (clearing and settlements) occur. This is often referred to as the payment process and it involves four basic steps:

1) Payment instructions are the information contained in a POS (Point of Sale) communication, a wire transfer or cheque. These instructions are from the payer and will instruct the paying bank to transfer value to the beneficiary through the payment network to the receiving bank.

2) Payment generation is when the instructions are entered into the system—printed on a cheque or transmitted via ACH or wire.

3) Clearing is the process where the banks use the payment information to transfer money between the relevant parties in order to fulfil the payer's instructions and to ultimately transfer the funds to the beneficiary.

4) Settlement only occurs when the beneficiary's bank account is actually credited and the payer's bank account is debited. Hence, the final settlement only occurs when the banks pass value from the payer's account to the payee's account, which is an important distinction. The time taken to actually fulfil the settlement of the payment process will depend on the type of transaction method that the payer and payee have chosen to use—or more often the case that is available to them through their financial institutions.

Payment Channels Processors (PCP) working with the payment systems can use different channels that have evolved over time to make a payment and each has different operating characteristics, local availability, regulations and settlement mechanisms. For example not all banks internationally or even branches of a bank nationally may be able to support electronic payments. This may be determined by local or national geography constraints, regulatory policy or the available technology infrastructure. However, generally, the most common types of traditional payment systems can be placed into one of the following four payment channels:

1) Paper-based systems such as cheques or Bank drafts where the payments are initiated when one party writes an instruction on paper to pay another. These systems are well established and some of the oldest forms of non-cash payment systems but the clearing and settlement process are still relatively misunderstood by the public. For instance, cheques will need to be manually processed via a clearinghouse which can take up to 5 working days. Furthermore cheques are only relevant forms of payment nationally and they are unlikely to be accepted internationally due to the settlement period likely taking months. Cheques were for many decades the most popular and common paper-based channel and are still widely used in the United States and a few other countries. In recent years, cheque clearing has been improved through the use of image recognition technology and A.I. algorithms which have greatly enhanced and automated the process of handling cheques, which speeds the clearing process. In addition, the ubiquitous presence of mobile phones with cameras allows the capture of the cheque image which can then be transmitted electronically. Sometimes the image is created at a retailer's point of sale where the cheque is scanned into the terminal and then processed electronically.

2) Wire Transfers – Cheques and bank drafts had several limitations the most obvious was the time

taken for settlement due to delays transferring the cheques in the mail. Hence there was a requirement for faster settlement especially for high value transactions and this is where the telegraph/telephone networks came into play. The RTGS (Real Time Gross Settlement) or High-Value Payments; called wire transfers were introduced in the late 1800s with the invention of the telegraph but did not become widely used until the early 1900s. High-Value Transfers are generally used between businesses when there is the requirement for fast, secure and final transfer of value. Frequently referred to as wires they are considerably more costly than paper-based or batch systems. The sender (payer) instructs their bank to wire money to the beneficiary (payee) using a wire transfer. The payer's instructions to their bank include the name of the beneficiary, the beneficiary's bank and other address details specific to the particular high-value system. In the case of Fedwire this would include the ABA number (American Bankers Association) of the banks being used along with the beneficiary's account number. The sender's bank would then use its direct access to the high-value system to instruct the beneficiary's bank to debit its account with the central bank and credit the beneficiary. The important part of wired transfers is the role played by the central bank, both in holding deposit accounts for other national banks and acting as a guarantor. For instance, the central bank provides the funds to the beneficiary virtually on an immediate basis therefore the central bank stands as a guarantor of the system to both banks. The receiving bank can rely on the central bank for the funds in the event that the sending bank fails to adequately cover their account with the central bank. This element of RTGS systems adds considerably to their cost but they are extensively used in business even though the making of high-value payments is a bit more complex on their part. Consequently many technologies and processes have been developed to help businesses communicate wire payment instructions to their banks. These include bank-proprietary systems, ERP (Enterprise Resource Planning) file transfers through SFTP (secure file transfer protocol) and third-party payment systems, such as payroll processors. How the sender structures its message to the bank will determine the time to settlement, cost and risk with which the bank can complete the transfer. Interbank transfers use the SWIFT network to communicate the payment instructions but that can still take several days, especially for international transfers, as not all systems are Real Time Gross Settlement Systems (RTGS). There are still a few non-RTGS systems in operation in which case the instructions and value are transferred between the sender's bank and the beneficiary's bank on a periodic basis perhaps even via a clearing bank. This will reduce the immediacy of the settlement but not the finality. Because RTGS systems are important for global financial stability, non RTGS systems are in a state of permanent—and rapid decline. Fedwire, the U.S. based high-value transfer system, is an RTGS system and there are similar public and private large-value transfer systems in most countries around the world. Examples include CHAPS in the UK, LVTS in Canada and CNAPS in China.

3) Batch Payments - Automated Clearing House (ACH) batch payments or RTNS, (Real Time Net Settlement) systems were introduced in the early 1970s and were designed to replace cheques by introducing the concept of electronic payments. Batch Systems such as the ACH (Automated Clearing House) in the US and BACS in the UK, were designed to handle large volumes of relatively low value transfers, where immediacy was not a requirement. Therefore, banks would exchange batches of transfers on a daily basis settling the transfers the following day. Like high-value systems, the payers, which are called originators in the ACH domain, provide their banks or what are termed the ODFIs (originating depository financial institutions) with payment instructions. Unlike high-value systems, there are usually multiple payments in each instruction sent

to the ODFI, for example a payroll. The ODFI processes the instructions and sends a file of all customer instructions to its ACH Operator. The ACH Operator then distributes all of the payments in all of the batches to the appropriate RDFIs (receiving depository financial institutions) which then credit the individual receivers (payees). The distinction in syntax between payers (originators) and payees (receivers) is at first a little unclear but it is due to the little known fact that it is also possible within the ACH—and many other batch systems—to send instructions to debit the receiver's account. This is how the Nigerian email bank scams work, the scammer asks the victim to establish a test payment where they will deposit a small amount into the victims account but then they use the same details to request a large debit, and clear out their victim's account. It is for this reason that the terms originator and receiver are used rather than sender and beneficiary as in a debit instruction the terms payer and payee would be reversed. To remediate this issue ACH is designed to transfer batches of low value payments, and there a considerable range of checks and balances that apply to these payments. These mechanisms include debit filters and blocks, which will restrict somebody that knows a firm's ABA routing code and account number from withdrawing money from the account using the ACH. Batch systems via the ACH systems have typically been used for domestic transactions but are also a way of transferring money between countries and currencies using cross-border ACH transactions. ACH has typically been a next-day payment system where it takes a day from initiation of the payment for the value to transfer to the receiver's bank. However, the demand of the internet era has made several countries such as the UK offer a same-day payment system known as Faster Payments Service (FPS). In the US financial institutions are wary of this as it could detract from the revenue stream they receive from RTGS payments and this is a typical example of the cannibalization conundrum where banks must be wary of new products eating into the revenue streams of existing high value products.

4) Card Based Payments - Card based systems, which include both debit and credit cards, are the fastest growing form of payment and bank-issued cards are the most widely used. The distinction between the two forms, credit or debit, are that a credit card is issued against a line of credit that the institution or bank has extended, whereas a debit card is issued against a deposit account held by a business or consumer. There are also third-party vendor that may issue credit or debit cards, such as retailers, supermarkets and governments that offer credit or stored value cards, such as gifts, payroll or welfare cards. These are a special

type of debit card that do not access a specific bank account but are pre-funded at the time of issuance. Some stored value cards can be "reloaded", that is they can have funds added to the available balance, to extend their usability. The following diagram shows the participants in a typical card transaction. The cardholder presents a card for payment to a merchant. The merchant captures the transaction information and sends it to its merchant acquirer, typically a bank, for authorization. The merchant acquirer queries the issuing bank for authorization for the transaction via the appropriate card network which it then returns to the merchant. If the transaction is denied, the payment is cancelled. If the transaction is approved, the payment is completed. The merchant then sends the final transaction information to the merchant acquirer, either at the time of transaction or more typically in bulk at the end of the day. The merchant acquirer presents the transaction to the issuing bank, again using the appropriate network. Each card network net settles the day's card transactions between all of its member banks, typically through a separate batch payment system such as the ACH in the U.S. or BACS in the UK. The issuing bank charges the card holder's account and the acquirer credits the merchant's account net of any transaction fees. The way the transaction fees are calculated and subsequently deducted from the merchant's payment is complex and varies dependent not just on the brand of card, Visa, MasterCard, Discovery or American Express but also on the privileges or status of the card, with high end prestige gold and platinum card fees being higher. The merchant however is obliged under the terms of use to accept all cards of that brand and must not under any circumstance apply a surcharge to the customer for accepting payment using a brand's card.

To see how settlement works with card payments we need to understand how the business model operates and how the fees associated with accepting payment via a credit card are distributed. For the card holder there should be no additional fees payable and the merchant is strictly forbidden from trying to pass their fees onto the card holder. The merchant's fee or discount which is typically 2% of the transaction value is the cost of doing business by accepting a credit card as payment. Secondly, this fee, which consists of a percentage of the transaction and a set fee per transaction, is divided among a few different parties (not just the card network (Visa, MasterCard, etc) and the card issuer (the customer's bank):

1. The Issuing Bank – The bank that issued the card to the customer, the bank name will be on the card as the contract is between the customer and the issuing bank, Bank of America, Chase, RBS, etc… are all examples. The issuing bank receives the largest part of the fee charged to accept your card. In the payment services industry these fees are known as "interchange".

2. Card Associations – This is Visa, MasterCard, Discovery and American Express. The card processors which are the brands essentially receive approximately 0.01% – 0.09% or $0.02 per transaction for supplying an operating the network.

3. The acquirer bank – receives the remainder of the fees charged. This is entity that does the majority of the work for the merchant. They settle the funds to the merchant's bank account and are generally available 24/7 for questions in relation to charges and supply the rental POS

equipment (card readers/terminals).

During each payment transaction that the merchant accepts it is assessed for an appropriate merchant discount fee, a percentage (with some potential flat fees) of the total transaction volume that needs to be paid to the various companies that enabled the transaction. The merchant discount can be broken down into three component parts: Interchange (Card Issuer Fee), Network Fees/Assessments, Acquirer/Processor Fees for supply of terminal/settlement service – and this is why the card holder should never be passed this ≈ 2% merchant fee.

The interchange is the fee that the card issuer receives. Interchange is nuanced. It is determined or set by the network (MasterCard/Visa) but paid to the card issuer. This key fact often confuses people. Interchange comprises the single largest component of the merchant discount. Networks set various different levels of interchange ranging from just under 1% (debit cards) to up to around 3% (highest end credit cards). Again, this percentage is determined by the Networks but paid to the Issuers (Chase, Bank of America, Citibank, etc.)

The network Fees/Assessments are the fees charged by the Networks (MasterCard and Visa) to facilitate the transactions through their systems as they charge basis points of the transaction in the range of around 0.05% with fluctuations of several basis points in either direction. They have the smallest cut but they can afford that with circa 32 million transactions a day or 74 billion a year.

The Acquirer/Processor fees are charged by the merchant processor/acquirer and are highly variable. They are normally in the 10s of basis points (i.e. 0.10%-0.70%) as a percentage of a transaction.

To put this all together within a hypothetical example, consider that Citibank is the card issuer, MasterCard is the network, First Data is the processor/acquirer. Furthermore, the retail transaction value is $100 with a merchant discount of 2%. Hence, the merchant only has to pay that 2% or rather they will have that amount discounted from their settlement payment by their processor, First Data in this case). Hence, First Data the processor, upon initially receiving the transaction data passes this information to Visa who then allocates the $2.00 the following way:

- Interchange (assume 1.65%) --> $1.65 to Citibank (set by MasterCard based off of the credit card used in the transaction)
- Network Fee (assume 0.05%) --> $0.05 to MasterCard
- Processor/Acquirer Fee (assume 0.30% --> $0.30 to First Data

There are often several other parties involved charging additional fees such as gateways and additional types of merchant processors making the dynamics of a transaction layered with many companies each taking a sliver out of the merchants 2%. Additionally the interchange levels set by the networks are complex documents with discounts, fees and assessments applied to various merchant classes, geographies and card types.

Cardholders can typically dispute charges assessed to their accounts for anywhere from 60 to 120 days after the originally transaction. These disputes may result in a charge-back to the merchant unless the merchant can provide proof of the original transaction, e.g. a signed transaction receipt in the case of credit cards.

The banks make their money from supplying the credit card to the customer and managing the account hence the lion's share of the merchant's fee. It is important for the transaction fee to be split the way it is – in favour of the issuing bank – in order to encourage the banks to use the credit card service.

Debit card transactions can be either signature based in which case they are processed through the merchant's normal credit card networks and the card-holder signs a receipt at the time of the transaction. Alternatively, debit cards can be PIN-based in which case they are processed through an EFT or ATM network and the customer enters a personal identification number, or PIN, at the time of the initial transaction. There are a number of variations on standard card payments, including procurement cards, single use card and virtual or ghost cards. Each of these is an attempt to improve the security of the basic transaction, but all use the same clearing channels as regular debit and credit cards.

Mobile Payment

Mobile payments have become extremely popular recently as these are conducted using a smartphone such as an Apple iPhone, and Android Pay but they are really just another form of a credit or debit card transaction. It the case of Apple Pay, Android and Samsung Pay the phone's inbuilt near field communication sensors are utilised to transmit the payment details to the Point of Sale sensor in the same way as a plastic contactless card. Samsung Pay, in addition to supporting NFC-based terminals, can also use Magnetic Secure Transmission (MST) technology. Samsung has put in a magnetic coil inside some of its recent Galaxy smartphones, and the field created by that coil, combined with the Samsung Pay app, can be used to transmit payment signals to normal credit and debit card terminals. In essence, Samsung Pay makes those terminals think they are being accessed by a normal magnetic strip found in credit and debit cards.

Regardless of the contactless technology used in the smartphone it is still basically an embedded credit card account by a Card Issuer but in a different style of user interface. Hence, everything regards the transaction for all the parties - the user, merchant, and the banks is the same with regards the payment and settlement process.

There are other forms of mobile banking but again these are just plays on the established forms of internet banking so instead of using a PC browser the customer uses a laptop, smartphone, or tablet. An alternative payments method for both online and mobile payments is through eWallets, which are prefunded debit accounts typically held by Fintech firms or vendors such as Google but which can be used for transferring funds to others with immediacy so have gained popularity with those requiring a quick, regular mechanism for transferring funds or making regular but variable-value payments or remittances in close to real-time. We summarise some of the most popular mobile payment systems below and in no particular order;

Apple Pay - This is Apple's mobile payment system and it uses near field communication (NFC) technology to communicate payment credentials from the phone to the Point of Sale contactless reader. Apple Pay is designed for in-store customers to pay by holding an iPhone or Apple Watch close to a POS contactless reader. A security feature that Apple Pay uses is the Touch ID fingerprint sensors in the iOS devices to authenticate the user and to approve transactions.

Apple Pay's has been extremely successful with widespread adoption as Apple Pay launched mobile payments with the major card-issuing banks, supporting American Express, MasterCard, and Visa.

ogle Wallet is Google's mobile payment system for in-store and online payments. This is also built upon NFC technology for contactless payments which allows users to store credit and debit cards, as well as loyalty and gift cards on their mobile phone. An interesting feature of Google Wallet is that it is integrated with Gmail allowing payments to be sent as email attachments.

Venmo a PayPal subsidiary is another mobile peer-to-peer payment system which is popular with millennials. The premise of the Venmo system is to make payments social in so much as you can pay anyone that has a phone number or an email account, whether or not they have Venmo. The ability to pay instantly using money you have in Venmo, or link a bank account or debit card in seconds is the attraction. There is a 3 percent fee per payment for credit cards and non-major debit cards. However, receiving money on Venmo is always free.

Facebook Messenger is another of the tech giants getting involved in the mobile payment market launching a new feature for peer-to-peer payments. In order to initiate a payment a Facebook user simply taps the $ icon and enters the amount to send but it will require the user to add a debit card to send or receive money. The addition of this feature is another example of the tech giants' developing interest in bank payments and how they can leverage their social networks to market mobile payments.

Samsung Pay uses both NFC and a Magnetic Secure Transmission technology which also allows users to pay at in-store payment terminals where normally a card is swiped. The benefit for merchants is that no special equipment is need for merchants to accept payments magnetic card readers suffice. Again with Samsung Pay the payer loads credit or debit cards onto the phone or store the cards in the case provided for magnetic transmission to enable a source payment account.

Square Cash is Square's peer-to-peer solution to exchange money electronically. However it is finding a niche in small business as it's a lightweight solution to accept debit card payments. With Square Cash for personal use, there's no fee to send, request, or receive money. Payments are deposited directly to the registered debit card.

Tilt is another peer-to-peer mobile payments system but with Tilt there is also a feature that allows for crowdfunding. For example, users create a project and set the amount needed. Contributors pay the organizer, and the organizer tracks the payments. Companies can also use Tilt Open for open-source crowdfunding pages and the Tilt API to add crowdfunding or group payments to an application.

As can be seen from just a small sample of the offerings on the market for mobile payments there is a solution for just about anyone's requirements. However it should be noted that in many cases these are not actually mobile banking and the user should be clear that funds that they store on these digital wallet are at their own risk. This is because most of these companies do not fall under financial regulators as they are non-banking entities; as such these mobile payment apps are not required to be federally insured. Consequently, consumers should be aware that not only are their funds not insured or protected they are also providing unsecured loans to these app provider companies. The exception at present is Google Wallet which has applied to be FDIC-insured, hence securing its system with the same federal protection of regular banking institutions. Google's action could be an essential step forward toward a more reliable and regulated mobile payments marketplace.

For true Mobile Banking we are actually just using a mobile optimised version of the bank's browser-based PC internet service. The advantages of Mobile Banking are best described as a type of remote access/service as it makes it possible to perform any operations remotely with an online bank account and a mobile phone. Therefore you can do the following from anywhere you have a secure internet connection:

- Make utility payments, pay fines, credits;
- Find current information on your available credit or debit card;
- Convert funds, exchange currency;
- Make payments and transfers.

Apart from the advantages described above, you can perform any financial transactions in a matter of seconds. Credit or other payments will be accepted at the banking account immediately. Besides, due to the automation of calculations, online rates are lower than commissions you have to pay when you go directly to the bank.

Finally, all payments in an online banking system are encrypted from being hacked and other fraudulent actions, since all clients' data is stored safely on the bank's server. Thus, online banking can be a real virtual assistant.

Types of online banking

There are some different types of online banking:

- Informational type: which is a service, which provides information regards the customer's bank account. The customer can monitor the account balance, history of payments and manage expenses. The constraints are that they cannot make payments, transfer funds or buy currency;

- Accounts management: The customer will have access to information and control of their account and hence they are able to make payments, transfer funds or buy currency. As a result the customer can remotely pay for bills for electricity, rent etc as well as make payments in stores;

- Finances management: this is the full gamut of mobile banking services in online mode typically offered by FinTech startups – where the customer can make payments, transfer funds, get loans, short-term over-draughts, sell and buy securities and so forth.

Thus, online banking is a technology for managing banking accounts via the Internet using a smartphone app. It embraces all ranges of banking services available in the bank except for cash transactions.

However the proliferation of the smartphone throughout society along with the near ubiquitous WiFi has disrupted many industries and banking along with financial services in general has been no exception. Hence we can see a new breed of bank and a new type of service evolving from the more traditional models and these are built upon mobility and innovation.

The new breeds of service that have emerged are typified not by the customer end-products but more how the products are sourced, constructed and delivered to the customer. For example, the producers of these new services are not banks but technology companies, and this niche is termed FinTech. What is of interest is that these technology companies are bringing innovation and modern services to their customers but are riding on top of the traditional banking networks we have discussed earlier such as ACH/BACS, and the Credit Card clearing and settlement networks.

What makes these services new and different is that they are delivered often independently of the customer's bank indeed that is often the catalyst as it enables the FinTech developers to offer competitive products and services from third parties. By being able to view the customer's financial data and transactions will allow the algorithmic software at the backend of the mobile app to offer unbiased financial advice based upon price and suitability over a catalogue of alternative services from completing banks and institutions rather than on purely in-bank products and commission.

These FinTech firms have proved to be very adept at raising capital and marketing as they have emerged quickly to gain a small but significant market especially among the millennial demographic. If we consider some of the more well know brands on the market it will better explain the niche banking that they address.

Mint: This is possibly the most well known of the mobile financial services as it is an effective all-in-one resource for creating a budget, tracking spending and making payments/remittances. In essence it can connect all the user's bank and credit card accounts, as well as all their monthly outgoings, even if you have accounts in different banks i.e. no more logging in to multiple sites as Mint can collect and present all your financial data in one convenient place. In addition, Mint sends notifications when bills are due and based on spending habits Mint can tailor specific advice to let the user gain more control over their budget.

Another FinTech developed product that has come to attention recently is the You Need a Budget (YNAB) mobile app. YNAB claims that its technology will help you stop living paycheck to paycheck, pay down debt and "roll with the punches" if something unexpected comes up. There is nothing really innovative about YNAB except that it goes back to real world kitchen table economics as You Need a Budget forces you to live within your actual income, it will not let you budget for income that you forecast but you do not have. The built-in "accountability partner" monitors the user's bank accounts and incoming an outgoing funds and based upon these patterns its algorithms can suggest different tactics to balance the budget.

Another traditional banking segment which is less often targeted by FinTech firms is saving but Acorns addresses this niche in the market in an extraordinary way. Acorns, is a payment processor and handles direct payments but also aims to harness the benefits of saving through good financial behaviour. What that actually means is that every time the apps user makes a purchase with a card connected to the Acorns app, Acorns rounds it up to the next highest dollar and automatically invests the difference in a portfolio of low-cost exchange-traded funds (ETFs) that is user selectable based on risk tolerance.

What all three of these examples demonstrate is that for the services to work the companies would need access to the client's bank accounts and or their payment history. Very few banks allow access to third parties to such confidential information even with the customers consent. However an old technique has gained a fresh lease of life and purpose. FinTech firms with the customers consent and using their security credentials utilise a technique called screen-scraping to gain access to the banks online-banking websites. This importantly allows them to not only scrape the bank for the customer's account details, such as balances, transaction records, direct debts, but more importantly it can use this technique with any bank with an online customer service. They can consolidate information from diverse accounts residing at several banks. We will revisit screen-scraping in detail later but for now it is sufficient to know that this is how most of these mobile financial apps gain access to the customers bank accounts.

Authentication and Anti-Fraud Measures

In the preceding section we covered how credit cards are cleared and settled as payments however credit cards can be used in two distinct ways 1) card present and 2) card not present the former being the way payments are done in person and the latter when carrying out payments on the internet. With regards 'card present' transactions originally only a signature was required similar to a cheque as the method of authentication and perhaps for larger value items a further item of identity such as a driver license. However online purchases are far more problematic as the card is not present so other mechanisms were require to authenticate the card as being in the possession of the payer. Initially this took the form of an CV2 code stamped on the reverse side of the card which could be used to authenticate the transaction by either checking the number matched the card or by checking the CV2 number against both the card and the cardholders address and postcode in what was termed an AVSCV2 check. Unfortunately this was only effective for a time as with the advent of mobile phone cameras it became all too easy for a card and any supporting ID to be surreptitiously photographed capturing all the required details. These stolen details could then be used safely online to make successfully authenticated but fraudulent purchases. Credit card companies in order to thwart the increasingly high levels of online fraud introduced a process of two factor authentication, which was commonly used in ATM transactions. It was called two-factor, because the customer was in possession of something, the card and had knowledge of something, the PIN. Following on from this the credit card companies introduced a small integrated circuit into their plastic card which could store security credentials this was called Chip&PIN. So successful was this method that it became the standard secure method for credit cards for both card present and card not present transactions.

3DSecure

The latest secure method that the major cards use is a system called 3-D Secure, which is an authenticated payment system to further enhance and improve online transaction security and encourage the growth of e-commerce payments. Collectively Visa, MasterCard and AMEX secure systems are brand identities of the 3-D Secure Cardholder Authentication Scheme.

In order to further protect merchants from online fraud the credit cards use their own systems to verify an authenticate cards and hence guarantee the purchase. These systems such as MasterCard SecureCode, Verified by Visa and Amex SafeKey provide the merchant with additional assurance and the confidence to accept payment by card. This method effectively shifts the liability for 'chargebacks' from the merchant to the issuing bank. The way it works is that the user registers a password against the card which can be verified at the time of purchase. The system uses Three Domain and SSL Technology to provide a standardised and secure method of performing transactions over the internet. These systems are in place to protect all parties including the merchant, card holder and the banks of the cardholder and merchant against unauthorised use. The way it works can be seen in the diagram below:

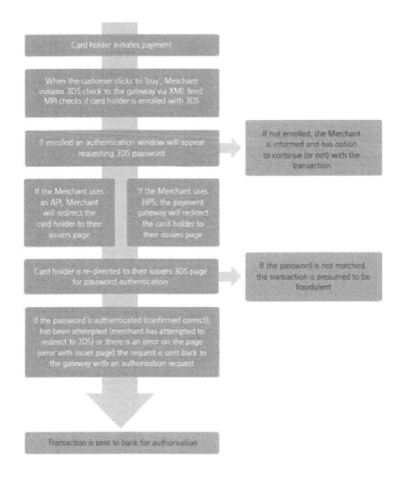

In general 3D-Secure is an extra layer of protection as the name suggests. It is also called the third factor of authentication.

The basic concept of the protocol is to tie the financial authorization process with an online authentication. This authentication is based on a three-domain model (hence the 3-D in the name). The three domains are:

- Acquirer Domain (the merchant and the bank to which money is being paid).
- Issuer Domain (the bank which issued the card being used).
- Interoperability Domain (the infrastructure provided by the card scheme, credit, debit, prepaid or other type of finance card, to support the 3D-Secure protocol). Interoperability Domain includes the Internet, MPI, ACS and other software providers

As mobile phones have become extremely popular around the globe and hackers more informed and consequently more dangerous, new ways of authentication have become essential. An interesting point regards 3D-Secure is that despite its effectiveness in keep fraud at very low levels merchants are very reluctant to use it with many opting not to in favour of their own transaction risk analysis. This is partly because of the high levels of abandoned transactions due to an extra verification step which is added to the process, I.E. entering the password. The creation of version 2.0 of the 3D-Secure by EMVCo, addressed the needs for a protocol designed for secure online payment authentication, as well as the need to improve the user experience associated with 3D-Secure.

3-D Secure 2.0 now uses token-based and biometric authentication, instead of static passwords. In addition it also supports extended data during a transactions, which enables risk-based decisions regards whether to authenticate or not. The consumer experience will also be simplified and enhanced, starting with the elimination of the initial sign-up process and removing the need for cardholders to use static passwords. It is hoped that merchants will see fewer abandoned shopping due to the simplified customer journey.

Despite this new simplified model merchants are still wary of strong authentication mechanisms deterring customers and reducing sales conversions and also because many merchants feel that when it comes to handling risk and fraud their experience and transactional risk analysis is a good if not better than the card companies or the issuing banks.

Transaction Risk Assessment

TRA as it is known is how traditional and online merchants evaluate the levels of risk when contemplating an online transaction in a card not present scenario. There are many mechanisms available to the merchant dependent on their size and budget and these can range from gut feeling manual guesswork to multi million dollar AI and machine learning networks. However basically they work in the same way, and if we look at the criteria that may be considered we can get a good idea how the risk assessment works. Some of the checks the online merchant or the TRA system will make are;

1) Is this the customers usual device
2) Is it coming from the usual location/region/country
3) Is it the typical time of day
4) Is it the usual browser and language
5) Is it a typical purchase product/price range
6) Is it being made in the usual currency
7) Is it being shipped to the usual address
8) Is the shopping browsing pattern typical

More advanced systems will be able to look at a lot more behavioural metrics and data to assess the risk but either way merchants do have considerable faith in their TRA and as we will see later when we discuss PSD2, they are not to keen to have other strong and invasive forms of authentication forced upon the customer as they believe these are often 'sales conversion-killers'.

Alternative Payment Systems

For most people the payments for services or products are only considered at a high level – is there sufficient funds in the account - they have little perspective or interest in the underpinning infrastructure and rules surrounding the payment, clearing and settlement process. Therefore, most payments today for small retail purchases are made with a debit card, which can be swiped—or waved—past a terminal with charges taken directly from the user's bank account. The marginal cost of these payments is very small and it is only when something goes wrong that these issues are given consideration. Credit card clearing and settlement goes through the Card Association networks but debit cards, which use a variety of networks and are issued under a variety of brands, are ultimately settled through a wire or ACH/BACS type system.

However, the need to transfer value is not something exclusive to highly developed economies with their sophisticated payment networks, regulated processes and consumer protection schemes. Indeed, there is, and has been a necessity to transfer funds globally especially to under developed nations. This requirement has existed long before postal mail let alone electronic communications. Indeed the first money transfer systems date back to the Crusades, where Knights instead of carrying their wealth around with them would have funds made available along the route to the Holy Lands. Some of these early primitive systems still prevail today due to their simplicity and easy access.

Hawala, is such a system, an informal money transfer network, which predates all of the banking systems such as paper cheques or telegraphic wires. In its modern form, Hawala is a way for payers and payees that have no access to banks to transfer money. As an example of how the Hawala system works it is very similar to how descendents such as Western Union and other foreign remittance specialist firms operate. For instance if we consider that a person in one city/country wants to transfer some money to their family in another city/country. Neither party has a bank account or access to one. Therefore the person wishing to transfer the funds uses a trusted agent, known as a Hawaladar to act on his behalf. The person wishing to make the transfer brings an amount of cash to the local Hawaladar and explains his intentions. The Hawaladar provides the person with a code that their family will use to obtain the counter value of cash from a local agent situated close to their location. The code is duly provided to the family along with the name and address of a Hawaladar agent close by who will provide the cash when the appropriate code is presented. The Hawaladar then exchange details about the transaction in a way convenient to them and move the appropriate amount of money between them using the banking system. This trust-based system is very effective and reasonably cost-effective for the participants. And these two attributes make it very popular for those with limited means and access to the formal banking system. The Hawaladar function as banks, aggregating a number of small transactions, which are ultimately settled through the formal banking system.

Unfortunately, the Hawala, albeit centuries old is looked upon with suspicion by governments today as it has characteristics that also appeal to those operating outside of the law such as money launders and terrorists. For example, a transfer of money might possibly be flagged as suspicious and as a potential money laundering transaction and be rejected by a bank but this would not be flagged by a Hawaladar. Furthermore, Hawala and the agents are unregulated so consequently Hawala is not looked upon with favour by regulators and other government officials. However, that does not diminish the importance and relevance of the Hawala system as it is fundamental to many payment and remittance systems new and old.

A more regulator-friendly, transparent and modern technological version of the Hawala can be seen in action through Western Union and other money remittance firms. They work in a very similar fashion to Hawala with the key difference being that Western Union operates the network in full-sight to both customers and regulators. Nevertheless, it is based upon the same Hawala model Western Union connects all their agents in a global network that ensures an almost immediate availability of a cash transfer anywhere in the world. The physical cash doesn't transfer immediately but the cash value does as one agent will pay out from their local pool of cash upon receiving a request from another agent to fulfill a transaction. The way it works is that each money transfer agent (or Western Union) agent, needs to work with his/her own money. So in order to be a Western Union agent, WU will require that an agent will have their own money pool to fund the daily transactions. So for the purpose of explanation if we suggest this condition to be set at a daily float of US$ 5,000 which would mean everyday, the Western Union agent needs to have US$ 5,000 cash at their location.

The way that the Western Union foreign remittance works is that it uses non-bank agents that cooperate over a trust network underpinned by the traditional banking network. So for example, an ex-pat worker wishes to send money to his family in the Philippines from his location in Dubai. He will visit a local Western Union agent and he fills out a form that has essentially three pieces of information:

1: His personal information (Remitter Information)

2: Information about the person sending money to (i.e. their name, contact telephone number, which is required and optionally maybe some ID # of the Passport or Driving License of the beneficiary). This is the Beneficiary information.

3: The amount of money being sent.

Upon receiving the form and the cash the WU Agent in Dubai will inform him he needs to pay $10 more (as fees). So the remittance will now be a total of US$ 510.00 in total for transferring US$ 500.

The WU agent in Dubai will forward this information into the WU's back-end system for agents. The WU system will give back to the agent, an MTCN (Money Transfer Control Number). This unique MTCN is a number that is unique and used only once. The number is immutably linked to the transaction detail of the transfer for that day for a particular amount for a particular beneficiary.

For the Western Union system to work the expat worker will need to somehow forward that MTCN number to their family typically through a mobile text message. However once that has been accomplished the beneficiary named on the transfer can go to any WU Agent in the Philippines and provide them with the MTCN Number. The WU Agent in the Philippines will access the WU Computer System via usually the Internet and the system provides the WU Agent with the full name of the beneficiary and the amount and whether ID is required. The WU Agent then using "their" US$ 5,000 float they are supposed to have at the start of each day counts US$ 500 and settles the transaction.

Now lets assume 1 US$ = 100 Units of Philippines Currency. So for $500 that the expat worker sent home, their family should get 500 x 100 = 50,000 Philippines Currency Units (as per the Official Rate). But, Western Union can set their rate to be lower than the official transaction rate, for example, to be 1US$ = 97 Units of Philippines Currency. So the beneficiary, upon conversion would get = US$ 500 x 97 = 48,500 Philippines Currency Units, and the difference of 1,500 is kept by Western Union.

The reason for this difference can be due to currency fluctuations, etc. but the reality is this is how WU make money, on the tiny foreign exchange differentials over millions of daily transactions. The difference between the official price and the cash-out price is the income for Western Union.

So the transaction is relatively simple on how the 'money' or rather the value gets transferred from Point A, to Point B. But the actual money that the expat worker sent is still with WU Agent in Dubai and the WU Agent in the Philippines is now short US$ 500.

Each Agent (on both locations) is supposed to have two things:

1. Cash at hand (US$ 5,000)

2. Deposit Balance with Western Union (US$ 5,000).

Total investment = US$ 10,000

Therefore the WU Agent has US$ 5,000 (Opening Balance) + US$ 500 (from the expat worker) + US$ 10 (an easy made-up example of the Fees paid). At the end of the day, the Dubai WU Agent has:

US$ 5,510.00

Out of this he will deposit to Western Union: US$ 502 (US$ 500 payment and US$ 2 for Western Union's Fees).

Western Union earns US$ 2 from this transaction from Dubai to the Philippines.

WU Agent (Dubai) earns US$ 8 from this transaction ($10 fee - $2 to WU).

However, the WU Agent in the Philippines has:

US$ 5,000 (Opening Balance) - US$ 490 [US$ 10 was deducted as fees in the Philippines].

End of Day balance = US$ 4,510, out of the US$ 10 deducted as Agent fees, US$ 2 needs to go to WU for their Fees.

Therefore, the End of Day Balance for the WU Agent in the Philippines is

US$ 4,510 - US$ 2 = US$ 4,508

The Next day two things will happen.

The WU Agent in Manila will get a credit to his account for US$ 500

Thus:

US$ 4,508 + US 500 = US$ 5,008.

Income earned: US$ 8.

Businesses that become the front-end agents have to pre-fund themselves as WU does not provide money to them. Western Union itself nets off all the agents accounts in a given country, and then nets off all the countries on a daily basis. This is a tried and tested model for foreign remittance and is the basis for many other seemingly high-tech FinTech solutions using modern devices such as mobile technology.

PayPal

The explosive growth of the internet during the early to mid nineties brought a similar surge in credit card usage as it was the only way to conduct business on the ecommerce sites that flourished at the time. Similarly, as freelance work also blossomed upon the framework of the web a need for ways for people to transfer small cash amount between parties that did not end up decimated by bank charges arose. Hence, the need and interest of individuals to find low cost ways of transferring small sums of money should not be viewed as only of interest in the third world. PayPal, a system that came to prominence in the early days of the ecommerce and.com boom is a good example of a system that is low in cost and quite efficient. Essentially PayPal operates as the web interface between the originator and the receiver. PayPal handles the payment process and other banking functions and settles the transaction using the ACH network to transfer funds between the originator's bank and the receiver's bank.

Furthermore, PayPal is international as it can handle multiple currencies as well as credit and debit card payments, while remaining efficient and low in cost. The differentiator in PayPal's business model which allows it to utilise yet still compete with the bank networks is that PayPal is not a bank and so does not fall under the same regulatory scrutiny or obligations as opposed to those of a conventional national bank Banks are highly regulated and operate with sophisticated compliancy, cyber-security and capital adequacy requirements. Regulatory compliancy alone can run to 10s of millions of dollars even for the small banks so being an unregulated FinTech 'nonbanks' can be extremely advantageous. Moreover, from a banks perspective, should a payment go missing and the payer has complied with the bank's requirements and processes, any loss or other problem is generally absorbed by the bank or their insurers. PayPal does not have either of these operational overheads and so is able to operate at significantly lower costs that make it appear more consumers friendly.

But PayPal has been around for nearly twenty years and has been highly successful in that time but has not significantly disrupted the banks operation in money transfers or payments. This appears to be because each has their own type of service and thus their own type of customer and the correct payment approach will depend on the context of the payment and the amount.

Bitcoin

Any discussion on alternative payment systems must include Bitcoin as it is a true modern day innovation, a cryptocurrency that has massive disruptive potential. For Bitcoin is not only a value transfer system that is independent of any treasury or central bank, it is also a currency in it own right. Bitcoins can be traded and purchased using a conventional currency or providing goods or services with the payment denominated in Bitcoins. The holders of Bitcoins can then transfer them amongst other Bitcoin holders using an extremely clever and secure process. If everyone used Bitcoins it would be very difficult for conventional payment systems to compete. In the near-term there are two aspects of Bitcoin that make this highly unlikely. Public acceptance is still extremely low and most people would not know what to do with one if they were offered a Bitcoin as payment. This is due to lack of awareness as how to acquire or dispose of Bitcoins for a conventional currency for as with conventional currencies, the rates vary. However, unlike conventional currencies the factors that drive this variance are unknown and as a result there are spurious meteoric surges in prices followed by equally bizarre crashes. This is because there is no national central bank supporting the currency, which can intervene in the market to ensure stability and protect investors. Second is the way Bitcoin accounts for the holdings of its participants. While the technical aspects of Bitcoin are extraordinarily elegant, secure users of Bitcoin have little recourse if something happens to their holdings. The recourse that users have with conventional currencies and payment systems such as through the banks and central banks is not available in the Bitcoin world. Another significant issue is that there is artificial scarcity designed into the Bitcoin model – it emulates scarcity of a natural resource - in order to maintain as with any currency an inherent value, and possibly one day those limits will be reached and no further mining will be possible.

However, those fears have not stop Bitcoin flourishing and developing a niche market on its strengths of an independent currency with distributed ledgers that make transactions immutable and irrevocable.

The one thing that is clear from looking at alternative payment systems from Hawala to Bitcoin is that the desire for alternatives to conventional systems is strong and technology enables some technology firms, Fintech to enter the payment service market with truly elegant ways of meeting this demand. Therefore, the future is likely to see additional innovations and technical developments in order to address some of the issues and leverage the many opportunities inherent in alternative payment systems.

Real-Time Payment Schemes

Summary Payments are a critical part of modern commerce that is simple conceptually, as there will always be a sender and a receiver and both will need bank accounts. The complexity arises however when we consider the implementation and application of such payment systems. As banks holding the accounts will need to have a method of exchanging payment instructions and money amongst each other. In order to resolve disputes or ease competitive friction Central banks will be needed to not only adjudicate but offer and operate the payment systems or at least act as guarantors of the systems. Consequently, just because the technology may change, it may change for the better of all parties, but there are still underlying frictions, competition and suspicion that will require to be overcome before a payment system will find market acceptance. Hence, there are many obstacles and inertia to overcome before change can be accepted, as some high levels of inertia is deliberately introduced into the payment systems for it benefits several key players.

As opposed to real-time payments with eWallets and smartphones, transferring money between banks or cross-border payments often takes several days to be processed. It is for this reason that the EPC (European Payment Council) decided to introduce SCT Inst (SEPA Instant Credit Transfer) scheme: a real-time payment system where inter-bank transactions will be cleared within maximum 10 seconds at any time of the day and 365 days of the year. Similar schemes were already successfully put in place in other states (e.g. Denmark, Sweden and the UK).

The characteristics of the new SEPA Instant Credit Transfer Scheme, SCT Inst, are the following:

- SCT Inst is proposed by the EPC, and is hence not a mandatory scheme
- it is a 365/24/7 available (no down time)
- it is near real execution time (maximum 10 seconds, and some communities try to reduce this execution time)
- there are real time failure notifications of the beneficiary
- the funds are immediately credited and reusable by the beneficiary
- a very important feature is the irrevocability of the payment. Once the payment has been initiated, it cannot be revoked, except in case of fraud
- the scheme only covers a single transaction – there is no batch processing
- currently the scheme limit is set at 15.000 euros, but this limit is expected to increase later on

The scheme should be operational in November 2017, but in some countries it is already live (e.g. Finland and Spain). Besides the processing, an important aspect is to ensure that the beneficiary is advised. Hence, from a cash management, and from a treasury perspective, Instant Payments open many new possibilities both for FinTech, merchants, and corporates.

Thanks to its irrevocability, the SCT Inst will also be a disruptor for existing nonbanks Payment Service Providers (PSP) such as PayPal and Amazon Pay as it is expected that the banks will charge lower fees than them and have the immediacy of the transfer. We might also expect that this scheme would also challenge in the cards market, where new players could benefit from both PSD2 and SCT Inst to offer more competitive payment schemes. However the card operators and card issuers might also take stock of the situation and proactively react to the changing competitive environment by adapting their prices and/or offering additional new services.

For the banks, merchants, and the payment industry more widely, the PSP (Payment Service Provider) model is at the forefront of innovation in the payment services industry and this will have a significant impact on the way in which consumers and merchants transact in the future. Unlike the traditional four-party card model, customers would "push" cleared funds to merchants, with faster ACH\BACS transactions replacing the current card CSM (Clearing & Settlement Mechanism). This will significantly simplify the existing payment model, with fewer players and interactions involved and crucially it will provide lower barriers to entry for competitors.

However an even more seismic shift within the European payments industry is likely post-2018 when the EU Payment Services Directive 2 (PSD2) a revision to the existing PSD regulations comes into effect. The rationale behind the Payment Services Directive (EU) 2015/2366 (PSD2), is that it aims to increase competition, bring into scope new types of payment services, enhance customer protection and security. PSD2 is seen as being an important step towards harmonising regulations across all member states in order to provide a Digital Single Market in Europe. PSD2 is expected to lead to Open Banking, which is a major conceptual change in terms of the accessibility of customer data to authorised third parties when the customer has given their explicit consent. Banks and other financial incumbents will be required to provide access to customer accounts to third parties thus customers will be able to use payment initiation services and account information services where their payment accounts are accessible online, making internet and mobile payments easier and helping customers to manage their accounts and make better comparisons of deals. We will discuss the PSD2 directive in detail in the following chapters but for now this drawing illustrates the model quite well:

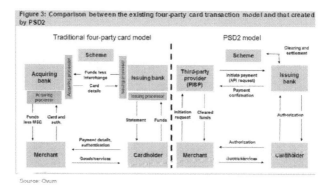

Figure 3: Comparison between the existing four-party card transaction model and that created by PSD2

SOURCE: *OVUM – Instant Payments and the Post-PSD2 Landscape*

The Cashless Society

There is also considerable expectation in the industry that due to the introduction of these new schemes and competitors, the use of cash will decrease, although many others believe that cash will remain important for the foreseeable future. The public have been raised on the concepts of a cashless society for many generations and still cash is ubiquitous. Furthermore physical cash is accessible to all which importantly means those who do not have a bank account. It enables immediate settlement without intervention of a third party. Cash is the only payment instrument that currently guarantees the user's privacy and anonymity, while all electronic transactions are traceable. However privacy and anonymity are not the classic reasons for cash's popularity. Merchants prefer cash as it saves them on card or other mobile payment fees – even though some show great initiative in attempting to pass those fees onto the customer. But for the customer, cash is a great inhibitor to spending as it is inordinately more difficult to look at the bank notes in their possession and then consider handing them over as they can clearly see what little will remain. Cards and other exotic flavours of mobile payments distance the customer from the transaction making them more compulsive buyers. Hence, until the proponents of the cashless society can provide a model that benefits all parties and not just themselves cash is likely to be around for a very long time.

Chapter 2 – Introducing PSD2 & Open Banking

In chapter 1 we considered the various types of payment systems and the underlying clearing and settlement networks and processes. In this chapter we will look at how a new European directive on Payment Services will affect the industry, the banks, payment processors, merchants and the customers.

Two new types of Payment Service Players

PSD2 is a game changer for digital payments and commerce in Europe and will have a significant global impact. The aims of the new PSD2 revision are to provide stronger customer security and authentication and to provide a level playing field for competition that will encourage innovation in the Finance industry.

As the PSD2 scope aims to encourage new players to enter the payment market, it mandates the retail banks to "open up the customer's bank account" to external parties subject of course to the customer's informed and explicit consent. Furthermore, the PSD2 legislation envisages two additional players called Third Party Players (TPP) of two types:

1. Account Information Service Providers (AISPs)

2. Payment Initiation Service Providers (PISPs)

In addition, PSD2 introduces another new definition: "account servicing payment service provider" (AS PSP) to distinguish the provider where the customer's payment account is held typically the bank. The PSD2 text makes it clear that customers have a right to use PIS and AIS where the payment account is accessible online and where they have given their explicit consent.

According to the PSD2 text AISPs are providers of a service which that can connect to bank accounts and retrieve information from them. A typical example of this would be an investment recommendation service: the service will be able to see how much money a user is saving each month from his income, and provide tailored an importantly neutral advice based on his spending patterns.

On the other hand there are also PISPs, which are also third party players that can initiate payment transactions. This is a radical change in the payment services industry, as currently there are not many payment options that can take money from a customer's account and transfer that amount elsewhere. Currently the only instruments that have this capability are (SEPA) Credit Transfers and debit cards, which are both offered only by the account holder's own bank. In the future under PSD2 there will likely be several different payment options that can move money directly from the customer's payment account to a merchants account, without the need of using an electronic wallet (e.g.: PayPal) or a pre-paid card.

These two new types of service provider reflect the recent market trends and growth in internet based payment and banking services. The prevalence of FinTech firms offering internet and mobile payments as well as the adoption of new technologies has led to customers having relationships with multiple account providers. The way this may work in practice is that a merchant may integrate a payment initiation service provided by a PISP into its online checkout process. This alternative service would enable the merchant to offer the option of online credit transfers as an alternative to card payments. The advantage to the merchant being that they will evade the 2% bank charges on credit card transactions and for the customers it provides an alternative mechanism for payment for those that do not have or want to use a credit card.

On the other hand an Account Information Service is designed to allow consumers and businesses to obtain a consolidated view of their all their financial accounts and to use tools to analyse their transactions and spending patterns with one or more financial institutions, which are typically banks or in PSD2 lexicon an ASPSPs. Again the way this could materialise as a practical service is through a long term relationship between the customer and the AISP whereby the customer delegates the AISP to manage its accounts. The AISP could then provide an automated portal that displayed all the information in one convenient dashboard that was updated automatically. Alternatively, the customer may use the AISP for single operations and provide their consent for one-off access in order to enable, for example, an affordability check to be carried out when applying for a mortgage or loan. Due to the limited nature of their operations PSD2 defines a lighter prudential regime for AISPs, which are treated as payment institutions but are only subject to some of the provisions regarding transparency, information, rights and obligations.

One caveat though is that PISP and AISP are distinctive entities with very defined roles in so much as an AIS can query, retrieve and store information as well as post and edit updates to information but it cannot initiate a payment or transfer funds. Conversely, a PISP can initiate a payment and transfer funds but cannot other than check an account for sufficient funds - and receive a binary response (yes or no) - it cannot query for account information such as a balance let alone a history of recent transactions. In addition another important restriction is that PSD2 only applies to payment accounts.

Hence most FinTech firms will most likely need to be registered and licensed as both entities, for example as an AISP and as a PISP for being just one or the other is somewhat restrictive.

However, any PSP subject to having the appropriate authorisation and a license, including importantly an ASPSP, could potentially offer payment and account information services. In that case the joint service provider could interrogate a customer's accounts across various ASPSPs and based upon that information move funds between accounts.

In order to facilitate the interconnection between the banks and third party providers the PSD2 mandates that the European Bank Authority (EBA) is obliged to develop, operate and maintain a publicly available electronic central register containing information drawn from the public registers in each Member State, identifying the payment services for which each payment institution is authorised or for which an AISP is registered. Hence, PISPs and AISPs can rely on the authentication procedures provided by the AS PSP to the customer but there are customer protection conditions in place. The TPP must ensure that the personalised security credentials are not shared with other parties; in addition they must not store sensitive payment data; and they are obliged to identify themselves to the AS PSP each time a payment is initiated or data is exchanged. In turn, AS PSPs are required to treat payment orders and data requests transmitted via a PISP or AISP "without any discrimination other than for objective reasons".

The scope and potential of the PSD2 initiative reaches far beyond those basic explanations but they serve to introduce the scale of the changes being foisted onto the banks. The magnitude of these changes should not be underestimated as PSD2 requires financial institutions to transform not just their processes and procedures but their platforms and systems. These changes will require significant investment as well as a strategic shift, as banks are forced to consider how they can balance the requirements of security, compliance and trust against opening their customer accounts to external third parties.

In addition, not only do banks and other Payment Service Providers (PSP) need to work toward compliance, they will also need to define their strategy regards their competitive position in the market. Simultaneously, the banks as PSPs will also need to align the somewhat competing demands of rapid innovation while maintaining vigilant security over their and their customers assets (account data) as they continues to battle cybercrime. To compound matters there is the significant looming presence of the EU General Data Protection Regulation (GDPR), which also shares the premise of giving the customer control over its data but its approach is very different.

To understand why the revisions to the existing legislation were deemed necessary it is beneficial to view its background and brief history. The original Payment Services Directive (or PSD1) came into force in 2007 and was a set of initiatives aimed to bring competitor payments companies (also known as Payment Institutions) to market and compete on the same level as banks, without the need for a bank charter. That was back in 2007 when the European Parliament voted for the adoption of PSD1 the original legislation that simplified payments and the processing of payments across the European Union, as well as increased competition by lowering the barriers to entry for new entrants to come to market. In addition PSD1 provided a market for Single Euro Payments (SEPA).

A feature of EU legislations is that the directives have an in-built review date so that they can be assessed for effectiveness and to see if they remain fit for purpose. This is essential in environments that experience rapid change or in volatile markets. An example of which was the MiFID directive for Markets in Financial Instruments Directive of 2007 which was required to be revamped and updated as a result of the significant changes introduced to financial services since the banking crisis in 2008. The revised directive will come into effect as MiFID II in January 2018.

When reviewing the PSD in 2012, the European Commission found that the original PSD legislation had introduced a number of benefits:

• An increase in competition and choice by facilitating market entrance for regulated non-bank players (i.e. payment institutions);

• Improved economies of scale while providing the foundation for the operational implementation of the Single Euro Payments Area (SEPA);

• Enhanced transparency as information requirements for PSPs are now set and the rights and obligations linked to payment services, such as execution time, refund rights and the liability regime, have been reinforced.

However, there is a need to ensure that legislation remain relevant, and partly as a result of the PSD's own effectiveness in lowering the barriers to entry and in increasing the quantity and quality of the competition in financial services, the industry is experiencing rapid change. Indeed as markets develop and grow, especially in the payments segment, advances in technology encourage the customers' needs to evolve, however there are significant barriers to meeting these expectations that are impeding innovation and the creation of advanced products and services. Thus although many young firms encouraged by the PSD emerged that were developing these new products and services much of their ingenuity was focused upon defeating obstacles and circumventing existing legislations for example by using screen-scraping robotic techniques to access customers' accounts. Consequently, it was recognised that as customers were showing a willingness to consent to their data being accessed and indeed were willing to delegate responsibility to FinTech firms to manage their bank accounts that there may well be a case for more open banking. Subsequently, after an industry review it was decided that PSD needed to be updated to keep it relevant in these times of volatile technological change and to future proof it for the new breed of FinTech PSPs that are becoming increasingly active in the pan European market.

The approach taken when revising the PSD was to retain all of the benefits it presently bestowed but also to incorporate further technological innovation, enhancements and protections into law. Hence the aim of the second Payment Services Directive is to ensure a harmonised pan-European market across all EAA member states that protects customers and encourages lower prices, while encouraging a competitive playing field, but without exposing individual consumers or businesses to undue risks.

Aims and Motivations of the PSD2

The European Parliament adopted the revised Directive on Payment Services (or PSD2 In early October 2015); with the aim of harmonising the regulation across the EAA market. Further motivation behind the extension to the directive known as PSD2 was to simplify the payment process in general and to further open up the market for innovation and competition. The aims and tactics implemented by the PSD2 legislation are shown in the following table.

PSD2 Aims & Motivations	PSD2 Extensions
Increase the geographical/territorial scope and the currencies used.	► PSD2 extends the provisions relating to transparency and information requirements for ► 2 leg in non-EU currency transactions ► 1 leg out transactions in

	non-EU currency
Increase the scope for types of payment services and exemptions.	▶ Introduction of new payment services ▶ Exemptions have been restricted and/or clarified for: ▶ commercial agents, ▶ limited networks, ▶ telecoms, ▶ ATM operators, and ▶ the waiver regime - for "small" payment institutions. ▶ The use of the limited network exemption will also impose an obligation on firms to report to the regulator where transactions utilising this exemption exceed EUR 1,000,000 within a 12 month period.
Increase the customer's rights to access to payment accounts	▶ A customer will have the right to use a payment initiation service where their account is accessible online and their consent to the payment may be given via the

	payment initiation service.
	▶ Similarly, new account information services will afford consumers a consolidated view of their accounts, enabling access with a single online login.
	▶ Authorised payment institutions must be able to access payment accounts on an objective, non-discriminatory and proportionate basis. Where access is refused the customer must be informed (where possible) before denying access, and the regulator notified so that it can monitor the grounds of refusal.
Increase the security of payments	▶ New frameworks to control and manage operational risks, including security risks relating to payments; payment services providers will need to have a security policy document, a description of their security incident management procedure and an explanation of their contingency procedures.
	▶ New reporting

	requirements for major operational and security incidents. ▶ New obligations to notify customers of data breaches without undue delay where it may impact their financial interests. ▶ Strong customer authentication. – The validation of the identification of a person based on the use of two or more elements categorised as ▶ Knowledge – something only the user knows (PIN; password) ▶ Possession – something only the user has (CVV number; PIN entry code) ▶ Inherence – something only the user is (fingerprint; voice print) This is to be used when accessing a payment account on-line, initiating "an electronic payment transaction or for any action, through a remote channel, which may imply a risk of payment fraud or other abuses.

	▶ The European Banking Authority (EBA) will issue guidelines and regulatory technical standards to support the new requirements. However, timelines are problematic.
Provide for new liabilities & consumer protection	▶ Liability cap for unauthorised payment transactions reduced to 50 EUR. This will not impact payment service providers that do not apply this to customers. ▶ New rules on liability allocation as between the bank and payment initiation services. These rules will be mandatory, meaning that payment service providers cannot make the agreement of a different allocation of liability a condition of permitting access to their customers' accounts. ▶ Payment service provider liability where strong customer authentication is not provided or accepted. ▶ Unconditional right to a refund for a SEPA direct debit.

	This is already available in some countries and in the UK through the direct debit guarantee scheme, but it will now be put on a legal basis.
Provide for Non-discriminatory access to payment systems	▶ Access to payment systems to be objective, non-discriminatory and proportionate, and not to inhibit access to payment systems other than to safeguard settlement risk. Sponsor banks will need to review policies and agreements for compliance with the non-discrimination provisions.
Redress	▶ Out of court redress system – a full response within 15 business days.

The key changes introduced by PSD2 can be grouped into four main but complimentary themes: market efficiency and integration; consumer protection; competition and choice; and security.

Notably the territorial reach has been expanded to include currencies other than the euro as well as covering one-leg transactions were only one of the parties is in EU territory. Hence from Jan 2018 Non-EEA currency payments between EEA-domiciled PSPs; and One-leg transactions (where one of the PSPs is located outside of the EEA) in any currency will fall under the auspice of the directive. In addition the directive is also increasing its influence over the EEA market by setting more stringent operational, security and capitalisation requirement for third party payment processors who in addition will also require professional indemnity before they will be authorised and licensed. There has also been the creation of the new types of payment providers and business institutions which will have the same rights to access account information and under the same conditions, given customer consent, as the customer they represent would have using the banks online services. That aspect of PSD2 may be the most controversial and has already been covered at length earlier in this chapter. Nonetheless, these are the more significant tactical moves that the PSD2 utilises to try and open up the market in order to level the playing field and lower the barriers to entry for FinTech firms so that they can bring innovation and fresh approaches to benefit customer payment services. This is quite inline with the core principles of PSD2 as it places strong emphasis on protecting the consumer, as can be demonstrated through some of the key customer-centric provisions introduced under this revision.

PSD2 will increase consumers' rights in a number of ways. For example:

1. Payments sent or received where one of the PSPs is located outside the EEA will be covered, as will payments in non-EEA currencies.

2. The amount a payer could be obliged to pay in an unauthorised payment scenario has reduced from € 150 to €50 – except in cases of fraud or gross negligence by the payer.

3. PSD2 provides a legislative basis to the unconditional refund right (for a period of 8 weeks from the date when the funds were debited) which already applies under the SEPA Core Direct Debit scheme. Member States may require or retain even more favourable refund rights in non-euro direct debit schemes. In the UK this is already the case regarding the UK Direct Debit scheme in terms of its unlimited guarantee.

4. In the context of the pre-authorisation of card payments, where the final amount of the transaction is not known in advance, e.g. when renting a car or booking a hotel, the payee will only be able to 'ring fence' funds on the payer's card account where the cardholder has approved the exact amount that can be blocked. The payer's PSP is required to unblock those funds without undue delay once information about the exact final amount is received and, at the latest, after having received the payment order.

5. PSD2 will ban surcharging for the use of payment instruments covered by the Interchange Fee Regulation and payment services covered by the SEPA Regulation.

6. PSPs must put in place dispute resolution procedures and will be required to respond to payment complaints within 15 business days of receipt. In exceptional circumstances a holding reply can be provided, explaining the reasons for the delay, with the final response being received within 35 business days.

7. Member States are required to designate competent authorities (such as the FCA and Financial Ombudsman Service) to ensure and monitor compliance with PSD2 and to handle disputes between PSPs and customers.

Customer Benefits from PIS

The PSD2 provides the consumer with extended protection more aligned with the internet and the global market place. Nonetheless, as beneficial as these extensions to the articles are in protecting the consumer's interests it is in the way they experience the changes that will ultimately affect their perspective.

From a customer's perspective the PSD2 will simplify the payment process and provide choices of payment methods that were previously limited to cards or pre-paid wallets.

The way that this is envisaged working in a real world scenario is that the extensions to the payments directive would allow consumers and retailers to streamline online and mobile payments. For example: A customer shopping online might complete their transaction using a bank debit or credit card which in this scenario let us consider that e-bay are the 'merchant' and they use a broker such as First Data that in turn utilities the banking network to take money out of the customer's bank account and settle the transaction by placing it into eBay's account.

This is shown in the diagram below:

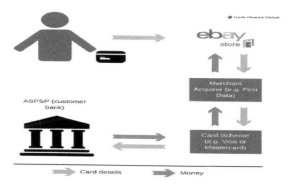

Diagram 1 – PAYING ONLINE WITH A DEBIT OR CREDIT CARD

Now let's consider how this transaction may proceed when PSD2 is active. Once the new directive is in force the consumer will have a choice so rather that being limited to a credit or Debit card, the consumer may if they wish delegate the merchant's payment processor to carry out the transaction by directly accessing their account on their behalf via a token and an API. The key change is that PSD2 allows the Payment Initiation Service Provider (PISP), to manage the payment transaction with the explicit consent of the customer, via direct access to the customer's bank account which is held by the Account Servicing Payment Provider (ASPSP), i.e., the customer's bank.

This payment path is known as Access to Accounts or XS2A (access to account). The original PSD2 suggested that this would be secure because the retailer (PISP) and the banks can communicate with each other through an API, an open Application Programme Interface. An API was suggested as being ideal as the interconnection would make for significant improvements in efficiency and speed of transaction. However in the autumn of 2017 the final SCA RTS technical document distanced itself from prescription standards and specifications in favour of a technology-neutral stance and instead determined it was up to the banks to decide on the interconnectivity mechanism.

For the majority of customers, online transactions will go largely unnoticed, as they have become accustomed to one click shopping through online stores such as Amazon but they will no longer require having a credit or debiting card, just a payment account in their bank and so payment transactions are unlikely to significantly change a customer journey on ecommerce checkout. It is the ease of use and improved customer experience that online stores such as Amazon offers which the PSD2 strives to facilitate but also to balance against its own stringent objective for secure customer authorisation. And here is where some conflict potentially rises for PSD2 is built upon the premise of strong customer authentication, i.e. 2 Factor Authentication and that is the antithesis of one-click payment. Consequently in an effort to balance the need for convenient frictionless online payment with the need for stringent authentication with robust anti-fraud mechanisms the PSD2 exempts online purchases of below €50 from requiring SCA. Similarly low value transactions for parking and travel have also been made exempt from the requirement for SCA.

Customer Benefits of AIS

Although payment is the primary focus of the PSD2 directive it also provides another benefit for the customer through the Account Information Service Provider (AISP), which allows companies to consolidate information from many different Account Servicing Payment Providers (ASPSPs) such as bank accounts, loans, mortgages at different banks. Hence, for customers such as those who multi-bank or small businesses that have bank accounts spread across several banks, this would allow them to view their entire financial situation in one common portal. Interestingly, the PSD2 envisaged AISPs as being financial institutions but it's likely that fintech firms will position themselves as Account Information Service Providers, in order to leverage the potential of the data collection and aggregation facility. If this occurs as is likely it may pressurise high street banks to also register as AISPs in order that their customers can login to their main bank account and see the aggregated information from all of their other bank accounts simultaneously.

The customer benefits are delivered through better protection, lower prices and extended freedoms of choice but they are not the only major beneficiaries. The potential benefits for the merchant means cost of sales are significantly reduced as they no longer need to pay a bank transaction fee on a debit or credit card, which means that they can make significant savings and perhaps pass some of these along to their customers. It of course remains to be seen if they exercise the same vigour, imagination and ingenuity when finding ways to pass on subsequent savings as they so ably demonstrated when passing on the bank charges to their customers.

Although most players in the payment ecosystem seems to benefit to some degree perhaps at the expense of the banks and the credit card companies, the major beneficiaries however are likely to be the Third Party Players the FinTech firms that enter the payments market in order to take advantage of these new freedoms of access to customer data. As a result of forcing the banks to open up and share their customers data that was previously closely guarded, many fintech startups will develop solutions and create APIs which will enable innovative payment solutions. *Or that was the way it was supposed to be but as we will see later that is not how it is turning out.* It was also expected that the large technology firms could leverage their own vast customer networks and become PISPs, in order to leverage their social media networks and customer base to send payments. It is predicted that up to 9% of revenue for retail payments could be lost to traditional banks and payment services by 2020 due directly to the introduction of PSD2. Such forecasts should be contemplated with caution however as recent studies into the explosive growth of FinTech in the US within the payments and loans segment has failed to show a correlation or a corresponding drop in the income generated by the incumbent banks through the same activities over the same period. This may tend to suggest that the FinTech firms were creating a new customer base perhaps engaging with customers that the banks would not entertain rather than acquiring customers and their business from the banks.

However it is not all bleak news for banks as they also have opportunities based upon their large retail footprint, customer database and the high trust in which they are held. Few FinTech business models focus on taking cash deposits and for a good reason, it is highly regulated, would require a bank charter and high levels of capitalisation. Consequently FinTech firms tend to want to enter the payments and loan segments where technology can be a major differentiator and their fresh young brands are attractive to their target audience. The major banks on the other hand hold a distinct advantage when it comes to trustworthiness and that ultimately decides where a customer banks their salary. Banks therefore could look at positioning themselves as AISP and developing customer centric applications which use data analytics to examine spending behaviour, inform customers of appropriate products or cross/up sell services or products to their customers. HSBC UK has proved itself to be an early mover in this regard announcing the arrival of their open banking platform that will allow customers to see all of their accounts on one screen, even if they are with a rival bank. Within the HSBC Beta platform, customers can add current, savings and mortgage accounts from up to 21 different banks, including Santander, Lloyds and Barclays.

Moreover, it may be that time was catching up with the banks anyway so regardless of PSD2 coming into force it seems that the bank's days of segregating their customer's data from the outside world was coming to an end. As Kevin Hanley, director of design and services at RBS explains. "You see the disaggregating of banking services, the disintermediation of banking services, banking becoming more unbundled, more modular. We are moving from an era of physical banking to a connected bank of digital services. This starts to re-frame banking and our role in it as much more of a composite where we both provide services and link to other services. So we become a platform for our customers to navigate around "

Indeed several countries, which are independent of the EU PSD2 initiative, have already started their own Open Banking projects, which amount to much the same thing and interestingly they foresee that banks opening APIs will eventually prove to be beneficial as they will remain in control of the services and functionality they present to the world.

Summary of the Aims and Objectives of the PSD2

The original objective of PSD, which was adopted in 2007, was to create a single-market for payments within the European Union. Therefore the legislation set out to:

1) Create the rules and guidelines for modern payment services in the European Union

2) Simplify payments and payment processing across the European Union

3) Aim to promote competition by opening payments up to new entrants

4) Advocate payment efficiency, innovation and reduced costs

5) Provide the legal platform for the Single Euro Payments Area – SEPA

The revised Second Payment Services Directive (PSD2 – EU Directive 2015/2366) was proposed by the European Commission in 2013, and the objective was to create a level playing field by:

- Standardising, integrating and improving payment efficiency in the European Union

- Offering better consumer protection

- Promoting innovation in the payments space and reducing costs

- Incorporating and providing clarity on the use of emerging payment methods such as mobile payments and online payments

- Create a equal playing field for payment service providers - enabling new companies to get into the payments space

- Harmonise pricing and improve security of payment processing across the European Union

- Incorporate new and emerging payment services into the regulation

The banks are naturally concerned because it will require a lot of investment, reduce their existing revenue streams, increase risk, and introduce a whole new wave of disruptive competitors into an already competitive market space.

Furthermore, the opportunities that open up to competitors, retailers and customers will transform the payment services industry as they include:

- With PSD2, the Directive will allow retailers to 'ask' consumers for permission to use their bank details. Once given permission, the retailer will receive the payment directly from the customer's bank – no intermediaries, no fees

- PSD2 introduces an entity called an Account Information Service Provider or AISPs, which will allow customers to view all of their multi-bank details in a single portal.

- The direct connection between retailers and banks will be enabled using industry standard Application Programming Interface or public APIs

- A strong customer authentication system – Two Factor Authentication will reduce fraud

- Ban on surcharging (additional costs) for card payments benefits customers

- Better consumer protection against fraud, capping any potential payments if a unauthorised payment is made to €50

o   Improved consumer protection for
payments made outside of the EU or in non-EU currencies

Introduction to the world of Open Banking

The technology of the Application Programmable Interfaces or more commonly APIs has become almost synonymous with PSD2 despite the fact that it is not even mentioned within the Regulatory Technical Specifications. This is because APIs are deemed by many experts to be the logical way for banks to open up their systems and platforms to the third parties. Consequently, APIs are now the almost de facto standard interface for what is termed open banking, which is the provisioning of an interface to a third party in order to permit access to information or to consume a service. Contrary to what you might expect, PSD2 was not the instigator or even the catalyst behind the concept of allowing third parties access to customer's data – with the customers explicit consent or strongly redacted – as there have been open banking project and initiatives from banks within the EU and some out-with the EU for some time predating the PSD. Incidentally, it is also erroneously believed that FinTech firms lobbied strongly for API access – but that as we will see later was well of the mark. Despite this the open banking projects have been catching on with banks around the world. For example there is regulator movement in the USA, Asia, Australia and the Middle East. However as diverse as these projects may be with banks operating solo the common denominator does appear to confirm the experts predictions that the technology of choice for the communication channel interconnect between the banks and the authorised third party is a bank supplied API.

The use of API's is exciting because it enables third party companies to connect to financial institutions directly and interact with a customers account. This is potentially highly beneficial as AISPs, and not necessarily banks, can consolidate their clients account information in one place. However it also means that they can acquire insightful data about the customer, which would present very lucrative cross-selling opportunities but also the potential for abuse through monetisation via direct marketing. There is also the very real threat that if FinTech firms or even the traditional banks are not very diligent they may come under the beady eye of the GDPR regulators – an all that entails. Furthermore, the gift of the APIs bestowed upon them by the PSD2 may not actually be much of a gift at all it might in reality is a poisonous apple - as we will see later when we consider the details.

Nonetheless, the Open Banking Standard proposes open APIs be built as open, federated and networked solutions, rather than as a centralised system. This echoes the design of the Web and will allow the widest scope for innovation. It is further proposed that Open APIs will be available under a licence that enables free use, reuse and distribution. The use of Open APIs will encourage banks to deploy existing standards, datasets and structures, which will enable code to be reused. It is also seen as being important to keep the barriers to participation deliberately low in order to encourage and to cultivate a sizable developer community. For their part the Open Banking Standard will ensure that there is an implementation register that lists API providers that have implemented the Open Banking Standard and this will be publicly available on the Web along with the relevant documentation, development code and reference implementations. Providing access to information will help developers understand the services being exposed by the banks an encourage them to engage in collaborative projects that build and develop services of mutual benefit (e.g. sandbox environments for secure testing)

However, the open API model has also come in for its fair share of criticism as a consortium of 70 leading European financial technology companies banded together recently to protest a provision in the PSD2's draft Regulatory Technical Standards (RTS) that would ban the technology commonly known as screen-scraping. These companies argue that banking APIs, while well intended is an unproven method of consumer data sharing. In fact, limiting data sharing to APIs could threaten the very same consumers that PSD2 was originally designed to help—by mandating a shift from a reliable data sharing method. In addition the fintech firms claim that APIs effectively hand over control of digital financial services to banks, instead of consumers. They have concerns that for instance, a bank could decide to restrict availability of certain data fields needed for critical consumer use cases using the ambiguous 'sensitive payment information" and data privacy concerns as an excuse. Furthermore, there is a consensus of opinion within the consortium that the banks may not maintain their API infrastructure for third parties, favouring direct customer access over access via a third party.

However there may be an even bigger issue with the API model as proposed by the Open Banking and PSD2 initiatives and that it is back-to-front in its design regards the priority of authentication, over authorisation against a standard data set. The banks and of course the regulators want to build into the design of inherent strong authentication, so that they can determine who is accessing customers' data. That is perfectly correct approach as security must be paramount as a key design principle. But if we hold true to the premise of Open Banking - that the customer owns their data - then when it comes to data access and sharing, it should be the consumers and not their bank, who determines 'Authorisation' and what data they wish to share with third parties. For this reason, it's more useful to standardize the data set layer, for authorisation rather than authentication. At the data layer, standardization would provide consumers with much finer granularity when determining the minimum amount of data and permissions necessary to provide access to third parties for a specific purpose. PSD2 has actually reversed these priorities—focusing on payments it makes authentication paramount and is less concerned with the actual data sets. By the industry lacking a standard data architecture FinTech firms will need to build specific APIs for each individual bank, hence consumers might find that they're unable to access the data they want for a given purpose, such as applying for a mortgage or a loan. As we will see in subsequent chapters these issues were only early indicators that all might not be well in the FinTech camp regards APIs as they were still was awaiting the release of the Regulatory Technical Specifications, the draft would be released in February 2017 along with the FinTech outrage.

The Rise of FinTech

Digital transactions have had a huge impact on the evolution of the fintech industry as niche products and services have emerged to fill the crevasses left by larger financial institutions. These include services for the unbanked and underbanked, instant insurance, crowdfunded loans and global online remittance. Fintech operators have been able to rapidly innovate for many reasons. For example they have not been hamstrung by legacy back-end systems, yet have benefited from lower regulatory oversight, obligations, rules and thus less scrutiny. Moreover, large financial institutions have unwittingly become the enablers often providing the FinTech firms with the required network access to clearing and settlement networks such as ACH or BACs with minimal benefit to themselves.

The PSD2 legislation and Open Banking regulations are set to create more disruption within the banking segment with major opportunities arising as both financial institutions and new providers compete to drive smarter revenue from customer payments. With open banking, the banks and financial institutions are becoming increasingly at risk of losing their direct relationship with their customers and being relegated to a back end utility provider. On the other hand, new providers could emerge, in the customer interaction and facing services which enables customers to access their banking services from a common portal, without having to ever log into their bank. These portals may also enable the customer to get services à la carte from a menu of banks. However this scenario overlooks the fact that there is nothing stopping banks becoming AISPs and providing these services to their customers, which they are well positioned to do. Subsequently, new payment platforms that support revolutionary payment and banking ecosystems may emerge from the open banking disruption that leads to new business models but not necessarily from Fintech firms it might well be the banks that leverage their reliability, repute and trust that comes out on top. Hence, it will be critical for established service providers such as the banks to decide how to take advantage of the opportunity proactively and very importantly to realise that they are still in the prime position to control information flow as it will be their APIs and ultimately their services that others will consume.

Open Banking however is not just about technology the concept is far more nuanced and the bulk of the work in implementing and promoting the Open Banking Standard are around governance, security, liability, standards, communications, regulation and legal. These are areas where the traditional banks excel and FinTechs lack experience. FinTechs will require the support of independent authority that has the ability to ensure standards and obligations between participants are upheld. The PSD2 already has this but the Open Banking initiatives will require this independent authority to be established and to be responsible to govern how data is secured once shared and to ensure the security, usability, reliability and scalability of APIs. Its responsibilities would also extend to assessing and vetting third parties, accredit solutions, maintain a whitelist of approved firms and create the necessary frameworks for handling complaints and redress. These are the critical issues that need addressed to win over customers and allay their fears as currently the two issues that hinder customer acceptance of open banking are a perception of a lack of sufficient security controls and mechanisms for redress.

A consequence of PSD2 is that the requirement for clearing and settlement networks is removed or at least greatly reduced thus opening up the banks to new entrants into the Payments Segment called PISP (Payment Initiation Service Providers). These new FinTech firms will in effect represent consumers and act as delegated financial administrators of their bank accounts, offer them financial advice and provide them with more competitive offers for loans, over draughts, credit cards, mortgages or high interest savings accounts. The Open banking Standard believe UK consumers could save around £70 if they changed their current account or up to £140 if they changed to a more suitable over-draught facility. In theory this seems wonderful but as can be clearly demonstrated within the investment and wealth management segment advice is not always in the best interests of the consumer hence the MiFID II directive requires asset managers and other financial advisors to record and store for 5 years all communications with their clients. This is not currently on the PSD2 radar but customers will need to have protection and a mechanism for redress should FinTech firms engage in activities that promote products that benefit themselves rather than providing impartial advice.

PSD2 also looks to provide greater transparency over charges, improve consumer protection and the security of payments. Banks, customers and third party providers will be required to address these issues and provide more direction on the key issues identified and exploring what these will mean in practice. Hence there is an onus on the banks, FinTech firms and the regulatory authorities to ensure the education of the customer. At the very least individuals, businesses and governments must have an awareness of their rights and responsibilities when sharing or handling personal identifiable data. Importantly the FinTech firms must understand and be clear on what informed consent means and why it is so important especially today in the ubiquitously connected one-click transaction world. The app designers must ensure that the customer should be fully aware of the purpose when they give their explicit consent each and every time they share specific data. Moreover, service providers should be aware that the customer must be able to revoke access at least as easily as they grant it. Platforms must be transparent and proactive in how they use and store customer data (for example, to not hold data for longer than they need to). As two of the biggest challenges in encouraging consumers to share data are (1) helping them to fully understand what is happening and (2) helping them to feel confident that their data is secure so that they are able to provide informed consent there has to be much more effort invested in both data literacy and security by both the banks and FinTech firms.

Open Banking and FinTech

The recent concept of a shift towards open banking makes the incumbents face the prospect of operating in a more competitive environment with the introduction of the Payment Services Directive (PSD2) in January 2018. EU regulators want to increase competition, improve customer service, and promote the development of online and mobile payment systems.

The key feature of the directive is that banks provide Third Party Providers (TPPs) access to customer online accounts / payment services through a dedicated communication interface that many believe to be an open API (Application Programming Interface) when account holders provide consent. This will allow third parties described as Payment Initiation Service Providers (PISPs) to directly access customer accounts by connecting directly through the dedicated communications interface such as a standard API or whatever interconnection the bank provides to the TPP. (The RTS leaves the choice of technology to the bank)

PSD2 is a parallel progression towards Open Banking as in the UK the Competition and Markets Authority (CMA) published a report in 2016 advocating greater competition and reforms, with retail banks required to implement Open Banking by early 2018. This timeline and parallel development of somewhat similar projects has proven to be rather fortuitous for the Open Banking Working Group which has aimed to develop their standard APIs to comply with the PSD2 suggested standards based upon Rest and JSON. Now that the EBA (European Bank Association) have decided not to prescribe a standard API and to leave the decision up to the banks it places the OBWG in a good position to provide a standard API template for all the European banks.

The PSD2 and the open banking initiatives were penned to ensure that the nascent FinTech community continues to flourish but the RTS proposal to ban the FinTech firms existing screen-scraping techniques has turned that on its head. Consequently, the banking landscape will not be so easily disrupted by these new technology startups which many though as being inevitable indeed many if the RTS ban remains may well go to the wall or have to rely on cooperation from competitor and mobile only banks such as Atom Bank, Starling and Monzo. In addition, non-bank service providers such as PayPal and Google Wallet are also entering into the market but whether these technology firms take much share of market from the incumbents remains to be seen. Where the Technology giants will have a huge effect is on card payments as they are sure to push their customers to pay through their banks and thereby save the tech firms vast amounts on card payment fees. Prior to PSD2 FinTech companies have been growing steadily in markets in the US and the EU but have not had any significant impact on the incumbent's market share even though they have had access to the customer accounts through aggregators such as Yodlee and latterly Mint.com. This has led to speculation that the FinTech firms are actually creating new niche markets rather than disrupting the existing market share held by the incumbents. In contrast to some of the mature Fintech firms that fear that being forced to use the bank's APIs will prevent them from running the services that they have built over the last decade, the new Fintech entrants that are willing to embrace the API, may find the PSD2 is an opportunity to provide new innovative services and perhaps to create new niche markets. Gaining legitimate access to the customer's accounts could well lead to greater customer acceptance of the concept of open banking as they would no longer have to share their bank account passwords ala screen-scraping. Overcoming the considerable customer resistance to the open banking model would provide the much needed boost in confidence and provide a platform for future development of apps that may further entice customers with enhanced insight into their spending habits and products along with services that will allow them to manage their financial affairs and make decisions that fit their lifestyles. There is a known demand for these advanced services as the mature FinTech firms have been servicing this niche for fifteen years or more but bringing the service to the mainstream will only be feasible through the adoption of secure and trusted API technologies.

From the banks perspective PSD2 has unsurprisingly raised concerns amongst some incumbents who are fearful about future profits and the loss of direct customer relations. As a result, there has been considerable effort by banks lobbying MSPs in Brussels to get some of the requirements of PSD2 diluted or removed. However, it appears that there might be sea change in perception and the fear that they will be usurped by FinTech upstarts has morphed into a reluctant acceptance of the challenges ahead. Perhaps as incumbents of all sizes begin to recognise that PSD2 and Open Banking present as many opportunities as threats and importantly the strong resistance from FinTech amply demonstrates that they will certainly not have it all their own way. Banks are beginning to realise that their imminent demise has been greatly exaggerated and are beginning to explore these new opportunities with renewed vigour and lease of life. But the opportunities to monetise APIs may also have been overplayed as FinTech firms are adamant that they will not pay to use APIs so perhaps the better opportunities lies with leveraging account payment data to develop new financial products and services of there own through data analysis and extracting insights.

The initial burst of hype surrounding the open banking initiative has led to increased competition and has encouraged many new FinTech firms to enter the market, which in turn accelerated the adoption of Open Banking initiatives. The subsequent change in perception and attitude towards Open Banking has certainly not dulled the appetites of new entrants as many sign up for the Open Banking Initiative's API sandbox so it may create an environment of networks where banks or system integrators will adopt a platform strategy, opening up their technology to fintech firms and other financial service providers. How the incumbents respond to this challenge and manage to monetise the opportunity will determine whether they stay at the apex of the industry.

It was initially envisaged that for the FinTech firms the availability of APIs to third party developers would provide them with legitimate access to the banks customers' accounts. This level of unprecedented legitimate access would allow them to build products and services over the top of a bank's existing infrastructure – enabling them to create valuable services and products for their shared customers.

Unfortunately that view overlooked the fact that through advanced screen-scraping techniques many mature FinTech had been operating unrestricted and unregulated for over a decade. Indeed for them the risk is that the PSD2 takes away an awful lot more access than it gives them. For example prior to the PSD2 FinTech firms used screen-scraping to perform all the functions that they will likely be able to do using the banks APIs. Indeed they will now be restricted to only functions opened up by the banks and to compound the problem they will be restricted to action consistent to their role as an AISP or a PISP – under their screen-scraping there was no limitations they had the freedom to do both. It is possible to be licensed and regulated as both an AISP and a PISP but that may well be financially beyond most firms.

A significant advantage that FinTech still has over incumbents is rather than provide all the services that a bank does, PSD2 allows new challengers to provide specialist financial services more efficiently and cost effectively. As Fintech firms will as AISP or PISP require licensing and now have the burden of regulatory compliance which doesn't come cheap then their advantage may not be so clear cut. Regulatory compliance is expensive but banks can dilute the effects due to their economy of scale however smaller banks and Fintech firm are often disproportionately effected.

Despite that Fintech should still hold a key advantage albeit a smaller one and this is where perhaps the established incumbent banks will need to consider which services they can still deliver competitively, and importantly what new products they can deliver which will not cannibalise their existing product lines. Open banking will provide the banks the opportunity to offer a selection of APIs to third parties in a similar way in which apps are presented on smartphones. New business opportunities will exist if incumbents can make their APIs attractive, available and accessible to third party developers who will be prepared to pay for them or more likely bring alternative value through commission sharing or partnerships. Access to the customer's data is at the heart of this development and providing data is fully accessible through the bank's APIs, new tailored services can be delivered to bank customers to specifically meet their needs. Examples include the development of new apps which allow customers to aggregate, visualise and manipulate different sources of financial information in ways that previously have not been available to them.

Open Banking will potentially transform the relationship between banks and their customers, especially if the ECB ratifies the RTS and bans screen-scraping in European law. This would represent a significant power shift from established and mature FinTech's back to the traditional bank and their customers. With this alternative development, incumbents will need to reconsider how they create the same value as the mature FinTech firms created for their customers and it will require banks to adopt a more customer centric and data centric view on how they do business. Increasing levels of regulations have driven up costs and often capped fees into the bargain making monetising products and services difficult without bundling services to obfuscate their fees.

The Payment Accounts Directive

In order to make basic payment accounts obtainable to every citizen and the bank service charges more visible The Payment Accounts Directive has been implemented in the UK by the Payment Account Regulations 2015. It seeks to improve the comparability of fees related to payment accounts, facilitate account switching and improve access to payment accounts with basic features. Consequently, the payment service providers will have to provide consumers with a document listing all the fees for the most common payment services provided and the fees charged for each of them. Payment service providers must also offer a switching service for Payment Accounts that are denominated in the same currency and provide assistance to any consumer who wants to open an account in another EU Member State. Furthermore, there must be non-discriminatory access to payment accounts in the UK so that consumers legally resident in the EU have the right to open and use such a payment account, irrespective of their place of residence. Moreover, nine payment service providers have currently been required to offer a payment account with basic features to consumers. A basic bank account must be provided either free of charge or for a reasonable fee.

Open Banking Use Cases

The new challenger banks and FinTechs are providing
incumbents with the best examples on how technology and
data can support and enhance the customer experience in
Open Banking. A common strategy is for banks to partner or
purchase startups and FinTechs. Spain's second largest bank
BBVA is at the forefront of fintech acquisition and digital
transformation. They are a major shareholder with British
startups bank Atom Bank. They have also acquired Holvi,
Finnish based API based fintech innovator who specialise in
small business payments. In 2014, BBVA purchased US based
fintech Simple which uses APIs to help customers analyse
their financial activity. BBVA has been leading the way by
exposing a range of its APIs to approved developers. Their
APIs include, customer profile data, key account data, money
transfer services, and aggregated card purchase data. In
Germany, Fidor Bank is not only a digital bank but also an
innovative digital banking platform, providing an API enabled
platform for third party developers and other market entrants
wishing to offer bank services.

For incumbents seeking guidance, opening up APIs requires having an appropriate API strategy and governance in place. This will allow them to confidently open up their core data so that it can be utilised by other parts of their business and by third parties. The speed of execution for such strategies and governance will vary depending upon the organisation. To fully embrace Open Banking, incumbents must move beyond the current mind-set of merely complying with PSD2 as the regulation is more than just compliance – at its heart is the aim to increase competition. Open Banking is an opportunity to deliver an improved customer service and experience and at the same time represents both a clear opportunity and a threat to the bank.

The future of banking will likely see more fragmentation with customers prepared to spread their business around, choosing different financial providers for different services. PSD2 and Open Banking are about making it easier for customers to do this. Customer experience is now at the heart of the new business model needed for Open Banking.

Some banks are embracing the concept of open banking and have established open channels that enable data sharing or are eager to position themselves as leaders in the new digital financial marketplace. AIB Group, Bank of Ireland, Barclays, Danske, HSBC Group, Lloyds Banking Group, Nationwide, RBS Group and Santander are all currently working together to create that open API standard. In practice this should look like a set of documentation, development code and reference implementations that anyone can use, dramatically bringing down barriers for participation in financial services.

The advantage of this, as the CMA itself defines, would be: "Reliable, personalised financial advice, precisely tailored to your particular circumstances delivered securely and confidentially."

HSBC UK has proved itself to be an early mover when it comes to PSD2 announcing the arrival of their open banking platform, which will allow customers to see all of their accounts on one screen, even if they are with a rival bank. The bank will do this through a new test and learn mobile banking platform ahead of introducing a new app for customers in early 2018. HSBC believe this is the starting point ahead of the launch of a range of new open banking-enabled features. This includes Safe Balance, which shows customers how much disposable income they have before the next payday, and a Spend Analysis tool, which categorises spending, adds tags, notes and photos to transactions and analyse patterns for more informed decision making.

The Royal Bank of Scotland (RBS) is also a pioneer in experimenting with open banking and it wants to position itself as a market leader in the digital financial market as the "the bank of APIs". RBS see the disaggregating and the disintermediation of banking services happening already as service catalogues become unbundled, more modular and the future as they see it revolves around a digital marketplace connecting an array of digital financial services and hence banks will realistically become the platforms hosting this digital market. The way it is envisaged is that customers will connect to and navigate around the marketplace selecting the best of breed solutions that meet their criteria. That may sound very attractive almost like a supermarket for financial services but it overlooks the basic fact that most people do not understand financial instruments so there would be a requirement for freely available neutral advice and robust consumer protection.

Open banking is not confined only to Europe, in Asia and Australia there are digital players emerging as open banks for example China's first online-only bank is a joint venture led by gaming and social network group Tencent Holdings. WeBank is one of five institutions to be granted a licence under a government pilot scheme to establish privately operated banks, as part of moves to open up China's banking sector. Banks licensed under the scheme are expected to focus on expanding access to finance for small and micro businesses, and individuals. Tencent operates the highly popular mobile messaging and social media app WeChat — one of China's largest social networks, with 549 million monthly active users (as at first quarter 2015). WeChat already offers customer's financial services in the form of a bank card linked to their WeChat account and Tencent's wealth management platform, offering customers the opportunity to invest in third-party investment products via their smartphones.

In Australia, which is the latest major market to join the open banking spotlight the National Australia Bank (NAB) announced the introduction of APIs for third-party data sharing. In addition, a Parliamentary Committee introduced a new regime which will oblige Australia's four largest banks to enable open API access for customers by 2018. Indeed, the national government has budgeted AUS$1.2 million for the Treasury in 2017-8 to assess what the open API schema should look like.

Banks that are embracing the digital market like RBS, BBVA and Fidor have a perception of what financial services provision may look like in a digital economy and are adjusting their strategies to reap the potential benefits. Individual banks will also have a choice to make on how they want to approach the conundrum of open banking in the digital age. It is easy to say that financial institutions need to view PSD2 as an opportunity but that rings rather hollow when contemplated along side a recent report by McKinsey titled 'A Brave New World for Global Banking', which estimates that banks in Europe and the UK currently have $35 billion, or 31 percent, of profits at risk because of digitisation in general. Furthermore, the report forecasts that "More severe digital disruption could further cut their profits from $110 billion today to $50 billion in 2020, and reduce returns on equity in half to one to two percent by 2020, even after some mitigation efforts." However, the banks ultimately might not have a choice as the market forces drive the demand for digital banking and enshrine the principles of data as a commodity. Digital disruption and technological innovation are unlikely to be just a fad, a product of over imagined hype. Hence, rather than trying to stem the tide and stifle this development, incumbents should seek ways to take advantage of it.

What do PSD2-API's mean for Fintech?

The PSD2 makes direct connections between retailers and customer's bank accounts possible with the use of an API or Application Programming Interface. The technical term API is a template with a set of rules and required parameters that can be utilized to fetch or change data in an existing database or to act as preconfigured software which is tailored to meet specific needs without changing the overall host system's source code. This opens up all sorts of possibilities and opportunities for FinTech developers to take advantage. An open API, for example, would enable the use of congregated data that can be targeted to individual customers as well as retailers without compromising security. Classic examples include card-linked marketing in which consumers can receive targeted assistance from their financial institution at the point-of-sale.

This form of realtime directed marketing may include incentives to buy or not to buy, provide alternative perhaps cheaper offers, or provide cross or up sell opportunities. All of these can be made available digitally on the consumer's mobile device at the point of purchase. FinTech's are clamouring for these rich data sets that traditional banks have stored in their customer account records and all of these treasure troves will soon be available with the customer's informed consent throughout the entire European Union. That loosening of the banks hold on their customers' financial records and affairs will allow fintech firms to engage more effectively with the banks' customers. The customers will still retain their bank accounts and affiliations but now they can delegate access to their account to a TPP to obtain third party financial services.

It is tempting to contemplate the emergence of FinTech as some disruptive, revolutionary and unstoppable force that will transform customer retail banking and usurp the stuffy old-fashioned incumbents with their fat cat bankers. However, banks are far more resilient that most other industries and there is an awful lot of work required to overcome customer inertia. As a report from Accenture indicates two-thirds of consumers in the UK won't share their financial data with third-party providers such as online retailers, tech firms and social media companies. And that shouldn't really be surprising.

The research by Accenture, which surveyed 2,008 UK consumers during August 2017, found that 69 percent of respondents would not share their bank account information with these third-party providers. More striking still was that 53 percent of the consumers said 'they will never change their existing banking habits and adopt open banking'.

Security will be the Biggest Challenge

Security will be a serious concern for FinTechs looking to enter into this market as it has always been for the banks. Therefore, these new companies will not just be allowed access to the banks services and APIs as they will need to meet some stringent security measures as required by The European Union as well as the host country regulator. Further more to obtain insurance which will also be a requirement for access they will have to prove to the insurance company that they are a competent and low risk firm, which already has competency and tight personal, cyber and financial security measures in place. This obviously includes compliance with regulations such GDPR, Know Your Customer, PCI-DDS, as well as being skilled in implementing IAM (Identity and Access Management) and OTP (One Time Passwords). Hence, it is not going open the floodgates for unqualified startups as there will still be significant barriers to entry. However for ambitious competent FinTech firms within this highly regulated and specialised field the PSD2 has lowered the barriers to entry considerably.

How will PSD2 affect the payments industry?

The definition of PSD2 for banks is: free-market competition.

Two new competitors in the form of service providers will open up to the banks: Account Information Service Providers (AISP) and Payment Initiation Service Providers (PISP). AISPs are the new entrants who will aggregate and collect the data of customers' banking habits like how much they spend, when they spend, and where they spend and turn that data into a profitable material. However AISPs will need to tread extremely carefully if harvesting customer financial payments data is their business model. The redaction and pseudo-anonymisation of the data they collect and share will be a necessity and it is imperative they do so diligently if they wish to not fall foul of the GDPR regulators. Thus AISPs will need to be careful what data they collect and to whom they share that data as they do no have the freedom to use that data for any other purpose than the purpose for which the customer consented. Interestingly, several FinTech companies are already advertising so called APIs (they are actually screen-scrapers) which will connect to most banks that support online banking, if the customer credentials are provided. They described the process to potential AISPs as *"connect to the API, collect customer data, profit!"*

That is certainly not the spirit in which the PSD2 legislation has been brought into law in the EU and if FinTech's are not providing benefits to society and the customer, then it is unlikely they will last long. PISPs on the other hand are the ones who will initiate the bill payments or P2P service on behalf of the financial institution's customer. The PISP is very likely to be seen in a better light as they are providing a visible service for the customer, that the customer clearly wishes and provides their consent and delegates access to their account. Hence, PISPs are likely to be the public facing marketing brands of Fintech, which provide the innovative services and technology the customers' crave.

In either case, the two new competitors will have fewer costs than traditional banks and be much more agile in delivering technical solutions. Banks conversely will see increased costs in their tech teams as well as compliance and security personnel for they will have to build, maintain and support the use of their banking APIs. The end result will likely be increased costs, which will be deferred to account holders in terms of creative fee structures and costs. Unfortunately, there is also the threat of unintended consequences whereby the PSD2 regulations will force the banks to increase their prices to offset their additional costs. Yet that also comes at a time when consumers will be able to shop around for their financial services creating a volatile market where the costs of compliance drives prices up, and culls the low priced affordable services leaving the low end customers with less rather than more choice.

All that said there will be unique opportunities for the traditional banks to collaborate and even partner with fintech companies and for each to take advantage of their mutual strengths. Some banks are already doing this through participating in sandbox environments, participation in fintech conferences, and through business acquisition.

The aims and the spirit of the PSD2 legislation, as envisaged by the European Parliament were to provide the customer with more control over their data and to enhance the consumer's security when conducting payments. Therefore the EBA (European Bank Association) were mandated to author the Regulation Technical Specifications for Strong Customer Authentication (SCA) report. This is an area of the PSD2 where the RTS takes a rather pragmatic approach to authentication of the customer during a transaction. For example to lessen the burden for two or three part authentication of transactions they have exempt payments under 30 euros, which is a major advance as it means cards are practical methods of payment once more for parking, or more importantly on commuter bases and trains were the authorisation process must be at a absolute maximum sub-second for these and other quick high-throughput unattended payment stations. However, for payment greater than that they now enforce two part authentication as a minimum. In theory that should benefit consumers by reducing fraud through making the whole process more cumbersome and awkward for both retailer and customer - but it will work.

The new RTS guidelines also sought to increase the standards of security, authentication and encryption and to provide a consent-based method for customers and banks alike to delegate permissions for TPP access to customer's accounts or bank services. Furthermore, PSD2 also ensures better accountability on surcharges for payments. The European Parliament has also vowed to improve the ease and security of EU payments online through non-EU affiliated vendors using currencies other than the euro and that significantly increases the territorial scope of the regulation to include payment transaction where one party is a EU resident or citizen an again this relates to greater consumer protection especially for online payments. In addition the increase in territorial scope also brings the non-EU tech companies that offer products and services in the EU under the PSD2 regulations, which for now includes Google, Facebook and Amazon amongst others of the technology world which will be keeping a close eye on all that potential customer data to feed their algorithms and boost their direct marketing advertising revenue. They may even see themselves as AISPs or a PISP in order to reduce the amount of fees they pay on processing credit cards.

Interestingly enough not everyone is convinced that this initiative will have the desired effect and it's not just the banks pushing this viewpoint. In fact, several FinTech firms have spoken out robustly about their concerns that the banks will not provide APIs that actually provide them with full customer access to the data. To that end they demand there must be a fall back contingency plan for times when the dedicated link provided by the bank should be unavailable or unacceptable and hence they are intending to carry on with screen-scraping the data for themselves. The fact that the European Council have seemingly taken their side and stepped back from banning screen-scraping altogether and are now allowing it in all but name is an indication that they also have doubt about the levels of cooperation and trust between parties. Furthermore, the EU council's perspective of PSD2 is that it revolutionises the payments industry and provides customer's access to their data which they can delegate to a third party which is their prerogative. However this is not as radical as might first be thought as consumers have been able to do this for years. Many FinTech firms have upon receiving customer consent, i.e. their online banking login credentials; been able to act as fully authorised delegates for their customers through mimicking them while accessing their online accounts. Therefore it has not been the ability to share that has held customers and FinTech back it has been the consumers' natural reticence in divulging their bank account passwords. What PSD2 allows is for customers and TPP to continue this practice but in a more secure manner through an API whereby the customer must still provide explicit consent but will not have to divulge their bank login credentials. Where customers will benefit is not just through stringent security but through the PSD2 aim to suppress surcharges and fees on payments. In addition, the customer should benefit from more open competition provided that is how it works out in practice. Opening up the bank's customer accounts through APIs has vast potential for creating fast efficient payment systems with potentially lower fees but will we also see a drop in service levels, performance and security?

What about PSD2 in the United States?

The PSD2 or Open Banking model cannot simply be replicated as a fintech solution into The United States. In the United States today, there is a thriving ecosystem of security-focused, third-party data sharing benefiting tens of millions of consumers, enabled by trusted intermediaries. Hence although the PSD2 stance on banning screen-scraping technologies may have been well intentioned it actually may have been premature. In The US for example FinTech firms such as Plaid is just one in a thriving ecosystem of Fintech firms that uses screen-scraping technology as an access method which is critical for enabling an ASIP style financial system. Therefore, there is not the same customer demand as their banking requirements have been satisfied through third party firms using screen-scraping techniques for a decade at least.

Another issue is that the demographics differ to the EU as the United States has a fragmented consumer banking landscape, compared to many other markets. The US has over 9,000 banks and credit unions, many of which have substantial customer bases, yet aren't large enough to have resources to introduce as API model. In comparison to two of the most eager proponents of open banking, the UK's Big 5 and Australia's Big 4 banks support an estimated 80+ percent of consumer bank accounts in each country.

However, in the US because there is a "long tail" of small and medium banks any effort to restrict data access methods such as screen-scraping would have consequences that would severely impact consumers as rather than increasing choice it would be more likely to restrict service offerings as smaller banks would struggle to implement and support appropriate APIs.

Still, with the scale of experimentation in Europe and Australia there is a replicable model to consider or at least learn from. After all there's much to learn from the approaches to financial data access unfolding internationally especially in the early adopter nations such as the UK and Australia. The U.S. should perhaps take the path where they heed PSD2's lessons and put consumers first while piecing together its own consolidated and regulated data sharing model. Given the costs involved and the additional regulatory compliance issues that the financial institutions that are already mired in a regulatory national patchwork of state and federal regulations would have to take onboard its unlikely they would be enthusiastic on such ambitions. Also, some of the world's largest financial powers are based in the US and given their influence and the power of lobbying it might be far-fetched to suggest that open banking will be the next financial experiment.

What can the US Banks do to avoid a PSD2 of their own?

The regulators in the US have been keeping a keen eye on the recent developments in Europe, and of especial interest is the open banking phenomenon. This sea change, which has largely been accelerated and thrust into prominence by the revised Payment Services Directive — known as PSD2 — requires European banks to share data with financial technology companies if their mutual customers request they do so. The regulation is based upon giving the customer more control over their data and by doing so it aims to stimulate competition. The motivation is that by giving fintech companies legitimate access to customer data - data that they have been collecting surreptitiously for years much to the chagrin of the banks - it will foster an era of innovation, remove much of the friction in payments and promote healthy competition.

There are signs U.S. regulators could take a similar approach. Last year, the Consumer Financial Protection Bureau signalled its intention for mandating that banks allow access to the sharing of financial data. But U.S. banks and FinTech firms have been working together albeit reluctantly for a decade or more as FinTech firms established a foothold in the financial services marketplace using the same covert techniques to gain access to their client's accounts, namely screen-scraping. The difference being that the US customers appear more acceptant of the practice and are more willing to delegate full permission to FinTech firms to access their accounts for the purpose of supplying a superior service and the banks seem to have accepted this. The banks have gone along with this symbiotic relationship perhaps cognizant of the fact that preventing these covert methods of access to the customer accounts is nigh on impossible both technically and legally. The FinTech firms are using the customer's login credentials and hence their explicit consent but even if they could stop the practice the banks fear the alternative is actually worse if it is an open API mandate. The worry is that an API mandate would require heavy investment in development, maintenance and support and also in onboarding and mentoring the FinTechs which shifts all the costs but none of the benefits onto the banks.

The US banks may be wise to resist the fate of the EU banks and avoid such a mandate because it could force them to share data with fintech companies to use in delivering in-demand payment services but lose out on capitalizing from those services. Currently the FinTech firms need the banks to provide their clients with online accounts for their services to work so having their customer accounts with banks that provide the online access to data works well for them and there is no incentive to either appropriate the customer from the bank or get them to move, in fact the opposite is more likely. As a result as long as the banks provide the online access to customer account data everyone is reasonably content.

How the US banks avoid such a regulatory experiment by the CFPB might sound counterintuitive but Banks need to share more data. Banks should start selectively sharing financial data with third-party companies now in order to reduce the demand for regulatory measures such as PSD2. Some banks are aware of this and have experimented with secure application programming interfaces API for example Citigroup and Capital One. This forward thinking and data-sharing strategy gives banks the option to give fintech companies a test environment where they can access non-real customer data on which to build apps and provides a collaborative laboratory for testing new products and services. This selective data-sharing model can help banks stay competitive by retaining the negotiating advantage with fintech firms.

It could also be argued that the model works in the consumers' and the regulators interests as banks are better equipped to safeguard sensitive personal information than nonbanks. In addition the data-share model provides the capability to vet participating fintech firm security without a full regulatory assessment but nonetheless measures the firm's security competence before the banks share any real customer data. Banks can even build informal standards for fintech security by sharing data with fintech businesses on the condition the fintech companies take pragmatic steps to validate the stringency of their cybersecurity measures.

Not all FinTech firms however embrace this model as many believe that the banks string them along take forever to make decisions if ever and sometimes even appropriate the shared ideas leaving the Fintech out in the cold.

There is also the real concern that the development of this business self-governing model could be hindered by a regulation like PSD2 that would force banks to deploy prescriptive technologies and standards while allowing FinTechs to easily access a consumer's identifiable information. As can already be seen from the introduction of the PSD2 regulatory approach the concepts of open banking may be attractive but the implementation in reality is fictitious and fraught with teething problems. For what was once thought to be legislation that hammered the banks and gave more than a helping hand to FinTech may in reality with the banning of screen-scraping be their death knell. Hence, the regulators may be wise to sit this one out and observe how the PSD2 unfolds before they rush into the US financial services market to fix something that isn't broken.

Chapter 3 – Regulatory Technical Standards – SCA

When authoring and proposing the legislation for the PSD2 the European Council produced the articles and legal recitals which layout the aims and motivations behind the extensions to the current directive. We have discussed at a high level the significant goals and key pillars of the PSD2 in the previous chapter. However as this book is predominantly aimed towards an audience with an interest in the technology that will be required in implementing the PSD2 aims and realising the EU's goals and motivations we must contemplate the key document that specifies the technical standards and mandates the requirements, which is the Regulatory Technical Standards – Strong Customer Authentication and Common Secure Communication (CSC). The RTS was drafted under Article 98 of the PSD2 by the European Banking Authority working alongside the European Central Bank (ECB).

In accordance with Article 98 of the revised Payment Services Directive (EU) 2015/2366 (PSD2),the EBA has developed working alongside the European Central Bank (ECB), draft regulatory technical standards (RTS) specifying the requirements of strong customer authentication (SCA) and secure communication standards (SCS), A major piece of this work has been identifying and rationalising the use-case that may be exempt from the application of SCA, In addition they have had to contemplate the requirements with which security measures have to comply in order to protect the confidentiality and the integrity of the payment service users' personalised security credentials, and the requirements for common and secure open standards of communication (CSC) while remaining technology and business neutral.

Defining the Players

In this chapter we will review the RTS and contemplate the requirements set out by the EBS and their justification for selection of any technical standards. However, first we have to clarify and define the players involved;

- Account Servicing Payment Service Providers (ASPSPs), - a bank

- Payment Initiation Service Providers (PISPs), - Payment processor

- Account Information Service Providers (AISPs), - Information Provider

- Payment Service User – (PSU) – Customer or User

- Payer, - the entity making the payment

- Payee – the beneficiary of the payment

- Payment service providers (PSPs). – The entity processing the payment

Introduction to the RTS

On August 12 2017, the EBA issued the long-awaited draft of the Regulatory Technical Standards (RTS) in the area of Strong Customer Authentication (SCA) and Common Secure Communication (CSC) Standards, which address the technical issues underlying the PSD2 Directive, implementing the comments and feedback that they had solicited and received from stakeholders regarding their previously published discussion paper, but also proposing new questions on issues still open.

The last mandate (Article 98) of PSD2 lays down that the European Bank Authority (EBA) shall develop the draft RTS addressed to Payment Service Providers (PSP) specifying:

a) [Set out the technical requirements for Strong Customer Authentication for electronic payments] the requirements of SCA when the payer accesses its payment account online, initiates an electronic payment transaction or carries out any action, through a remote channel, which may imply a risk of payment fraud or other abuses;

b) [Establish legal exemptions from payments that do no require Strong Customer Authentication] the exemptions from the application of Article 97 on SCA, based on the level of risk involved in the service provided; the amount, the recurrence of the transaction, or both; or the payment channel used for the execution of the transaction;

c) [Fstablish the security controls for ensuring Confidentiality an Integrity of customer data] the requirements with which security measures have to comply in order to protect the confidentiality and the integrity of the payment service users' (PSUs') personalised security credentials; and

d) [Establish the communications and security standards for the link between the banks and the TPPs] the requirements for common and secure open standards of communication for the purpose of identification, authentication, notification, and information, as well as for the implementation of security measures, between ASPSP1, PISPs, AISPs, payers, payees and other PSPs.

Thus the EBA in accordance with PSD2 article 98(2) has the following objectives:

a) ensuring an appropriate level of security for PSUs and PSPs, through the adoption of effective and risk-based requirements;

b) ensuring the safety of PSUs' funds and personal data;

c) securing and maintaining fair competition among all PSPs;

d) ensuring technology and business-model neutrality; and

e) allowing for the development of user-friendly, accessible and innovative means of payment.

When developing these particular RTS objectives, it soon became clear that the EBA had to make difficult trade-offs between at times conflicting or competing demands. For example, the objective of PSD2 to facilitate convenient and innovative payment services would suggest that the EBA should pitch the technical standards at a higher level, i.e. less detailed level, which would not place constraints on the industry and inadvertently stifle innovation. Hence, the EBA should encourage innovation that exploits technological advancements and responds to future security threats. However, this path may result in fragmentation where many diverse and incompatible industry solutions emerge across the EU, in particular for communication between the banks and the TPPs. This, in turn, could potentially lead to incompatible solutions being adopted across member states or other geographical or political lines, which would undermine PSD2's objective of harmonising the payment service legislation across the EAA. Harmonisation of legislation underpins the creation of a pan-European level-playing field which is necessary in creating a single digital market that integrates retail payments in the EU and facilitates competition across the EU.

The RTS on SCA and Secure Communications Standards

Bearing the above in mind the EBA set about drafting the Regulatory Technical Standards to address the following requirements of the PSD2 revision:

General Provisions

(1) *Payment services offered electronically should be carried out in a secure manner, adopting technologies able to guarantee the safe authentication of the user and to reduce, to the maximum extent possible, the risk of fraud.*

This is the basis for the underpinning the requirement that all electronic payment services require strong customer authentication or SCA and it is necessary to specify the requirements of the strong customer authentication that should be applied *each time a payer accesses its payment account online, initiates an electronic payment transaction or carries out any action through a remote channel which may imply a risk of payment fraud or other abuse, by requiring the generation of an authentication code which should be resistant against fraud.* The mechanisms deployed to deliver SCA should have the capability to monitor and detect fraudulent transactions especially in the case where a customers security credentials have been lost, stolen or misappropriated. Similarly the authentication methods used must ensure that the customer is who they claim to be and that they are providing genuine consent for the transfer of funds or for the access to their account information.

Article 1 Subject matter

 (a) apply the procedure of strong customer authentication in accordance with Article 97 of Directive (EU) 2015/2366;

(b) exempt the application of the security requirements of strong customer authentication, subject to specified and limited conditions based on the level of risk, the amount and the recurrence of the payment transaction and of the payment channel used for its execution;

(c) protect the confidentiality and the integrity of the payment service user's personalised security credentials;

(d) establish common and secure open standards for the communication between account servicing payment service providers, payment initiation service providers, account information service providers, payers, payees and other payment service providers in relation to the provision and use of payment services in application of Title IV of Directive (EU) 2015/2366.

Article 2 General authentication requirements

1. For the purpose of the implementation of the security measures referred to in points (a) and (b) of Article 1, payment service providers shall have transaction monitoring mechanisms in place that enable them to detect unauthorised or fraudulent payment transactions.

2. The transaction monitoring mechanisms shall be based on the analysis of payment transactions taking into account elements which are typical of the payment service user in the circumstances of a normal use by the payment service user of the personalised security credentials.

3. Payment service providers shall ensure that the transaction monitoring mechanisms takes into account, at a minimum, each of the following risk-based factors: lists of compromised or stolen authentication elements; the amount of each payment transaction; known fraud scenarios in the provision of payment services; signs of malware infection in any sessions of the authentication procedure.

4. Where payment service providers exempt the application of the security requirements of the strong customer authentication in accordance with Article 16, in addition to the requirements in paragraphs 1, 2 and 3, they shall ensure that the transaction monitoring mechanisms take into account, at a minimum, and on a real-time basis each of the following risk-based factors: the previous spending patterns of the individual payment service user; the payment transaction history of each of the payment service provider's payment service user; the location of the payer and of the payee at the time of the payment transaction providing the access device or the software is provided by the payment service provider; the abnormal behavioural payment patterns of the payment service user in relation to the payment transaction history; in case the access device or the software is provided by the payment service provider, a log of the use of the access device or the software provided to the payment service user and the abnormal use of the access device or the software.

(2) *As fraud methods are constantly changing, the requirements of strong customer authentication should allow for innovation in the technical solutions addressing the emergence of new threats to the security of electronic payments.*

Due to the rapidly changing security ecosystem it is a requirement that security and anti-fraud controls and measures are documented and are periodically assessed, and tested for relevance as well as being fit for purpose. To this end security controls should be assessed using a risk analysis based approach and there should be regular audits performed by qualified experts in the technology to ensure the measures are suitable to protect the confidentiality and integrity of the personal security credentials.

Article 3 Review of the security measures

1. The implementation of the security measures referred to in Article 1(1) shall be documented, periodically tested, evaluated and audited by internal or external independent and qualified auditors in accordance with the applicable audit framework of the payment service provider.

2. The period between the audit reviews referred to in paragraph 1 shall be determined taking into account the relevant accounting and statutory audit framework applicable to the payment service provider. Payment service providers that make use of the exemption under Article 16 shall perform the audit for the methodology, the model and the reported fraud rates at a minimum on a yearly basis.

Security Measures for the Application of Strong Customer Authentication

(3) *As electronic remote payment transactions are subject to a higher risk of fraud, it is necessary to introduce additional requirements for the strong customer authentication of such transactions, ensuring that the elements dynamically link the transaction to an amount and a payee specified by the payer when initiating the transaction.*

Electronic remote transactions (such as payments made over the internet or mobile phone) require an additional form of SCA, being the inclusion in SCA of elements which dynamically link the transaction to a specific amount and a specific payee. The concept of "dynamic linking" of an authorisation of a specific payment is new to PSD2 and represents another layer of authentication over and above that required by the Guidelines.

Article 5 Dynamic linking

1. Where payment service providers apply strong customer authentication in accordance with Article 97(2) of Directive (EU) 2015/2366, in addition to the requirements of Article 4, they shall adopt security measures that meet each of the following requirements: (a) the payer is made aware of the amount of the payment transaction and of the payee;

(b) the authentication code generated shall be specific to the amount of the payment transaction and the payee agreed to by the payer when initiating the transaction.

(c) the authentication code accepted by the payment service provider corresponds to the original specific

---

amount of the payment transaction and to the payee agreed to by the payer. Any change to the amount or the payee shall result in the invalidation of the authentication code generated.

(4) *Dynamic linking is possible through the generation of authentication codes which is subject to a set of strict security requirements. To remain technologically neutral these technical standards should not require a specific technology for the implementation of authentication codes.*

Dynamic-links can be protected by authorisation codes but technology-neutrality prevents prescribing a specific technology so the solution can be based upon any suitable cryptographic mechanisms, one-time-passwords or digital signatures so long as that they can deliver the required level of security and granularity of authorisation while dynamically linking a token/code to a specific payment transaction.

Article 5 Dynamic linking (2)

2. For the purpose of paragraph 1, payment service providers shall adopt security measures which ensure the confidentiality, authenticity and integrity of each of the following: (a) the amount of the transaction and the payee through all phases of authentication.

(b) the information displayed to the payer through all phases of authentication including generation, transmission and use of the authentication code.

(5) *It is necessary to define specific requirements for the situation where the final amount is not known at the moment the payer initiates an electronic remote payment transaction, in order to ensure that the strong customer authentication is specific to the maximum amount that the payer has given consent for*

In cases such as Hotel bills and car hire where the payee will block or reserve funds in advance it will be a requirement that the payer must agree the amount to be blocked and prior to the funds being blocked. In addition any blocked funds are to be released as soon as the final amount is known or at the very latest upon settlement of the bill.

Article 6 (3)

3. For the purpose of the requirement under point (b) in paragraph 1 and where payment service providers apply strong customer authentication in accordance with Article 97(2) of Directive (EU) 2015/2366 in relation to a card-based payment transaction for which the payer has given consent to the exact amount of the funds to be blocked pursuant to Article 75(1) of that Directive, the authentication code shall be specific to the amount that the payer has given consent to be blocked and agreed to by the payer when initiating the transaction.

---

(6) *In order to ensure the application of strong customer authentication, it is also necessary to require adequate security features for the elements of strong customer authentication*

The requirement is to define the required criteria used for establishing strong customer authentication. There should be always two out of three criteria established as Knowledge (something the customer knows, Possession (something the customer has, an Inherence (something the customer is biometrics) it is also required that the elements selected are independent and the compromise of one will not weaken or defeat the reliability of the others.

Article 6 Requirements of the elements categorised as knowledge

1. Payment service providers shall adopt measures mitigating the risk that the elements of strong customer authentication categorised as knowledge are uncovered by, or disclosed to, unauthorised parties.

    3.   The use by the payer of elements of strong customer authentication categorised as knowledge shall be subject to mitigation measures in order to prevent their disclosure to unauthorised parties.

Article 7 Requirements of the elements categorised as possession
1. Payment service providers shall adopt measures mitigating the risk that the elements of strong customer authentication categorised as possession are used by unauthorised parties.

2. The use by the payer of elements categorized as possession shall be subject to measures designed to prevent replication of the elements.

Article 8 Article Requirements of devices and software linked to elements categorised as inherence
1. Payment service providers shall adopt measures mitigating the risk that the authentication elements categorised as inherence and read by access devices and software provided to the payer are uncovered by unauthorised parties. At a minimum, the access devices and software shall ensure a very low probability of an

unauthorised party being authenticated as the payer.

2. The use by the payer of elements categorized as inherence shall be subject to measures ensuring that the devices and the software guarantee resistance against unauthorised use of the elements through access to the devices and the software.

Article 9 Independence of the elements

1. Payment service providers shall ensure that the use of the elements of strong customer authentication referred to in Articles 6, 7 and 8 shall be subject to measures in terms of technology, algorithms and parameters, which ensure that the breach of one of the elements does not compromise the reliability of the other elements.

2. Where any of the elements of strong customer authentication or the authentication code is used through a multi-purpose device including mobile phones and tablets, payment service providers shall adopt security measures to mitigate the risk resulting from the multi-purpose device being compromised.

3. For the purposes of paragraph 2, the mitigating measures shall include each of the following: (a) the use of separated secure execution environments through the software installed inside the multi-purpose device;

(b) mechanisms to ensure that the software or device has not been altered by the payer or by a third party or mechanisms to mitigate the consequences of such alteration where this has taken place.

Exemptions from Strong Customer Authentication

(7) *In order to allow the development of user-friendly and accessible means of payment for low-risk payments, it is important to allow for some exemptions to the principle of SCA*

Payments hat are considered exemptions to the SCA must be clearly and unambiguously defined.

Article 13 Trusted beneficiaries and recurring transactions

1. Subject to paragraph 2 of this Article and to compliance with the requirements laid down in paragraphs 1, 2 and 3 of Article 2, payment service providers are exempted from the application of strong customer authentication in each of the following situations: (a) the payer initiates a payment transaction where the payee is included in a list of trusted beneficiaries previously created or confirmed by the payer through its account servicing payment service provider;
(b) the payer initiates a series of payment transactions with the same amount and the same payee.

2. For the purpose of points (a) and (b) of paragraph 1 the following cases do not constitute an exemption: (a) In relation to point (a) of paragraph 1, the payer or the payer's payment service provider, provided that the payer gave its consent, creates, confirms or subsequently amends, the list of trusted beneficiaries.
(b) In relation to point (b) of paragraph 1, the payer initiates the series of payment transactions for the first time, or subsequently amends the series of payments.

Article 14 Payments to self
Subject to compliance with the requirements laid down in paragraphs 1, 2 and 3 of Article 2, payment service providers are exempted from the application of strong customer authentication where the payer initiates a credit transfer where the payer and the payee are the same natural or legal person and both payment accounts are held by the same account servicing payment service provider.

> **Article 12 Transport and parking fares**
> Subject to compliance with the requirements laid down in paragraphs 1, 2 and 3 of Article 2, payment service providers are exempted from the application of strong customer authentication where the payer initiates an electronic payment transaction at an unattended payment terminal for the purpose of paying a transport or parking fare.

(8) *Exemptions based on low-value contactless payments, which also take into account a maximum number of consecutive transactions or a certain fixed maximum value of consecutive transactions without SCA, allow the development of user friendly and low risk payment services and should be included in these technical standards.*

Exemptions to SCA should be available for low risk transactions such as payment at low value remote payment terminals such as parking or transport, payments to self, recurring regular payments to the same beneficiary and the same value.

> **Article 11 Contactless payments at point of sale**
> Subject to compliance with the requirements laid down in paragraphs 1, 2 and 3 of Article 2, payment service providers are exempted from the application of strong customer authentication where the payer initiates a contactless electronic payment transaction provided that both the following conditions are met:
> (a) the individual amount of the contactless electronic payment transaction does not exceed EUR 50;
> (b) the cumulative amount, or the number, of previous contactless electronic payment transactions initiated via the payment instrument offering a contactless functionality since the last application of strong customer authentication does not, respectively, exceed EUR 150 or 5 consecutive

individual payment transactions.

(9) *To improve confidence in transactions over the internet, these technical standards should strike a proper balance between the interest in enhanced security in remote payments and needs of user-friendliness and accessibility.*

In order to meet these requirements minimum payment amounts must be set for online purchases where SCA is exempt when purchasing good or services of low value

Article 15 Low-value transaction
Subject to compliance with the requirements laid down in paragraphs 1, 2 and 3 of Article 2, payment service providers are exempted from the application of strong customer authentication, where the payer initiates a remote electronic payment transaction provided that both the following conditions are met:
(a) the amount of the remote electronic payment transaction does not exceed EUR 30;

(b) the cumulative amount, or the number, of previous remote electronic payment transactions initiated by the payer since the last application of strong customer authentication does not, respectively, exceed EUR 100 or 5 consecutive individual remote electronic payment transactions.

(10) *In the case of real-time transaction risk analysis that categorise a payment transaction as low risk, it is also appropriate to introduce an exemption,*

It is a requirement that technical standards should set at the maximum value of such risk based exemption in a conservative manner ensuring a very low corresponding fraud rate, also by comparison to the fraud rates of all the payment transactions of the payment service provider, including those authenticated through strong customer authentication, within a certain period of time and on a rolling basis.

Article 16 Transaction risk analysis

1. Subject to compliance with the requirements laid down in Article 2 and to paragraph 2 of this Article, payment service providers are exempted from the application of strong customer authentication, where the payer initiates a remote electronic

2. For the purposes of paragraph 1 all the following conditions shall apply: (a) the amount of the electronic payment transaction does not exceed the Exemption Threshold Value ('ETV') specified in the following table for 'remote card-based payments' and 'credit transfers' respectively, corresponding to the payment service provider's fraud rate for such payment services calculated in accordance with point (d) of this paragraph and up to a maximum value of EUR 500;

Reference Fraud Rate (%) for:		
ETV	*Remote card-based payments*	*Credit transfers*
EUR 500	*0.01*	*0.005*
EUR 250	*0.06*	*0.01*
EUR 100	*0.13*	*0.015*

---

(11) *With the aim of considering new historical evidence on the fraud rates of electronic payment transactions, it is necessary that payment service providers regularly monitor and make available to competent authorities, upon their request, for each payment instrument, the value of unauthorised payment transactions and the observed fraud rates for all their payment transactions, whether authenticated through strong customer authentication or executed under a relevant exemption.*

It is a requirement that in the case of an exemption due to transaction risk analysis that the fraud levels must be continually assessed and where new information leads to a revaluation of the risk level thresholds that would require strong customer authentication the EBA should update the RTS.

Article 16 Transaction risk analysis (e-g)
(e) the calculation of the fraud rate and resulting figures shall be assessed by the audit review referred to in Article 3, ensuring that they are complete and accurate;

(f) the methodology and the model, if any, used by the payment service provider to calculate the fraud rates, as well as the fraud rates themselves shall be adequately documented and made fully available to competent authorities upon their request;

(g) the payment service provider has notified the competent authorities of its intention to make use of the transaction risk analysis exemption in accordance with this Article.

Article 17 Monitoring
1. Payment service providers that make use of the exemptions laid down in this Chapter shall record and monitor the following data for each payment instrument, with a breakdown for remote and non-remote payment

---

transactions, at least on a quarterly basis (90 days): (a) the total value of unauthorised payment transactions in accordance with Article 64(2) of Directive (EU) 2015/2366, the total value of all payment transactions and the resulting fraud rate, including a breakdown of payment transactions initiated through strong customer authentication and under the exemptions;

(b) the average transaction value, including a breakdown of payment transactions initiated through strong customer authentication and under the exemptions;

(c) the number of payment transactions where any of the exemptions was applied and their percentage in respect of the total number of payment transactions.

2. Payment service providers shall make the results of the monitoring in accordance with paragraph 1 available to competent authorities upon their request.

Confidentiality and Integrity of the PSU's Personalised Security Credentials

(12) *The measures that protect the confidentiality and integrity of personalised security credentials, as well as authentication devices and software, should limit the risks relating to fraud through unauthorised use of payment instruments and unauthorised access to payment accounts.*

The requirement to create and deliver securely the customers security credentials and have secure mechanisms in place for renewal or deactivation of the credentials

Article 19 General requirements
1. Payment service providers shall ensure the

confidentiality and integrity of the personalised security credentials of the payment service user, including authentication codes, during all phases of authentication including display, transmission and storage.

2. For the purpose of paragraph 1, payment service providers shall ensure that each of the following requirements is met: (a) personalised security credentials are masked when displayed and not readable in their full extent when input by the payment service user during the authentication;

(b) personalised security credentials in data format, as well as cryptographic materials related to the encryption of the personalised security credentials are not stored in Plaintext;

(c) secret cryptographic material is protected from unauthorised disclosure.

3. Payment service providers shall fully document the process related to the management of cryptographic material used to encrypt or otherwise render unreadable the personalised security credentials.

4. Payment service providers shall ensure that the processing and routing of personalised security credentials and of the authentication codes generated in accordance with Chapter 2 take place in secure environments in accordance with strong and widely recognised industry standards.

Article 20 Creation and transmission of credentials

Payment service providers shall ensure that the creation of personalised security credentials is performed in a secure environment. Payment service providers shall mitigate the risks of unauthorised use of the personalised security credentials and of the authentication devices and software due to their loss, theft or copying before their delivery to the payer.

Article 21 Association with the payment service user

1. Payment service providers shall ensure that only the payment service user is associated with the personalised

security credentials, with the authentication devices and the software in a secure manner.

2. For the purpose of paragraph 1, payment service providers shall ensure that each of the following requirements is met:

(a) the association of the payment service user's identity with personalised security credentials, authentication devices and software is carried out in secure environments. In particular, the association shall be carried out in environments under the payment service provider's responsibility and taking into account risks associated with devices and underlying components used during the association process that are not under the responsibility of the payment service provider. The environments under the payment service provider's responsibility include, but are not limited to the payment service provider's premises, the internet environment provided by the payment service provider or in other similar secure websites and its automated teller machine services;

(b) the association via a remote channel of the payment service user's identity with the personalised security credentials and with authentication devices or software shall be performed using strong customer authentication.

Article 22 Delivery of credentials, authentication devices and software

1. Payment service providers shall ensure that the delivery of personalised security credentials, authentication devices and software to the payment service user is carried out in a secure manner designed to address the risks related to their unauthorised use due to their loss, theft or copying.

2. For the purpose of paragraph 1, payment service providers shall at least apply each of the following measures: (a) effective and secure delivery mechanisms ensuring that the personalised security credentials, authentication devices and software are delivered to the legitimate payment service user associated with the credentials, the authentication devices and the software provided by the payment service provider;

(b) mechanisms that allow the payment service provider to verify the authenticity of the authentication software delivered to the payment services user via the internet;

(c) arrangements ensuring that, where the delivery of

personalised security credentials is executed outside the premises of the payment service provider or through a remote channel:

(i) no unauthorised party can obtain more than one feature of the personalised security credentials, the authentication devices or software when delivered through the same channel;

(ii) the delivered personalised security credentials, authentication devices or software require activation before usage;

(d) arrangements ensuring that, in cases where the personalised security credentials, the authentication devices or software have to be activated before their first use, the activation shall take place in a secure environment in accordance with the association procedures referred to in Article 21.

Article 23 Renewal of personalised security credentials
Payment service providers shall ensure that the renewal or re-activation of personalised security credentials follows the procedures of creation, association and delivery of the credentials and of the authentication devices in accordance with Articles 20, 21 and 22.

Article 24 Destruction, deactivation and revocation
Payment service providers shall ensure that they have effective processes in place to apply each of the following security measures:

(a) the secure destruction, deactivation or revocation of the personalised security credentials, authentication devices and software;

(b) where the payment service provider distributes reusable authentication devices and software, the secure re-use of a device or software is established, documented and implemented before making it available to another payment services user;

(c) the deactivation or revocation of information related to personalised security credentials stored in the payment service provider's systems and databases and, where relevant, in public repositories.

Common and Secure Open Standards of Communication

(13) *In order to ensure effective and secure communication between the relevant actors in the context of account information services, payment initiation services and confirmation on the availability of funds, it is necessary to specify the requirements of common and secure open standards of communication to be met by all relevant payment service providers.*

Article 25 Requirements for identification

1. Payment service providers shall ensure secure identification when communicating between the payer's device and the payee's acceptance devices for electronic payments, including but not limited to payment terminals.

2. Payment service providers shall ensure that the risks against misdirection of communication to unauthorised parties in mobile applications and other payment services users' interfaces offering electronic payment services are effectively mitigated.

Article 26 Traceability

1. Payment service providers shall have processes in place which ensure that all payment transactions and other interactions with the payment services user, with other payment service providers and with other entities, including merchants, in the context of the provision of the payment service are traceable, ensuring knowledge ex-post of all events relevant to the electronic transaction in all the various stages.

2. For the purpose of paragraph 1, payment service providers shall ensure that any communication session established with the payment services user, other payment service providers and other entities, including merchants, relies on each of the following: (a) a unique identifier of the session;

(b) security mechanisms for the detailed logging of the

transaction, including transaction number, timestamps and all relevant transaction data;

(c) timestamps which shall be based on a unified time-reference system and which shall be synchronised according to an official time signal.

(14) *Each account servicing payment service provider with payment accounts that are accessible online should offer at least one interface enabling secure communication*

The interface should enable the TPP to provide their identity to the bank. It should also allow the TPP to rely on the authentication procedures provided by the bank to the customer.

Article 27 Communication interface

1. Account servicing payment service providers that offer to a payer a payment account that is accessible online shall have in place at least one interface which meets each of the following requirements: (a) account information service providers, payment initiation service providers and payment service providers issuing card-based payment instruments can identify themselves towards the account servicing payment service provider;

(b) account information service providers can communicate securely to request and receive information on one or more designated payment accounts and associated payment transactions;

(c) payment initiation service providers can communicate securely to initiate a payment order from the payer's payment account and receive information on the initiation and the execution of payment transactions.

2. Account servicing payment service providers shall establish the interface(s) referred to in paragraph 1 by means of a dedicated interface or by allowing use by the payment service providers referred to in points (a) to (c) of paragraph 1 of the interface used for authentication and

communication with the account servicing payment service provider's payment services users.

3. For the purposes of authentication of the payment service user, the interfaces referred to in paragraph 1 shall allow account information service providers and payment initiation service providers to rely on the authentication procedures provided by the account servicing payment service provider to the payment service user. In particular the interface shall meet all of the following requirements:

(a) a payment initiation service provider or an account information service provider shall be able to instruct the account servicing payment service provider to start the authentication;

(b) communication sessions between the account servicing payment service provider, the account information service provider, the payment initiation service provider and the payment service user(s) shall be established and maintained throughout the authentication; and

(c) the integrity and confidentiality of the personalised security credentials and of authentication codes transmitted by or through the payment initiation service provider or the account information service provider shall be ensured.

4. Account servicing payment service providers shall ensure that their interface(s) follows standards of communication which are issued by international or European standardisation organisations. Account servicing payment service providers shall also ensure that the technical specification of the interface is documented and, as a minimum, available, at no charge, upon request by authorised payment initiation service providers, account information service providers and payment service providers issuing card-based payment instruments or payment service providers that have applied with their competent authorities for the relevant authorisation. This documentation shall specify a set of routines, protocols, and tools needed by payment initiation service providers, account information service providers and payment service providers issuing card-based payment instruments for allowing their software and applications to interoperate with the systems of the account servicing payment service providers. Account servicing payment service providers shall make the summary of the documentation publicly available on their website.

5. In addition to paragraph 4, account servicing payment service providers shall ensure that, except for emergency situations, any change to the technical specification of their interface is made available to authorised payment initiation service providers, account information service providers and payment service providers issuing card-based payment instruments (or payment service providers that have applied with their competent authorities for the relevant authorisation) in advance as soon as possible and not less than 3 months before the change is implemented. Payment service providers shall document emergency situations where changes were implemented and make the documentation available to competent authorities on request.

6. Account servicing payment service providers shall make available a testing facility, including support, for connection and functional testing by authorised payment initiation service providers, payment service providers issuing card-based payment instruments and account information service providers, or payment service providers that have applied for the relevant authorisation, to test their software and applications used for offering a payment service to users. No sensitive information shall be shared through the testing facility.

Article 28 Obligations for dedicated interface
1. Subject to compliance with Article 27, account servicing payment service providers that have put in place a dedicated interface in accordance with Article 27(2), shall ensure that the dedicated interface offers the same level of availability and performance, including support, as well as the same level of contingency measures, as the interface made available to the payment service user for directly accessing its payment account online.

2. For the purpose of paragraph 1, the following requirements shall apply: (a) account servicing payment service providers shall monitor the availability and performance of the dedicated interface and make the resulting statistics available to the competent authorities upon their request;

(b) where the dedicated interface does not operate at the same level of availability and performance as the interface made available to the account servicing payment service provider's payment service user for when accessing its payment account online, the account servicing payment service provider shall report it to the competent authorities, shall restore the level of service for the dedicated interface referred to in point (b) without undue delay and shall take any action that may be necessary to avoid its reoccurrence. The report shall include the causes of the deficiency and the measures adopted to reestablish the required level of service;

(c) payment service providers making use of the dedicated interface offered by the account servicing payment service provider after reporting to the account servicing payment service provider may also report to the national competent authority any deficiency in the level of availability and performance required of the dedicated interface.

3. Account servicing payment service providers shall also ensure that the dedicated interface uses ISO 20022 elements, components or approved message definitions, for financial messaging.

4. Account servicing payment service providers shall include, in the design of the dedicated interface, a strategy and plans for contingency measures in the event of an unplanned unavailability of the interface and systems breakdown. The strategy shall include communication plans to inform payment service providers making use of the dedicated interface in case of breakdown, measures to bring the system back to business as usual and a description of alternative options payment service providers may make use of during the unplanned downtime.

(15) *In order to allow account information service providers, payment initiation service providers, and payment service providers issuing card-based payment instruments to develop their technical solutions, the technical specification of the interface should be adequately documented and made publicly available.*

An additional requirement is, the bank or ASPSP should offer a facility enabling the payment service providers to test the technical solutions and to ensure the interoperability of different technological communication solutions, the interface should use standards of communication which are developed by international or European standardisation organisations. To ensure technology and business-model neutrality, the account servicing payment service providers should be free to decide whether the interface they offer should be dedicated to the communication with TPP, or to allow use of the interface for it own customers online access

(16) *Where access to payment accounts is offered via a dedicated interface, to ensure the right of payment service users to make use of payment initiation service providers and of services enabling access to account information,*

It is required that the dedicated interface has the same levels of service and information levels as the interface provided to the banks online customers

(17) *In order to safeguard the confidentiality and the integrity of data, it is necessary to ensure the security of communication sessions between the ASPSP and the TPPs*

Securing the dedicated connection between the bank and the TPP is a requirement further it is particular necessary to require that secure encryption is applied between the TPPs and banks when exchanging data.

Article 30 Security of communication session

1. Account servicing payment service providers, payment service providers issuing card-based payment instruments, account information service providers and payment initiation service providers shall ensure that, when exchanging data via the internet, secure encryption is applied between the communicating parties throughout the respective communication session in order to safeguard the confidentiality and the integrity of the data, using strong and widely recognised encryption techniques.

2. Payment service providers issuing card-based payment instruments, account information service providers and payment initiation service providers shall keep the access sessions offered by account servicing payment service providers as short as possible and they shall actively terminate the session with the relevant account servicing payment service provider as soon as the requested action has been completed.

3. When maintaining parallel network sessions with the account servicing payment service provider, account information service providers and payment initiation service providers shall ensure that those sessions are securely linked to relevant sessions established with the payment service user(s) in order to prevent the possibility that any message or information communicated between them could be misrouted.

4. Account information service providers, payment initiation service providers and payment service providers issuing card-based payment instruments with the account servicing payment service provider shall contain unambiguous reference to each of the following items: (a) the payment service user or users and the corresponding communication session in order to distinguish several requests from the same payment service user or users;

(b) for payment initiation services, the uniquely identified payment transaction initiated;

(c) for confirmation on the availability of funds, the uniquely identified request related to the amount necessary for the execution of the card-based payment transaction.

5. Account information service providers, payment initiation service providers and payment service providers

issuing card-based payment instruments shall ensure that where they communicate personalised security credentials and authentication codes, these are not readable by any staff at any time. In case of loss of confidentiality of personalised security credentials under their sphere of competence, account information service providers, payment initiation service providers issuing card-based payment instruments and payment initiation service providers shall inform without undue delay the payment services user associated with them and the issuer of the personalised security credentials.

Article 29 Certificates

1. For the purpose of identification, as referred to in point (a) of Article 21(1), payment service providers shall rely on qualified certificates for electronic seals as defined in Article 3(30) of Regulation (EU) No 910/20144 or for website authentication as defined in Article 3(39) of that Regulation.

2. For the purpose of this Regulation, the registration number as referred to in the official records in accordance Annex III (C) of Regulation (EU) No 910/2014 shall be the authorisation number of the payment service provider issuing card-based payment instruments the account information service providers and payment initiation service providers, including account servicing payment service providers providing such services, available in the public register of the home Member State pursuant to Article 14 of Directive (EU) 2015/2366 or resulting from the notifications of every authorisation granted under Article 8 of Directive 2013/36/EU5 in accordance with Article 20 of that Directive.

3. For the purposes of this Regulation, qualified certificates for electronic seals or for website authentication referred to in paragraph 1 of this Article shall include in English additional specific attributes in relation to each of the following: (a) the role of the payment service provider, which maybe one or more of the following: an account servicing payment service provider; a payment initiation service provider; an account information service provider; a payment service provider issuing card-based payment instruments.

(18) *In accordance to Articles 65, 66 and 67 Directive (EU) 2015/2366, payment initiation service providers, payment service providers issuing card-based payment instruments and account information service providers will only seek and obtain the necessary and essential information from the account servicing payment service provider for the provision of a given payment service and only with the consent of the payment service user.*

Consent may be given individually for each request of information or for each payment to be initiated or for account information service providers, as a general mandate for designated payment accounts and associated payment transactions as established in the contractual agreement with the payment service user. Payment initiation service providers and account information service providers shall only request information on behalf of the payment service user with his/her consent.

Addressing the RTS requirements

Possibly the most notable standout article (27) introduced by the RTS draft is that in order not to constrain the future technological progress the EBA have determined that a centrally and shared single standard for the dialogue between the ASPSP, PISP and AISP will not be defined. In other words they will not prescribe an interface standard to be used between banks and the TPP.

Each ASPSP (Bank) will therefore be allowed to make their own appropriate communication interfaces available which the RTS recommends (but do not mandate in the interest of technical-neutrality) the adoption of the ISO 20022 messaging standard. Nevertheless, the interface or dedicated channel of choice must be exhaustively documented on the ASPSP (banks) website, and consequently it is then up to the PISP and AISP to customise their own applications for compatability with the supplied communications channel with the specific ASPSP. What this means in layman's terms is that the EBA are not going to set a standard open API specification, which has been what all the PSD2 hype has been around, instead they are going to leave it to the banks to decide on an individual basis how they will connect to an AISP or a PISP.

Initially this seems like a step back but the rationale for the EBA's decision is that prescribing, maintaining and enforcing a standard on the nascent process are more likely to stifle innovation rather than encourage it. Therefore the EBA feels it is wiser to leave the choice of interconnectivity up to the banks. Hence, with the technical specification of prescriptive solutions and technologies neatly sidestepped the EBA main contribution to the draft, are high level and are related to the discussion and definition of interfaces between ASPSP, PISP and AISP, and these can be summarised as follows:

Communication Interfaces

The EBA leaves the choice of the technical solution to the banks and the only requirement being the designs meet the goals of the RTS but it encourages the adoption of the ISO 20022 standard in the management and definition of interfaces, hence the ASPSP (bank) must:

1) make interfaces available that enable identification, authentication and implementation of the activities for AISP, PISP and for card-based payment services;

2) make free comprehensive technical documentation available on their websites, in order to allow the integration with TPP systems;

3) make infrastructures and support available to allow the test end to end of the TPP applications;

4) advertise any technical modification at least 3 months in advance of the production start.

In this regard, the RTS, seem to allude to some form of a "governing entity" responsible for supervising the design, development, maintenance and third party support of an interface as the standard form of communication. This governing entity shall ensure that service levels are maintained and information levels meet expectations. This is an important issue that needed clarification as several TPPs were concerned regarding the levels of commitment and support that they could expect to receive from the banks. As a result the RTS requires that the banks supply the same standard of service and information to the TPP as they do to their online customers. In addition there are requirements to the ongoing support levels such as;

Service levels - Service levels and related support shall be warranted as services directly provided by ASPSP to its customers (the AISP, PISP and en-users of their services) In other words the banks must provide on-going support to the AISP and PISP as a warranted service. There must also be in place similar contingency plans for restoration of service in the case of a service outage and a comparable and appropriate backup solution made available.

Information Set - The interfaces for PISP and AISP should ensure the same level of information is available to the TPP services directly via the interconnection channel as is provided to the ASPSP customers, with the exception of sensitive payment data. With respect to sensitive payment data, which has to be properly identified, categorised and excluded from the disclosure requirement traded to the TPP. What this means is that any information that can be accessed by the customer using an online service such as a website or portal must be made available through the communication channel the bank supplies. The exception being that if the bank identifies some payment data to be 'sensitive payment data' then it must be withheld from being sent to the TPP.

AISP Applications

The RTS also specifies that AISP (account information service providers, and data aggregators) applications must:

i. allow users to limit their queries according to the explicitly provided consensus;

ii. limit information requests not directly placed by the users to a maximum of four per day.

What these conditions relate to are i) the AISP must only request information or access to information where they have the explicit consent of the customer. The second condition ii) allows AISP systems to request or access data that is not directly as a result of a customer initiated action, but which they have consent, perhaps for the purposes of supporting the application, updating balances, reporting or maintenance but these independent queries are limited to 4 a day (it was only 2 in the draft).

ISO 20022

The EBA, though not explicitly saying so, also suggests the adoption of communication standards developed by European or International bodies and of ISO 20022 in particular. In the earlier draft the ISO 20022 was 'mandated in use' now it has been relegated to 'encouraged in use'. This is to remain consistent with the EBA's stance on he RTS being technology-neutral and business-neutral these terms appear regularly within the recitals.

The reasons why the EBA are keen to encourage the use of the ISO 20022 standard is for its capabilities with regards the conveyance of formal financial business messages. The standard is often used by financial institutions that want to streamline their communication infrastructure and associated costs by opting for a single, common "language" for all financial communications. By using a compatible financial standard protocol throughout will enable financial institutions to readily exchange communications regardless of the business domain, the communication network and the counterparty (other financial institutions, clients, suppliers and market infrastructures). ISO 20022 is targeted at these standards initiatives that are generally driven by communities of financial developers looking for more cost-effective communications to support specific financial business processes with a desire to increase interoperability with other existing systems and protocols.

What is ISO 20022?

ISO 20022 – Is a universal financial industry message scheme, which is the international standard that defines the ISO platform for the development of financial message standards. Its business modelling approach allows users and developers to represent financial business processes and underlying transactions in a formal but syntax-independent notation.

These business transaction models are the "real" business standards. They can be converted into physical messages in the desired syntax. At the time ISO 20022 was developed, XML (eXtensible Mark-up Language) was the preferred syntax for e-communication. Therefore, the first edition of ISO 20022, published in December 2004, proposed a standardized XML-based syntax for messages. The second edition of the standard, published in May 2013, included the possibility to use ASN.1 as well.

The standard ISO 20022 encourages the use of both XML (eXtensible Markup Language) and ASN.1 (Abstract Syntax Notation One) for the definition of data structures at a high level. This scenario, which is similar to what was implemented for EU SEPA systems, will lead to the adoption of compatible and structured data models for XS2A systems (Access To account) in the PSD2 perimeter. The data models are structured in three different levels:

Process Level - description of the operational processes and the related information used (facilitates the identification of the information contained in the communication between the parties)

Logical Level - definition of the set of expected data

Physical Level - physical representation of the messages defined in the logic level, based on a specific syntax and a certain standard message

The real power of the ISO 20022 however is the presence of a "dictionary" which contains the semantic description of the objects provided by the data model. Currently, there are around 700 financial business components and more than 300 "message definitions". These are standard financial business processes, rules and definitions, which makes it feasible to build interoperable applications using standard business logic. It also allows developers to carry out comparisons and find similarities on business models and concepts described in defined data patterns (although differently structured). This subsequently allows for mutual mapping with other standards used in the financial world which greatly simplifies the integration of systems, business processes and other financial standards. This type of mapping for example is evident with the big three financial payment services, Faster Payments, BACS and CHAPS are all working on or publishing documents that "map" ISO 20022 message interfaces to their native scheme interfaces. Similarly, MT103 and ISO15022 are used in swift and ISO 8583 is used for transactions with credit and debit cards.

Security

Security with regards the PSD2 environment will be discussed at length in a later chapter, however at this point we will only address the security points brought up in the final RTS report. Below are the main points of attention highlighted in the RTS, in relation to security issues:

The identification of TPP

The EBA aims to strengthen the security and confidence of consumers performing payment transactions using the electronic payment systems through strong customer authentication amongst other measures. Thus, as banks will now be required to securely communicate via dedicated channels with third parties it becomes necessary to mutually identify the authorised and licensed players involved, (ASPSP, AISP and PISP) which must take place through the use of trusted certificates. The draft RTS pondered over using industry standard identity authentication certificates (X.509) or to use e-IDAS and it appears that they have come down firmly on the side of the EU e-IDAS initiative – despite there not being at the time any authorised e-IDAS certificate authorities in existence. By utilising digital certified (notarised) electronic identities such as e-IDAS allows the generation of a list of authorised payment service providers. Underlying this principle would be the construction of a Public Key Infrastructure (PKI) as this would allow all the authorised (licensed) TTP to interact with around the 4,000 banks across the EU and provide an adequate level of safety. A prerequisite would be the establishment of root certification authority the e-IDAS, which would be the root of trust for all certificates it issued to the licensed ASIP and PISP.

e-IDAS

The eIDAS Regulation adopted on 23 July 2014 provides a predictable regulatory environment to enable secure and seamless electronic interactions between businesses, citizens and public authorities.

In this regard, the eIDAS Regulation:

- ensures that people and businesses can use their own national electronic identification schemes (eIDs) to access public services in other EU countries where eIDs are available.

- creates an European internal market for electronic trust services – namely electronic signatures, electronic seals, time stamp, electronic delivery service and website authentication – by ensuring that they will work across borders and have the same legal status as traditional paper based processes.

The eIDAS regulation complements the additional functionality which is brought in by the PSD2. AISPs and PISPs needs to interface with existing core banking systems in order to access relevant customer data and provide their services. Hence there is a need for a system such as eIDAS, which can meet the stringent PSD2 obligations regarding security, authentication, and document verification.

The way e-IDAS complements PSD2 is that it has certified members that have notarised eIDs (electronic IDs) which were issued by their host nation. These eIDs have been notarised against legal identity documents such as a passport or a driver's license, which provides the "high" level of assurance. These eIDs can be used across the EU to open a bank account digitally in any member country. The eIDAS regulation provides standardization for this process across the entire EU bloc. Therefore, combining the strengths and high levels of assurance supplied by e-IDAS with the PSD2 identification, authorisation and access management requirements makes for a good match.

As per the EBA, *"the qualified trust services provided by qualified trust service providers under eIDAS can also be of relevance for the identification between the AIS or PIS providers with the Account Servicing Payment Service Providers (ASPSPs), as well as for ensuring the integrity and correctness of the origin of the data transmitted between AIS or PIS providers and the ASPSPs."*

What this translates to in layman's terms is that the eID provided through e-IDAS can provide the identification required between the TPP and the banks as well as providing assurances as to the trustworthiness of the origin of the communication.

Furthermore, the qualified electronic signature (eID) will have the same legal relevance as a wet signature and a similar treatment is provided for electronic seals which can help with establishing the integrity and verifying the origin of the data as well.

Providing Confidentiality, Integrity, Availability and Authenticity

When opening up customers payment account details to TPP the protection of sensitive payment data and personal information of the users becomes paramount. The players will have to adopt technological solutions that guarantee confidentiality, authenticity and integrity of the data that are consistent with the principles of industry best practices for their technical solutions. Initially the requirement was to be consistent with the ISO 27001 standard but even that was removed as it conflicted with the goals of technology-neutrality.

ISO 27001

ISO 27001 (formally known as ISO/IEC 27001:2005) is a specification for an information security management system (ISMS). An ISMS is a framework and an ISO 27001 can be a structure of policies and procedures that includes all legal, physical and technical controls involved in an organisation's information risk management processes.

Accordingly, ISO 27001 was developed to "provide a model for establishing, implementing, operating, reviewing, maintaining and improving an information security management system."

Although not mandatory any more as any reference to ISO 27001 has since been removed from the draft RTS as some PSPs had never previously been required to conform to the security standard and once more it was viewed as a breach of technology-neutrality. Nevertheless it is still mandatory for the communicating parties to conform to the principles of confidentiality, authenticity and integrity of the data though to what standard is unclear. Further they must ensure this through widely recognised cryptographic techniques for data protection and for solutions enabling Dynamic Linking. This additional security control requires the protection of the "dynamic link" of the payment transaction to a specific amount and beneficiary. It is also expected that ASPSPs implement mechanisms to prevent, detect and block fraudulent transactions before the payment authorisation by the PISP. The practice today is widespread for card payments and the goal is to extend the application even to without-card payments. (3DSecure)

What is Dynamic-Linking?

The idea behind dynamic-linking is that the customer (payer) authorisation of the transaction should generate a token (an authorisation code) which is associated with that specific payment to a given specified criteria namely the payee and amount. Should for whatever reasons either the payee or the amount change then the authorisation will be void. This direct association between the token i.e. the authorisation and the specific payment is termed a dynamic link and as it is the de facto authorisation code for the payment it is required that it is encrypted.

In order to dynamically link the transaction, the draft RTS states the following requirements must be met:

- the payer must be made aware at all times of the amount of the transaction and of the payee;
- the authentication code must be specific to the amount of the transaction and the payee;
- the underlying technology must ensure the confidentiality, authenticity and integrity of: (a) the amount of the transaction and of the payee; and (b) information displayed to the payer through all phases of the authentication procedure (the EBA hasn't specified the nature of this "information");
- the authentication code must change with any change to the amount or payee; and
- the channel, device or mobile application through which the information linking the transaction to a specific amount and payee is displayed must be independent or segregated from the channel, device or mobile application used for initiating the electronic payment transaction.

Use of certificates & security controls

The RTS also contemplates where digital certificates could be used and what other non-prescriptive security standards or technology-neutral best practices could be deployed at each stage to improve security and provide higher levels of assurance. Certificates are required for the purpose of identification and must be in English and declare the TPP's defined and authorised roles;

"the role of the payment service provider, which maybe one or more of the following: an account servicing payment service provider; a payment initiation service provider; an account information service provider; a payment service provider issuing card-based payment instruments."

Communication Channels between ASIP, PSIP and the ASPSP

Certificates are required for identification and role for the parties using the dedicated communication channel

• Electronic ID & Trust Services (eIDAS)

• Public Key Infrastructure (PKI)

• eIDAS issued digital certificates for use with TLS mutual (client & server) authentication

Data exchange

• Confidentiality, Integrity and Authentication of the Data Exchanges are required using Security standards such as ISO 27001, and TLS if appropriate or alternative suitable standards that meet the technology requirements

• Sensitive payment data must be protected through encryption

Security measures

• Dynamic link encryption

• Intrusion & Anomaly Detection

• Fraud detection and prevention mechanisms

• Strong Customer Authentication

User authentication

As one of the primary objectives of the RTS is to specify the requirements of strong customer authentication (SCA), along with a limited set of possible exemption from SCA, the regulation contemplates the problem from several angles. Initially, the RTS clarifies the obligations and exemptions of the players involved, and, in relation to the theme of strong customer authentication, the Banks will have the burden to define the authentication procedures to be applied when a transaction is initiated through third-party services. While acknowledging the trade-off between SCA and usability, the EBA has decided to constrain the exemptions from SCA – roughly speaking, contactless card payments under €50, card not present transaction under €30, and payments to a payee that the payer has explicitly white-listed.

Interestingly, because the bank has the job of authentication this will leave no margin for discretion from the PISPs that could have chosen to smooth the customer journey by reducing the level of authorisation needed on transactions that they identify as low risk using TRA. This would have entailed on the part of the merchant or the PISP a voluntary "liability shift", whereby when the PISP chooses to bypass the Secure Customer Authentication for a transaction they consider to be low risk; but should that transaction turn out to be fraudulent, the responsibility for compensating the customer automatically lies with the PISP rather than the ASPSP. This kind of liability shift is used in the cards world to allow some discretion on the trade-off between convenience and risk. This may still be feasible as the RTS opens the possibility for the TPP to take charge of the authentication process but only in the case of a contractual agreement being in place with the Bank.

Repetitive authorisation to access to data

AISP's require information regarding the status of their clients' bank accounts hence they need access to the accounts in order to maintain current balances and time sensitive relevant information and they need this access on a regular basis with or without the end-clients initiation. This requires what is termed repetitive authorisation to access to data. Therefore the authorisation must be able to provide long term authorisation to an AISP, up to 30 days before the customer must authenticate and renew the authorisation. The requirement is to provide a method of access for a period of 30 days through the generation of an authentication code which would also allow the limiting of information access from TPP that are not initiated by the customer directly to a maximum of four (the draft said two) accesses per day.

The original draft acknowledged this requirement and set the limit to twice per day. This was an issue hotly contested by the relevant parties, with AISPs wanting hourly or even ad-hoc access to run batch jobs and on the other hand the ASPSP's insisting on retaining the control for managing the load and capacity on their networks and systems. One of the main changes introduced by RTS regards this issue is that an AISP can now access automatically a maximum of four times a day and for not more than one month after the last day in which strong customer authentication was carried out. This requirement suggests the generation of an authentication Token with temporary validity which, once verified by the ASPSP, enables the AISP to access services without further interaction by the user. Notably, there are no limits whatsoever to customer initiated access unless they are also limited on the online website.

Exemption from SCA

Another key objective of the RTS was to specify the electronic payments that could qualify for exemptions from the application of SCA, hence the RTS details the cases in which the adoption of measures of strong customer authentication is not required. In particular, the adoption of such measures is at the discretion of the institution in the event of:

Access to payment accounts – An exemption is allowed where the access to the information of the user account is for a process of consultation for example for an AISP. In this case first-time access authentication is still contemplated and will have a validity of one month maximum. However, for longer validity times re-authentication of the client will be needed; another, example of an exemption is with low value transaction using contactless electronic payment devices. In this case, where payments are made with contactless cards at retail stores with individual purchase amounts not exceeding 50 € and with a maximum cumulative value of 150 €;

Whitelist creation - There are exemption for transactions to beneficiaries included in a whitelist created with the Bank. The application of strong authentication measures is required in the process of the creation of the beneficiaries list and for any subsequent modification by the user; Recurring money transfer – There are exemptions for continuous transfers of similar transactions with the same amount and to the same beneficiary, for example a recurring payment such as a monthly standing order in this case SCA authentication is required for the first transaction of the series and in the case of any changes to the transaction details such as the amount and / or beneficiary;

1. Payment to self - Exemptions are also permitted where payment through a bank transfer is to self. For example when a transfer is made on current accounts of the same bank or at two different banks, that are made payable to the same person or entity

2. Contactless Card used at the Point of Sales – where that card is present at the point of sales there is an exemption up to 50€ per single transaction and accumulated sum of 150€

3. Payments <30€ - Payment via remote (online) channel with a maximum amount of 30 €, and the cumulative value of 150 €.

4. Parking & Transport – electronic payment transaction at an unattended payment terminal for the purpose of paying a transport or parking fare are exempt due to low value or safety concerns by causing a queue at a turnstyle

5. Transactional Risk Analysis - payment service providers are exempted from the application of

strong customer authentication, where the payer initiates a remote electronic payment transaction, identified by the payment service provider as posing a low level of risk according to the transaction monitoring mechanisms

The issues surround transaction risk analysis was possibly the most keenly contested single article as retailers especially took umbrage with what they considered low risk transactions not being exempt from SCA. Indeed many thought that the EBA had fallen into the classic trap of treating low value and low risk as being synonymous when they clearly are not. Indeed one of the key take away from the feedback that EBA received on their consultation paper was the determination of many of the retail players to do what they could to minimise the application of SCA. This might seem to be counter-productive as SCA works to reduce fraud and protect them however it may not be so surprising if we consider that many online retailers do not appreciate 3DSecure and go out of their way to avoid using it most notably due to its reputation as a conversion killer – i.e. customers appear to dislike it and abort the transaction because they are now accustomed to Amazon style one-click processing. Hence, many retailers, and they have support here across the board feel that they are caught between a rock and a hard place because if they apply SCA and secure the transactions they will at the same time annoy their customers, just like with 3DSecure. There is little doubt that SCA will help secure transactions but at what cost as online retailers know from bitter experience that customers seem to hate being messed around at the checkout – whether that be at a PoS or an online checkout - they want the payment model to be 'stored details' or a 'one-click' model.

Fortunately, the EBA consultation phase was not just a talking shop and they did listen and as a result TRA is allowed to an extent dependent on the individual's quality of their fraud detection and monitoring controls. In short the EBA have issued reference fraud rates for credit transfers and online remote payments under 500€. The table below shows the reference risk for both processes at amounts of 100, 200 and 500 euro.

ETV	Reference Fraud Rate (%) for:	
	Remote card-based payments	Credit transfers
EUR 500	0.01	0.005
EUR 250	0.06	0.01
EUR 100	0.13	0.015

Source: European Banking Authority Final Report on Draft Regulatory Technical Standards on SCA and CSC
The middle column in the reference table is particularly important. The Reference Fraud Rate is calculated by dividing the total amount of fraud by the total amount of all transactions over a 90-day period. This figure determines the fraud threshold that determines how banks and merchants handle SCA on e-commerce payments. The figure in the middle column is the precise targets fraud managers will have to hit to avoid using SCA and possibly annoying consumers with extra authentication steps. Hence if the ecommerce retailers can achieve a reference fraud rate of 0.01% – €1 of fraud for every €10,000 of transactions – then they will only be obliged to apply SCA on consumer transactions that are larger than €500.

For e-commerce merchants it means they may have to reluctantly adopt the schemes broadly known as 3D Secure – Verified by Visa, MasterCard SecureCode and American Express SafeKey though of course being technology-neutral none of these standards have been suggested. For issuing banks, particularly those that take a sophisticated risk-based approach it this will add another layer of complexity. Most, if not all online merchants, will now be focussing on how to beat the 0.01% reference fraud rate so that they can decide whether to ask a customer to authenticate themselves rather than be forced to by the PSD2 guidelines. However they will have to show due-diligence and perhaps demonstrate their fraud detection systems as they may be audited.

In practice this means that ecommerce retailers big and small will have to understand the role Transaction Risk Analysis and Transaction Risk monitoring plays. All payment service providers will need to use Transaction Risk Monitoring to deliver the reporting required by the regulation. However, PSD2 sets out specific parameters in reference to fraud rates that must be reported against. Hence, the PSPs must take care that these are understood and that they have the technology in place to report against them and this is required for each payment mechanism. Furthermore, the PSPs looking to avoid Strong Customer Authentication by using TRA instead will also require to understand the applicable parts of the PSD2 Regulatory Technical Standard and it's likely they will want to optimise their fraud rates for each payment mechanism to make the most of relevant exemptions.

Some other Issues with the RTS

The EBA's final draft RTS on Strong Customer Authentication (SCA) and Secure Communications is as expected a comprehensive document that covers a lot of ground and many contentious issues but ultimately its objectives are in accordance with Article 98 of the revised Payment Services Directive (EU) 2015/2366 (PSD2) in specifying the requirements of strong customer authentication (SCA), the exemptions from the application of SCA, the requirements with which security measures have to comply in order to protect the confidentiality and the integrity of the payment service users' personalised security credentials, and the requirements for common and secure open standards of communication (CSC) between the banks and the TPPs.

To be fair we should reiterate that the EBA had an incredibly onerous task in balancing the need for strong prescriptive measures and controls that would certainly have hastened implementation but these solutions would ultimately have been counterproductive as they would almost certainly have inhibited innovation. Hence, it is in this light that we can contemplate the effectiveness of the RTS and as comprehensive as it is it does leave many interesting ambiguities.

1. Cards are deemed initiated by Payer

Under PSD2 (article 97), SCA applies to a wide range of payment transactions where the payer:

- accesses their payment account online;
- initiates an electronic payment transaction;

- carries out any action through a remote channel which implies a risk of payment fraud.

Furthermore, the EBA interpretation of the scope is that card payments are electronic payments "initiated by the payer" through a payee and, therefore, within scope. To date, card payments have always been viewed by the sector as 'payee initiated' payments and the EBA view could challenge how firms apply other provisions in PSD2 which depend on whether payments are initiated by the payer or payee. For example it might be considered semantics but say the online merchant is also the PISP for instance Amazon. In his scenario Amazon which is the PISP will be initiating the payment but as they are also the payee, how can this be considered to be initiated by the 'payer'?

Another interesting point is what are the consequences of a merchant or PISP not applying SCA and using their own TRA? In a move designed to mitigate regulatory arbitrage, there are strict consequences for not adopting SCA under PSD2.

PSD2 is stricter than the current legislation in two respects: first, it places a strict liability on payment providers that do not require\accept strong customer authentication. This is regardless of whether that choice is made because of an exemption and arguably applies whether or not the payment is even within scope of the SCA requirements. Where the payee or the payee's payment provider does not accept SCA, then they must indemnify the payer's payment provider (who has the strict liability to its customer) for its loss; second, strong customer authentication is not optional – all payer payment providers must require it and payee payment providers must accept it. The EBA has made this clear in its Final Report.

What this means is that in practice the customer will see big changes in the way their payments are processed online. The SCA authentication requirements will be felt especially hard in the retail ecommerce sector. SCA will impact on consumers, payment providers and retailers alike and the debate surrounding it embodies a tension between providing frictionless customer experiences whilst also enhancing security. From a user and retailer perspective, SCA will have a particular impact for online payments. Increasingly, online merchants use pre-saved payment details to provide one-click payments. Unless an exemption applies, this frictionless consumer journey will now be interjected with two separate authentication requests. Similar annoyances will manifest for e-money products that simultaneously involve two payments potentially subject to SCA – the first payment being the card payment that funds the customer's e-money account, the second payment being the transfer of funds from that e-money account to the merchant.

From a payment provider's perspective, the required upgrade in technical capabilities to support SCA and investment in fraud monitoring capabilities should not be underestimated. SCA is also likely to change the competitive landscape for payment providers. Providers with the most sophisticated risk analysis tools will be best placed to utilise exemptions from SCA and deliver more convenient payment methods, but only if their ASPSP allows them to forgo SCA. On the other hand, there will be a demand from payment providers for a technology to deliver more seamless SCA techniques as these features will improve the customer journey.

2.   Banks define and own their interfaces

The EBA have decided to wisely take the non prescriptive route and have not tried to force upon the banks or the TPPs any detailed open standard for the suggested TPP APIs within the RTS leaving the method for interoperability up to the banks.

There are several good political and technical reasons for not taking the prescriptive route. For one, giving the banks the autonomy to define their own communication channels will ensure much needed buy-in from the banks, for if the banks do design, own and support the interfaces they will have to make sure they work. On the other hand if the EBA had prescribed a standard API then the banks may well have just gone through the motions implementing what was prescribed and no more. Secondly, a non prescriptive route encourages rather than stifles innovation and does not limit the technical scope.

As for guidance there are other banks that have already opened up APIs to Fintech partners also there are several working groups' active on parallel initiatives of Open Banking (e.g. Open Banking Working Group, Open Bank Project, Open Bank and the Berlin Group) producing proposals that would define a common standard interface or API.

However, the principles of technology-neutrality whilst levelling the playing field also leaves it wide open and this could lead to fragmentation whereby some banks align themselves with esoteric, diverse, proprietary or non-standard incompatible solution. An example of this can be seen already in the nascent Open banking community whereby a number of banks partnering with FinTech firms have already opened up their interfaces but using various diverse standards and technologies. Perhaps an area of concern is that most if not all of these solutions to date are proposing RESTful JSON APIs while the EBA RTS makes no mention of APIs but does encourage the adoption of the ISO 20022 standard that contemplates XML or ANI for financial business systems rather than JSON, which is prevalent in the mobile apps and FinTech world.

A more serious issue however for the banks and for the FinTechs is that if they are to build interfaces to support TPP then they will have to support them. This could be a very onerous and costly task as they would have to directly support onboarding of TPPs (RTS Article 27.6 mandates banks to provide "support, for connection and functional testing" which could be an extremely time-consuming and costly process if carried out for every new TPP).

A very interesting development that may well solve many of these interconnection issues is the emergence of several organisations that are offering "meta-aggregation" services. These platforms will act as multi-protocol gateways connecting many banks to a plethora of TPPs. This would certainly solve the issues of TPPs having to mesh with thousands of banks perhaps running diverse interface standards and data sets. However, if the platform was offering a single standard interface to Account Information Service Providers (AISPs) and Payment Initiation Service Providers (PISPs) then they would only have to concern themselves, similarly with the banks, with only one API interface. The meta-aggregator implements all the different interfaces to multiple banks, and handles the routing and conversion of messages between Third Party Providers (TPPs) and all of the banks.

However the real issue may be that banks presenting an interface is one thing and for the FinTech consuming the service another but receiving a standard response that is returned by a bank on a payment initiation API call, is a much bigger issue for TPPs and FinTechs. If this status does not imply a commitment of the bank that the payment is guaranteed, the PSD2 API is not suitable for purpose to pay for online and in-store purchases. (It is essential that the merchant knows that they are going to receive the money in order to hand over/send goods). Taking into account that one of the key reasons to launch XS2A by

ECB was to increase the competition on the card brands (besides the cap on interchange fees) then this is likely to fail. Without a guarantee of payment, it is very unlikely many merchants are going to accept PSD2 enabled payment instruments. But, why should this be of concern for nothing has changed as Fintech firms previously used screen-scraping to accomplish this XS2A style payments without a bank response to guarantee the merchant – we will see shortly how they managed this.

3. APIs, not screen-scraping

Another interesting strategic change of heart from the original draft RTS was the banning of screen-scraping and it appears that the European Council perhaps have realised the practicalities involved and softened their stance. Nonetheless, it was the European Councils political interference which proposed changes to the final draft RTS where the recital states that "screen-scraping will no longer be allowed". The EC proposals tries to over-ride the EBA and their RTS by allowing screen-scraping as a backup which contradicts the RTS by allowing a TPP to use the same interface as the customer should the direct TPP interface become unavailable. What this alludes to is that the TPP can return to screen-scraping as a contingency plan if there is loss of service on the main interface. Moreover, the EC proposals for change to the RTS clearly states that it should be optional whether a bank should develop a "dedicated" interface for the exclusive use of TPPs such as an API (though it is not mandatory). If they should decide not to build a dedicated interface for the

TPPs then the alternative the bank has is to allow TPPs to use the same interface offered to and used by the bank's online customers (e.g. online banking), which the FinTechs are already using through screen-scraping. There are some caveats though which might close some of the security holes associated with the practice. For instance, now the interface must allow TPPs to identify themselves to the bank (27.1.a), and that identification must take the form of "qualified certificates for electronic seals or website authentication" (29.1) as defined in the EIDAS regulation 910/2014. Therefore the TPP will no longer be allowed to masquerade as the customer using the customer's login credentials as they must identify themselves to the ASPSP.

There is another authentication anomaly whereby the RTS appears to indicate that a bank's customer may login using their bank credentials from within a PSP third party application or website. The issue being is that the RTS allows the "personalised security credentials and of authentication codes transmitted by or through the TPP" (27.3.c). This would in effect allow customers to log in to the bank via the TPP using the banks login credentials. If this is the case then the bank or any security monitoring tools would not be able to differentiate between genuine customer access and some TPP's robotic screen scraper albeit the TPP must now identify themselves – but who will police this. This does nothing to stop screen-scraping, in fact there is no technical way to prevent it that does not negatively effect the genuine customer's experience, but this does quite the opposite it all but encourages if not legitimises the practice.

4. **Payment security up to the banks**

The final draft of the RTS states that a PISP would only authenticate the customer in case of a prior contractual agreement between the PISP and the ASPSP, and that agreement would be outside the scope of PSD2. Recital 14 adjusts the EBA's stance on this point and now it is reworded as "PIS Providers have the right to rely on the authentication procedures provided" by the bank, and that "In such cases, the authentication procedure will remain fully in the sphere of competence of the ASPSP." This suggests that the PISP can always rely on the bank to authenticate the customer but this also implies that there are other cases where authentication does not rely on the ASPSP. But there is no case suggested whereby an ASPSP would have to accept an authentication performed by a PISP, so the onus is still on the ASPSP for authentication. However here lies the problem for the ASPSP to diligently authenticate their customer they must have confidence that the customer's security credentials have not been compromised i.e. disclosed to a third party. Without the full confidence that the customer's credentials have been passed to them under strict controls that guarantee the confidentiality and integrity of the security credentials the bank cannot possibly authenticate a customer, especially if they can detect that the customer's credentials are sometimes being used by a TPP software robot - to do so would be gross-negligence.

5. Authentication codes

Article 4.1 states that the 2 or 3 part authentication code is generated "based on two or more elements categorised as knowledge, possession and inherence" and it goes on to state that "The authentication code shall be accepted only once". This doesn't appear to make any sense as there are clear cases where the text suggests an authentication code (token) is reused. This seems to be down to the EBA's desire to be so technology-neutral that is has led to confusion between authentication codes and authorisation codes.

For example, contemplating the Article 13.1 there is a provision that allows for an exemption from SCA for "a series of payment transactions with the same amount and the same payee" – and SCA and the production of an authentication code is only required for the first transaction – presumably they mean the initial authentication produces an authorisation code (token) –which can be used until its validity expires i.e. 30 days. Likewise, for account information where an AISP can make up to 4 requests per day (31.5.b) for up to 30 days (10.2.b), presumably it will be the authorisation token and not the original authentication code that must be presented for all subsequent accesses.

Article 5.1.c now specifies that any change in amount or payee shall invalidate the authorisation code – as it should as those parameters are digitally signed, where as the previous requirement to just change the authorisation code seemed to be impractical. It's worth noting that the

Dynamic Linking of an authorisation code only covers the amount and payee, it is not specific to any other criteria for example the payment reference. For online payments the PSD2 feels that SCA is not sufficient and their also needs to be a dynamic linkage performed that directly connects the authorisation token to a specific payee and amount. The RTS only mentions Dynamic Linking for payment initiation that links a payee and amount, but it should also be required for consent to a specified set of parameters for AISP access. This could be applied when a customer provides granular permissions to a TPP to accesses their accounts, their frequency of access, and so on. It would be best to consider a powerful tool such as Dynamic Linking as a binding of the payer's consent for transaction(s), be they a single payment, series of payments or an enduring consent to access their payment transaction data.

6. Exemptions from Strong Customer Authentication (SCA)

This is the area of the RTS that has perhaps changed the most, and has been altered after due consideration based upon the feedback of stakeholders, which in turn has influenced the EBA to become more practical. The changes include:

• For contactless card payments, the single transaction value is raised to €50, and the option to count five consecutive non-SCA transactions has been added to provide balance to the previous impractical requirement to just accumulate payment values.

• A vital exemption is added for unattended transport and parking terminals has helpfully been included, but one should note in the TFL case, that the end amount is not known at the point of contactless exemption as the final billing is often calculated at the end of day based on all travel.

• No SCA is required for payments to trusted beneficiaries. Comment 79 also clarifies. The exemption for trusted beneficiaries only applies to payment transactions made on an online account by the payer. The PISP cannot on its own initiative create a list of trusted beneficiaries.

• The low value payment exemption is raised from €10 to €30, with a cumulative value of €100 or a cumulative count of five, aligned to the contactless exemption.

7. Whitelists

There are legal exemptions and then there is some limited support for 'whitelists' that the customer can create to exempt trusted parties from SCA. However, whitelist have a problem as creating the list of trusted parties would require SCA in order to authenticate the customer. For example, before applying the whitelist exemption, the ASPSP would need a high level of assurance that the purported payer is indeed who they claim to be. This would require some level of strong customer authentication of the payer therefore the suggestion put forward was the payer must only create or edit the whitelist from the ASPSP site, I.E. when they are logged in to the ASPSP, as this gives the bank assurance that entries to the whitelist are genuine.

8. Real Time Fraud Detection and Prevention

Whereas the previous draft RTS mandated real time fraud detection to prevent, detect and block fraudulent payments, the final draft is more practical and allows for a more nuanced risk analysis approach, with high risk transactions being blocked for bypassing SCA. There is also a specific approach with clearer reporting and processing procedures.

The final draft introduces exemptions from SCA based on Transaction Risk Analysis. The TRA exemption applies to transactions assessed by the merchant and supported by their PISP as being low risk, with a value limit depending on the type of transaction (remote card or credit transfer), and the PSP's own overall fraud rate, based on a rolling quarterly basis. If the transaction is determined to be low risk, i.e. the PSP can demonstrate that they have fraud rates lower than the threshold then SCA need not be applied by the ASPSP.

Unfortunately there is a caveat, as it is always the ASPSP prerogative to insist on SCA in the interests of protecting the customer, so regardless of the merchants or PISPs wishes the ASPSPS will always determine whether SCA is applied but they would have to document as to why as the TPP may complain about unnecessary friction being added to the regulator.

The banks though will rarely be concerned as it is difficult for a merchant or a PISP to gain an exemption as they must also ensure that an additional list of factors are considered and the list is extensive.

Article 2 mandates;

a) "lists of compromised or stolen authentication elements;

b) the amount of each payment transaction;

c) known fraud scenarios in the provision of payment services;

d) sign of malware infection in any sessions of the authentication procedure." For the SCA exemption to apply, additional factors must be considered including;

e) "the previous spending patterns of the individual payment service user; the payment transaction history of each of the payment service provider's payment service user;

f) the location of the payer and of the payee at the time of the payment transaction".

One interesting point is mentioned in Rationale 24, which says "both payees' and payers' PSPs could trigger such an exemption under their own and exclusive responsibility but with the payer's PSP having the final say."

This simply reiterates what we have said that the payee's PSP can request SCA exemption (with an assumed liability accepted by the PSP), but the payer's ASPSP can over-ride this and still present the challenge for SCA. Therefore it is at the banks discretion whether the SCA mechanism is bypassed or not and as the bank has little interest in the customer's experience at the online checkout but considerable interest in the rates of fraud it would appear unlikely that they will allow SCA to be bypassed.

Nonetheless, this exemption will be critical in delivering a frictionless customer experience, so PSPs that cannot agree a frictionless payment process with their bank and hence meet the criteria will lose out to those that can. Hence there will be a definite need for FinTechs to reach out to the banks to collaborate on creating a symbiotic and frictionless solution. Real time risk assessment is not easy and it's not something the FinTech firms want to have to be doing. However trying to come to an agreement or a contract with hundreds of banks is also an unrealistic or unsustainable business model so expect to see some innovation in payment risk assessment, the provision of a response to guarantee payment and also mutual liability contracts to be developed in the near future.

9. Sensitive Payment Data

ASPSPs must provide a service which an AISP can use that has the same reach of information from designated payment accounts and associated payment transactions that are made available to the payment service user, the customer, when directly accessing the information from the website;

"...provided that this information does not include display of sensitive payment data"

This is one of the strict rules defining the dedicated communication channel between the bank (ASPSP) and the TPPs however there is no definition as to what "sensitive payment data" is, this makes the wording not only ambiguous it also raises a barrier to interoperability. The information that banks currently make available to users varies widely, and banks could well – especially under the threat or the protection of GDPR – decide to play safe and to make more restrictive decisions about which data is considered to be sensitive and therefore which data must be redacted before release.

As an example a bank may decide that reference to a payment to a specific payee was potentially sensitive. Of course if they were to be over zealous in this approach the information being garnered by the AISP would be worthless. Consequently, as each bank may accept a different level of risk tolerance the TPPs would not be able to rely on a consistent set of data and services across all banks. This would result in the PISP being unable to optimise the data extraction method for a specific purpose and instead they will have to settle for the minimum common data sets or build unique apps for each bank.

Another issue with the RTS is that from an AISP perspective their right of access to customer information is limited by PSD2 legislations and that only covers customer Payments accounts. The problem for AISP, which are no longer free to use their screen-scraping techniques to access all the clients accounts, such as savings, credit cards, mortgage etc, means that their product and service portfolio will be severely limited to data accessible in the client's payment account. The bank under PSD2 has no obligation to make access available to any other customer accounts, other than a payment account, to a TPP AISP or PISP.

Similarly, PISPs may need some access to the customers payment account information for example a balance rather than just the binary yes/no response that PSD2 allows as it could assist them in selecting the correct account. Currently ASPSPs can only provide this information to AISPs, so presumably a PISP must apply as an AISP to get access to the information. This raises another question, as a PISP can also become an ASIP if they require the appropriate license and then presumably they can do both functions but can they do so concurrently i.e. on the same session? Presumably as there is no mention of such an entity with dual capability in either PSD2 or the RTS then there will have to be still some segregation of duties with AIS being performed under a different session/login to PIS functions. However using today's FinTech techniques of screen-scraping none of this is relevant as there is no segregation of duties.

10. Use of eIDAS authorities

With regards instilling stringent security and robust authentication of the main players and how the will authenticate to one another the EBA has put aside its doubts and firmly mandated the use of Digital Certificates issued under Regulation 910/2014, aka eIDAS. This is an interesting departure from the technology-neutrality stance but at least it provides useful guidance to all the players as to the certificate requirements albeit the most inconvenient option as all players would certainly already have X.509 issued certificates.

The choice of eIDAS over standard X.509 may be down to the RTS requiring that several pieces of data would need to be encoded in the new certificate, so field would have to be made available. These data fields would include a new TPP identifier as used on the register of PSPs in the organisation's home country, and an indicator of the role(s) of the TPP – ASPSP, AISP, PISP, PII.

What is interesting about the choice of eIDAS is there is at the time of the release of the final draft version of the RTS no such certificate issuing infrastructure in place in Europe. There are plans to implement a certificate authority before PSD2 comes into effect but there are serious issues regards certificates that require evaluating and addressing. For example, it is one thing to securely authenticate and notarise a TPP before a certificate is issued, similarly it is reasonably straightforward to maintain a database of all TPP and their identification codes, roles, by a single authority. However as can be seen with the X.509 system it is no trivial task to revoke a certificate and then somehow update the local certificate stores held by the other network members in a timely manner. Revocation lists we know do not work so online authenticate will be required to the central authority or to the TPP home registry, this in a closed network like the EAA so may not be such an issue but nothing is yet in place and PSD2 is likely to come into force in around eighteen months. Hence, there will be much to be done in the interim.

11. **Card Not Present requires Strong Customer Authentication**

Unless a card transaction falls under one of the limited exemptions, it must go through SCA. This could mean a 3D-Secure type process, but using two factors instead of the double knowledge factor(s) (e.g. Password + Date of Birth) being used by most banks currently. Vendors have rushed out solutions such as Dynamic CVV, where the CVV on the card changes regularly. Using this as one of the SCA components proves Possession, which along with

Knowledge satisfies the two factor requirement. The only alternative for online retailers wishing to bypass SCA is to use the Transaction Risk Analysis (TRA) exemption. The risk base exemption could potentially bypass SCA for companies whose transactions are mainly below the applicable TRA limit (€100, €250 or €500 depending on the PSP's historical fraud rate).

For those that do not their alternative is to adopt a mechanism that delivers SCA, and the card system 3-D Secure 2.0 should be able to meet these requirements. As well as browser-based payments, it will also support in-app, mobile, and digital wallet payments. Moreover it will support token-based and biometric authentication instead of static passwords, and will carry additional data such as device profile to support risk-based decisions and allow possible TRA-based bypass of SCA.

12. . Trusted Execution Environments for Multi-Purpose Devices

The security of mobile phones and similar personal devices casts a long shadow over the effectiveness of SCA. It appears that the EBA has recognised that neither the merchant nor the TPP software developer has the competency to alter the hardware and consequently the requirement for a "Trusted Execution Environment" is impractical. Instead the EBA reverts to using the term 'Secure Execution Environment' which is convenient but rather poor practice as the term has no current industry definition and hence allows any vendor to claim compliance.

There are still effectively only three ways to provide for 2FA (Two Factor Authentication) 'possession' element on a multi-purpose device:

1. Trusted Execution Environment – the gold standard for security and convenience, however many phones will not be enabled for this.

2. IMEI/USIM/ICCID/IMSI combination – which will cover all other non-TEE enabled phones if the manufacturer and/or operator will allow access to the SIM.

3. Whitebox Crypto in an App – this is the least desirable and lacks sufficient market exposure to provide confidence. An ASPSP would also have to have confidence that the end user the PSU was keeping the relevant software(s) and OS on their phone updated, but that is unrealistic.

Chapter 4 – FinTech Vs Banks

Much has been said about how FinTech is going to usurp the banks and revolutionise retail banking as we know it however the big question is who will actually benefit from the opening up of the banks? In order to contemplate such an issue we need to evaluate the business cases from both perspectives and there is no better forum than the EBA's collection of responses to their draft RTS proposals. For what is interesting is that the FinTech response was noted as being very cool initially which led some industry observers to question why they were not being more vocal in their support and gratitude for the PSD2 legislation. As it transpired as time slipped by it became obvious that the legislation was not all that it was made out to be as far as being beneficial to FinTech. Indeed, soon we were to witness that the FinTech response to the EBA's draft report on RTS was far from being quietly supportive, which publicly appeared to be the case, instead it has been anything but as they have been aggressively lobbying the European Commission to remove any suggestion of screen-scraping being banned in favour of bank supplied APIs.

Interestingly, this suggests that the imminent demise of the banks and the disruption that FinTech firms were sure to deliver as a result of the banks having to provide API access to customer accounts may be somewhat premature. There is also some considerable doubt whether the technology firms who will have to forego their existing technologies in favour of the API – should the EU uphold and ratify the RTS and ban screen-scraping in law - will subsequently be in a position to adjust and rebuild their operations and then scrabble to establish a foothold in the market. Indeed, it might be that it is they that may fall by the wayside rather than the more established banks.

The final draft of the RTS forbade the use of covert techniques such as screen-scraping which has been outlawed – or at least that was the intention – but that provoked a full blooded battle between the EC and FinTech on one side against the Banks and EBA, which at time of writing is still to be resolved. It is apparent from the dialogue between the three main parties to this dispute, the European Commission, the Future Fintech Alliance and the EBA that the situation is anything but clear but it is certainly divisive and poisonous and it is all the more so because the gist of the argument is theoretical. After all Fintech firms have been screen-scraping for a decade at least banks have been aware and turned a blind eye, customers in the minority may be willing to accept the FinTech services and the inherent risk, that is their choice whereas the majority of customers being risk averse will not ever consider sharing their banks login details online. It appears then that both the banks and Fintech want to have it their way the banks want to be able to choose which method they deploy, which is fair enough as it is at their expense whereas the Fintech want both options made available and then they will choose a preferred method. To dive deeper into this hotly contested dispute we need to consider the communications between the protagonists as it is within the text of their correspondence that we discover the true state of the industry and the protagonist's agendas:

For their part the European Council after heavy lobbying from Future FinTech Alliance announced in May 2017:

"... Another major objective of PSD2 is to bring about more competition and innovation in the retail payment market by including in its scope two new types of payment services, the so called payment initiation services and the account information services...

... PSD2 provides for this access, under strict and pre-defined conditions."

The ECB then went on to announce proposed changes to the draft RTS along with their reasoning behind their changes.

"...4. Contingency measures in case of unavailability or inadequate performance of the dedicated communication interface (Ref. Chapter 5, Article 28 of the EBA draft)

The proposed change is based on the following reasoning. The RTS shall ensure that an unavailability or inadequate performance of the dedicated interface does not prevent payment initiation services and account information services providers from offering their services to the users, where at the same time the user-facing interfaces operate without any difficulties and allow the bank to offer its own payment services.

In case of unavailability or inadequate performance of the dedicated communication interface, banks should offer secure communication through the user-facing interfaces as a contingency measure. Relevant provisions of PSD2 (Articles 65-67) should apply, including identification and authentication procedures. Payment initiation services and account information services providers should in particular comply with their obligations under Articles 66(3) and 67(2) of PSD2.

The use of the contingency measures should be fully documented and reported to the authorities by the relevant providers, upon request, including justification for the use of these measures. Once the dedicated interface is restored to full service, payment initiation services and account information services providers should be obliged to use it. Procedurally, under Article 10 of the EBA Regulation, the following options are available to the Commission: to endorse the regulatory technical standards without amendments, not to endorse them, to adopt them in part or with amendments. Endorsing the submitted draft regulatory technical standards without amendments is not recommended for reasons of legal certainty, verifiability, and for reasons of ensuring effective enforcement of specific obligations set out in the standards."

It seems clear from the European Commission Boards intent to revise and reverse the RTS decision to ban screen-scraping and to subsequently legitimise the technique as a contingency measure in order to allow the TPPs to continue using their existing screen-scraping technology albeit only in a fail-over scenario, but that has seriously weakened the EBA's position on a ban of screen-scraping. However the EBA was not taking this interference lightly.

The Response to the ECB regards the proposals to change the RTS

The EBA state that, "In its letter dated 24 May 2017, the Commission expressed its intention to amend the EBA's draft RTS ... and the Commission proposes that, in case of the unavailability or inadequate performance of a dedicated interface, AISPs and PISPs should be allowed to access information using the customer interface (Article 33 of the draft RTS as proposed by the Commission)
The Commission therefore proposes providing a fallback option that AISPs and PISPs can exercise in the event that the dedicated interface is unavailable for more than 30 seconds, or in the event that the ASPSP does not comply with the obligations applicable to interfaces under Articles 29 and 31 of the RTS. The Commission's proposed fallback option consists of AISPs and PISPs having a right to access account information through the ASPSP's customer-facing interface.
The EBA understands that, with this proposal, the Commission aims to ensure that ASPSPs comply with their obligation under PSD2 to share customer information with third party providers (TPPs) without any discrimination and in compliance with the security requirements of Articles 65-67 PSD2. The amendment is aimed at ensuring that AISPs and PISPs can access the data they need to provide services and effectively compete against banks and other PSPs.

The EBA shares those objectives and agrees that it is important to ensure discrimination-free access. The EBA also understands from a number of respondents to its Consultation Paper in August 2016, as well as from discussions with the European Parliament, that there are genuine concerns among some TPPs that ASPSPs will not deliver what is needed, especially in the case of a dedicated interface, where the ASPSPs may not have an incentive to provide the best possible interface to competitors.

However, the EBA is of the view that imposing such a fallback requirement would go beyond the legal mandate given to the EBA under Article 97 PSD2. The EBA is also sceptical about the extent to which the proposed amendment would achieve the desired objectives and efficiently address market concerns. Indeed, the EBA has identified a number of risks that would arise were PSPs to implement the Commission's proposal.

By way of background, the EBA notes that PSD2 imposes new security requirements that will change the way the market currently operates, and will do so for all existing providers. In this context, ASPSPs will be required by law to ensure that TPPs can access only the data necessary to provide a given service to their customers, that TPPs can identify themselves in the process and that TPPs can communicate securely with each other. This means that if ASPSPs were to choose to provide such access based on their existing customer interface, this interface would need to be modified to comply with PSD2. Current access approaches, often referred to as 'screen-scraping', in which the TPP impersonates the consumer and has access to all the consumer's data, rather than only the data necessary to provide payment services, would not be compliant.

"The EBA is of the view that a fallback option would have a number of negative consequences, which are summarised below.

"Negative consequences of a fallback option

"This section details the following: cost increases, increased fragmentation compromising the development of application programming interfaces (APIs), competitive disadvantage for new entrants, a lack of improved technical reliability, incompatibility with PSD2's security requirements, supervisory constraints, and unclear consumer understanding and consent. The EBA addresses each in turn... Cost increases

"In the new PSD2 era, an additional fallback option requiring ASPSPs to maintain an additional, PSD2 compliant customer-facing interface in case the dedicated interface fails, as proposed by the Commission, would have the following implications:

"- the compliance costs for ASPSPs would increase because, in addition to developing a dedicated interface and maintaining their customer interface, ASPSPs would have to develop, and continuously maintain, a PSD2-compliant customer interface to ensure that the fallback option also complied with the rules under PSD2; and

"- the compliance costs for AISPs and PISPs would increase, as they would have to pay to be able to access the dedicated interface and the customer-facing interface

"- Increased fragmentation compromising the development of standardised application programming interfaces

"The EBA is of the view that requiring ASPSPs to have a fallback option in place may lead to ASPSPs abandoning the route of dedicated interfaces altogether, opting instead for customer-facing interfaces that are PSD2-compliant. However, without ASPSPs developing dedicated interfaces, the achievement of an EU-wide communication standard is extremely unlikely, which in turn has a negative impact on one of PSD2's objectives: to standardise access across the EU Member States and create a single EU payments market.

"Eventually, this would compromise the development of standardised APIs across the EU, and would increase their fragmentation, along geographical or other boundaries.

☐ Competitive disadvantages for AISPs and PISPs wishing to enter the market

"As explained above, the requirement for a fallback option would weaken the ability to develop an EU-wide communication standard, for instance using APIs, and increase fragmentation.

"It would instead create:

"- a competitive disadvantage and market entry barrier for AISPs and PISPs that are not yet in the market, because they would need to develop a plethora of approaches to accessing payment accounts through different customer-facing interfaces; and

"- a competitive advantage for those AISPs and PISPs that have been in the market for many years, because they will already have developed those interfaces

☐ No improvement to technical reliability

"The fallback option is unlikely to guarantee a faultless and errorless interface, given that the modified customer interface would probably be based on the same technological infrastructure and would therefore have similar availability and performance risks to those of the dedicated interface. In short, a fallback interface would not be technically more reliable than the standardised interface itself.

☐ Incompatibility with PSD2's security requirements

"The new fallback option would probably negatively affect security and might in fact be incompatible with the security requirements set out in PSD2. Indeed, given the extremely short interval of 30 seconds proposed by the Commission, the ASPSP would not have enough time to assess the situation and safely activate any fallback solution without compromising security (for example in the case of a coordinated cyber-attack). The ASPSP would not be able to act and would not even be aware of any potential defect in its dedicated interface. This might result in ASPSPs treating any access to the customer interface as a security risk, thus blocking such access in compliance with PSD2.

☐ Supervisory constraints

"The proposed fallback requirement would also be extremely difficult to supervise, as competent authorities would not be able to conduct any checks or intervene in the ante, given the limited 30-second duration. Intervention ex post might be equally difficult.

☐ Unclear consumer understanding and consent

"It is likely that it would be very difficult for consumers to understand the multiplicity of ways in which they could access their account information, depending on the providers and/or the interfaces used by those providers, and therefore to understand the implications of giving consent.

"The EBA acknowledges the importance of ensuring reliable and continuous access for AISPs and PISPs, as well as TPPs, to be able to access the data required to execute a transaction when they need it. The EBA also agrees with the Commission's intentions, although it disagrees with the proposed fallback option for the reasons highlighted in the previous sections, and proposes an alternative approach in the paragraph below.

"The EBA's proposed alternative approach

"The EBA proposes the following four-fold alternative approach, which it believes will achieve the objectives sought by the Commission:
- to ensure that ASPSPs deliver reliable and continuous access to the data that TPPs need, the requirements set out in the RTS need to be reinforced;
- to build trust between competing actors, transparency needs to be increased;
- to facilitate a smooth transition from PSD1 to PSD2, cooperation needs to be facilitated by requiring ASPSPs to allow early testing of their interfaces; and
- to enable the EBA to review the practical implementation of the RTS, the EBA should monitor the performance of the interfaces.
"To those ends, the EBA suggests including the following requirements in the RTS:
- a requirement for ASPSPs to define transparent key performance indicators and abide by at least the same service level targets as for the customer interface, regarding both the availability and the performance of the interface, as well as qualitative measures to assess whether or not they are doing so (Article 31(2));
- a requirement for PSPs to monitor and publish their availability and performance data on a quarterly basis (Article 31(3));
- a requirement for ASPSPs to make the interfaces available for testing at least three months before the application date of the RTS (Articles 29(3) and 29(5)); and
- a review of the functioning of the interfaces as part of the review planned for 18 months after the application of the RTS under Article 36, to ensure information access and sharing is working as intended.
"The EBA is of the view that the suggested measures will ensure that ASPSPs deliver the information needed by TPPs to provide their services, do so in a reliable and continuous manner, and do so without jeopardising further standardisation across the EU or compromising security. The EBA is also of the view that by requiring ASPSPs to allow AISPs and PISPs to test interfaces before the RTS apply, the RTS will provide surety that all ASPSPs would have a working, efficient and reliable interface from the day the RTS apply."

The FinTech Response

Friction between the banks and the TPP is inevitable and so we must consider the positions each will take, for example the FinTech group does not necessarily feel the PSD2 legislation is at all beneficial despite the media hype;

"The Future of European Fintech Alliance – Commenting on EBA's opinion on the European Commission's amendments to the RTS on authentication and communication under PSD2;

"The Future of European Fintech Alliance (the Alliance), consisting of 72 European FinTechs, challenger banks and fintech associations, has reviewed the EBA's opinion on the RTS on authentication and communication dated 29 June 2017. The EBA disagrees with the European Commission's proposal to allow TPPs to use the customer-facing online interface of the ASPSP in case the dedicated interface offered by the ASPSP is unavailable or does not function as it should. The EBA instead puts forward an "alternative approach"

"We note that the European Commission adopts the same principle as the EBA in that the ASPSP (bank) can decide whether it wants to provide a dedicated interface or not; if a dedicated interface is offered, the TPP should use it. In our view, the optimal approach would be to reciprocate the ASPSP's free choice of providing a dedicated interface with the TPP's free choice to use it or not. While such symmetry has not been ensured, the revised RTS however do make clear that in case the dedicated interface does not perform as it should, licensed Fintechs and TPPs can rely on the customer-facing online interface as a fallback-solution. This extremely important amendment means that European Fintechs are not put at the technological mercy of their very competitors, but as a fallback can rely on an established interface which in any event is continuously maintained by the If a bank has the ability to monopolise the information flow to a TPP through a dedicated interface, then there will be no economic incentives to do it properly. On the contrary, there are several incentives for not doing it well, as a TPP can be seen in many instances as the bank's competitor. Will banks in general do their best effort to favour their competitors? Business logic simply does not support it. This is the reason many banks have been and are continuing to obstruct the services of TPPs in many EU countries. If, on the other hand, a bank's dedicated interface has to face the competition of its own customer-facing interface, then there is an incentive for doing it well. Naturally, banks are providing their customers the best possible interface to keep them happy, and this will be the benchmark for the dedicated interface if both are available to TPPs. If the TPP is not able to leverage the customer-facing online interface, then European Fintechs will be forced to idly stand and see their businesses die in case a dedicated interface has technological problems. The Future of European Fintech Alliance however also notes that the RTS on many topics leave significant room for interpretation. Clarifications in the following areas would be very welcome:

"TPPs must be allowed to verify on an ongoing basis that the fallback solution is working The TPP needs to be able to test the fallback/contingency interface at any time to ensure that the TPP can seamlessly use it when needed. The TPP could only switch back to direct access where it has a back-up system constantly up and running. Such a system cannot be built within a matter of hours or days but needs ongoing maintenance. Hence, without constant access at least for the purpose of testing and training, the "fallback" solution will not work. Constant access to the fallback-solution is also needed to allow the TPP to compare and know when a dedicated interface does not offer the same level of availability and performance as the interfaces made available to the payment service user for directly accessing its payment account online in line with Article 33 (3), Article 32 (1) RTS and to maintain technologies for fallback option access.

"ASPSP must not be allowed to force the TPP use a redirect-domain The current AIS and PIS solutions on the basis of direct access allows consumers to use the same TPP-provided interface throughout the entire session, i.e. TPPs are not forced to "redirect" their customers to a web page hosted by the ASPSP. This is absolutely crucial in order for TPPs to be able to provide a service adapted to different environments (desktop, mobile, in-app, watch, PoS terminal) and which is sufficiently user-friendly. If a PIS/AIS product was forced to redirect, the consumer would be moved between different websites - that are seldom optimised for every device - in a confusing and time-consuming way. TPPs need to be allowed to stay in control of their products.

"ASPSP interfaces must allow for both AIS and PIS to be used in the same session Article 30 RTS suggests that the interface should accommodate both AIS and PIS, but leaves open whether the two types of services can be provided within one session. It should be clarified that the same interface solution has to be available for PIS and AIS and combinations thereof in the same session. TPPs must not be forced to split their services into separate sessions for account information and payment initiation services, but need to be allowed to do both in one session.

"ASPSP should not provide less information on initiation by means of limiting the information provided to PSUs According to Article 30.1c of the RTS, PISPs shall receive „all information on the initiation of the payment transaction and all information accessible to the account servicing payment service providers regarding the execution of the payment transaction". This is an important principle in order for the TPP to be able to verify execution of the payment and must not be abused by means of the ASPSP deciding to provide the PSU with less information than before and using that as a benchmark for what information should be provided to the TPP.

"TPPs must be allowed to rely on the authentication procedures of the ASPSP also when using the fallback solution We note that Article 33.3b states that TPPs can only use the fallback solution when "they are enabled to rely on the authentication procedures provided by the account servicing payment service provider to the payment service user". This text must not be misinterpreted as if the ASPSP can somewhat block usage of the fallback solution by not "enabling" the TPP to rely on all authentication procedures; TPPs should as a general rule be "enabled" to do just that in accordance with Recital 30 and Article 97 PSD2.

"Same level of availability and performance needs to include data quality and functionality: Data quality should be the same as for direct access, i.e. the information has to be 100% synchronised in time and fully symmetric as to its content allowing TPPs to serve clients as well as they do today. We note that one way to ensure this principle and maximise probability for equivalent operating performance is if the dedicated interface offered by the ASPSP is based on the same API as the ASPSP's customer-facing mobile app application. Functionality should be the same as for direct access, i.e. the interface allows in the same way for new services and innovative designs, notably also for combinations of AIS and PIS. Thus, where a TPP proposes a new design to the ASPSP, but the latter cannot deliver the appropriate data or format via the dedicated access, direct access should be available.

"The fallback should be to the unlimited customer-facing interface Some banks are complaining that with the fallback option, ultimately they will be forced to maintain three different interfaces. The dedicated interface, the customer-facing interface and the fallback interface. We cannot see why this would be the case as in the fallback scenario TPPs "shall be allowed to make use of the interfaces made available to the payment service users for directly accessing their payment account online" (Art. 33 (3) draft RTS). Consequently, the real customer facing interface should only be modified to allow for the identification of TPPs. A "third" interface claimed by some banks would defy the purpose of a fallback interface as it would enable them to provide a different service level than for their own customers directly.

"TPP activities are supervised by competent authorities - not the ASPSP The extent of data accessed by TPPs is limited by (i) the explicit consent they obtain from the user, (ii) the stipulations within PSD2 and the RTS, and (iii) the ongoing supervision of competent authorities, e.g. based on data access logs, they may request. ASPSPs will no doubt monitor such data access, but it is not within their remit to deny it for any reason, once the TPP has identified himself properly as a PSD2-licensed PSP. Obviously, ASPSPs are free to challenge any TPP activity vis-a-vis the competent authority, but it must be clear that they cannot deny access based on their suspicions of non-compliance, e.g. lack of user consent.

"Standards of Communication must not be set by banks only It remains unclear what "standards of communication issued by international or European standardisation organisations" means per Art. 30 (3) draft RTS. It should be clarified that (i) this does not include idiosyncratic solutions that are neither "common" nor "open" in the sense of Art. 98 PSD2, and (ii) that bank-only organisations cannot be "standardisation organisations", because they do not represent/invite all stakeholders and do not provide for open and transparent procedures as stipulated, e.g., by DG COMP's Horizontal Guidelines on standardization agreements.

"RTS and PSD2 should accelerate security for access of Other Accounts and not restrict it In order to serve consumers' needs, TPPs today, with explicit consent of the user, collect data from different accounts including credit accounts, savings accounts, stocks, life insurance etc. and have innovated on such data since many years. It should be made clear that if users give explicit consent to TPPs to access data related to such accounts, and if such access is not specifically forbidden by Member States, TPPs should be able to use secure authenticated direct access to retrieve such data without discrimination.

"Services built on data and explicitly requested by the payment service user must be allowed It has come to our attention that some actors have interpreted Article 67.2 (f) PSD2 in a very restrictive way which would prohibit a third party to make use of data that has been retrieved by the AISP, even if the user explicitly makes the request and gives consent. This interpretation would go against the spirit of PSD2 as well as the GDPR and would severely hinder innovation. AIS have provided many additional services for several years that make use of aggregated data, with explicit user consent and following data protection rules. These additional services respond to consumers' needs, are key parts of the business models of AIS players and are already creating major economic value and benefits. It should be clarified that companies providing AIS services should be allowed to use, access and store account information data in order to provide additional services explicitly requested by the payment service user, in accordance with data protection rules.

" SCA managed by AIS every 90 days should be able to substitute SCA managed by ASPSP The forced SCA managed by ASPSPs every 90 days will seriously limit competition, innovation and user friendliness. SCA managed by ASPSPs during an ongoing use of AIS by users is a strong barrier in the user experience (as an example, the user may be sleeping when ASPSPs request an SCA at the AISP's connection). It should be clarified - in this particular case - that SCA managed by AISPs can substitute SCA managed by ASPSPs.

" Real time information are crucial for AIS's users While instant payments are not yet available, real-time information is already crucial for AIS to cover consumers' needs. The limitation to request information no more than four times in a 24-hour period erects an artificial barrier that will disable AISPs to provide services as good as ASPSPs. More concretely, ASPSPs will be able to push data to their clients in real-time while AISP users will have to wait for the next AIS authorized connection to be aware of financial movements on their accounts. It should be clarified that AISPs are allowed to always connect every time there is new information on ASPSP interfaces if users have actively requested once for all to AISP.

"The Fintech approach is summarised as being;

"Five years ago, the European Commission intervened to stop the banking sector's attempt to monopolise PIS and AIS. Then PSD2 was drafted to allow their TPP competitors' common practice of direct access to continue, albeit under regulatory supervision to ensure their security standards going forward. Exactly these core provisions of PSD2 are now getting undermined and contradicted through EBA's 2nd level legislation. The banking lobby appears to have good enough influence to drive it their way. The natural solution to the question about dedicated interfaces would be to make it symmetrical - ASPSPs' choice to offer a dedicated interface or not should be reciprocated by TPPs' choice to use it or not. This solution would ensure that the intentions of PSD2 would be achieved. The European Commission's proposal already compromises on this principle to the detriment of the TPP, saying that the TPP must as the general rule use the dedicated interface if provided by the ASPSP, and that the TPP can only use the fallback solution if the dedicated interface malfunctions. However, the EBA's approach is fully siding with the ASPSPs, removing all de facto possibility for TPPs to provide services in case the ASPSP has technological problems. This is utterly unacceptable. The EBA's approach is putting the existence of European TPPs at grave risk. TPPs are providing services based on direct access via the customer-facing online interface, an established technology perfectly compatible with PSD2. Why can the EBA not agree to the very easily understandable principle that in case an ASPSP provides a dedicated interface that does not work, then the TPP will be allowed to use the existing well-proven technology of direct access? This is why the Alliance call upon the European legislator to stick to the European Commission's compromise which has been crafted based on input from all stakeholders and to rebut the one-sided approach taken by EBA, which even falls behind its own proposal from earlier this year."

"However there are problems when considering an API solution and a case may be justifiable for a screen scraper solution if an alternative is not available. For example, in support of a screen scraper method there is the scenario where Banks are only partially cooperative and they have insisted that they are not willing to provide a payment execution guarantee, nor any other "risk-mitigation" data for free and PSD2 is not forcing them. However, the payment initiation is useless if merchants cannot get a realtime confirmation on the payment transaction, which is their banks prerogative, but when awaiting and checking execution (possibly overnight) or arrival of the funds (next day at the earliest) is not good enough.

"For the past 15 years, this dilemma was resolved by PISPs using screen-scraping via the user interface and then using the clients credentials to initiate the payment automatically, but prior to that retrieve some data, e.g. overdraft allowance, previously declined transactions, etc., was also harvested to identify the risk of non-execution. Therefore FinTech firms could base their TRA on that appropriation of sensitive data, supply merchants with a sufficiently risk-mitigated, realtime "payment confirmation".

"The alternative is that unless PISPs want to engage and sign thousands of contracts with all the banks in Europe and pay for their execution guarantee or risk relevant data, then they will have to maintain screen-scraping as the method of access. However why should the banks feel obliged to supply data that they generate through algorithms and methods– albeit based upon the customers data – which is not directly owned by the customer. After all even the strict GDPR acknowledges that data generated by a company belongs to them, and this would include risk assessment and other analysis of the customer data.

"This is not about restricting customers to share their own data, but restricts them to share the bank's generated data with third parties. Should the customer wish to share their bank details with then t is likely to bring them into potential conflict with the terms and conditions of their bank account. FinTech firms may well argue that by divulging their bank account credentials to licensed and supervised PISPs, they may avoid sharing it (bank or card details) with the unlicensed and non-supervised merchants they want to buy from, However that is rather disingenuous as handing over your accounts name and number does not in any way equate to the risk of surrendering you username and password. FinTech firms are adamant that by providing a third party (them) with your login credentials reduces payment risk and fraud potential significantly but that must be highly questionable as the customer is not just passing over an account name and number for example to Amazon but also their login credentials."

The Banks Perspective;

The bank as the ASPSP will still have the responsibility for authenticating any transaction that has been confirmed within the PSD2 legislation. The banks also hold and protect the customer's financial records however the consensus these days is that the data belongs to the customer and therefore it is their prerogative to share. Nonetheless there are issues that arise regarding access to the customer's account information such as what mechanisms are permitted and what data is accessible. For example there is customer data – records of prior transactions and balances etc – however there is also bank generated data such as risk assessment data which albeit is constructed based on the customer data - is the banks data and hence not available to be shared. The GDPR recognises the difference between customer data and data generated by a third party's algorithms working on the customer's raw data. Data generated by a company through algorithms or analytics is the property of the company, so is exempt from PSD2 or GDPR legislation.

The conundrum of who owns what data is ably demonstrated in other industries, such as the travel business where Airlines would spend vast amounts advertising and promoting their deals but took exception to screen-scrapers collating pricing and availability in order to profit from presenting this information to prospective customers. Yes the information is in the public domain in so much as the pricing is made public but they do not wish their offerings to be compared like-for-like with competitors. As a result the diverse levels of acceptance is unclear, for example some of the low cost airlines would actually cancel bookings made through travel firms that were known to screen scrape the airlines websites and as we have witnessed in the enterprise and ecommerce market the technique is far from being unilaterally accepted. Indeed there isn't even a consensus on the technique's name as it is referred to as screen scraping in ecommerce, in the financial services segment (FinTech) it will be called direct-access and in the Insurance segment as being referred to as rate-rape.

The banks quite correctly find the trespass into their systems to be unacceptable as would any enterprise where security, confidentiality and trust are paramount. They have been unable however to prevent FinTech firms using such techniques because a browser is effectively a screen scraper as are the Google robots that evaluate and catalogue websites. Consequently, the banks just like the majority of other enterprises that would like to put an end to third parties screen-scraping their websites, have to face the unpalatable truth that there isn't really a lot they can do to prevent them. Consequently, banks have tended to turn a blind eye rather than implement features that might also have a negative effect on their legitimate customer's user experience. Despite this, banks are still frustrated that FinTech firms use customer online credentials to pull data from their websites. The banks feel it is a breach of trust, contract and service as the customer willingly shares their online credentials with the FinTech business despite this being strictly forbidden within the Terms of Service. On the other hand the customers that do share their credentials are likely to be high value customers for they are the ones most likely to benefit from a FinTech's services. This will be especially true post PSD2 with AIS and PIS services on offer. In addition high value clients are perhaps more accustomed to delegating permission over their finances for example to an accountant so are less resistant to sharing with a FinTech they trust. This makes it nigh on impossible for the bank to suspend the customer's access to the online service for persistent or flagrant abuse of the service. Consequently the banks have collectively gone along albeit reluctantly and turned a blind eye to the abuse of their systems and services. As we will discuss later FinTechs believe they have, given the customer's permission and their delegated authority, an entitlement to the same rights and permissions as the customer, and this makes sense if you ignore the fact that the customer has no right to share his credentials or delegate there authority under the Terms of Service. The banks also feel aggrieved that FinTech firms build their competitive businesses riding on top of the banks own server and network infrastructure, relying on the banks security, servers and bandwidth to deliver their products to the banks customers.

The Retailers View

From the perspective of the retailer things become somewhat complicated as it would initially appear that free trade without card charges would be beneficial. However there is a caveat, for with a card or bank authorised payment the retailer can have the assurance of payment before they release the goods. The issue with SCA is that although the transaction may well be authorised and authenticated there is still the lack of real time confirmation – I.E. the payer's bank sending a confirmation. This is because this TPP payment model does not involve the bank as such, indeed it's a competitor to the banks issued credit cards.

Without a confirmation or assurance of payment the retailer is unlikely to want to use such a payment instrument and this is a big problem. Banks are not required to respond to a payment initiation by a PISP for example by sending a response that would guarantee the payment to the retailer. Furthermore the banks are not also obliged to supply free of charge risk assessment data on a given transaction which is the basis of the assurance or payment guarantee response that the bank sends on credit\debit card purchases.

Consequently, if a bank does not respond to a payment initiation with a guarantee or settlement it is highly unlikely that many retailers will utilise the FinTech or TPP system. Secondly, retailers have been surprisingly resistant to protection systems such as 3D-Secure as it is perceive to be a conversion-killer, meaning it puts people of converting a shopping cart into a sale. The reasons for this, is that many online shoppers appear to be against the extra steps required by them to authenticate and hence secure their transaction. Consequently, many retailers have ignored 3D-Secure and have taken aboard the risk using their own Transaction Risk Assessments in order to minimise and smooth the customer journey. If this is indeed the case that the retailers are willing to except higher risk rather than lose potential sales through unwieldy and unfriendly customer payment services. Then the additional hoops that PSD2 will make the customer jump through for SCA will also be a conversion-killer.

The Customer Experience

Customers love 'one-click' or 'details stored' and all the other simplified payment mechanisms. The convenience and ease of use is paramount to delivering a good customer experience. However it is also essential that the payment system can authenticate and protect users especially when conducting business online. To this end the PSD2 legislation strives to secure consumer payments while reducing the friction that is inherent in strong authentication mechanisms.

Consumers that are accustomed to one-click payments will likely find SCA just like 3D-Secure credit card authentication a troublesome turn-off. Hence it appears that much education and coaching will be required in order to produce a smooth transition.

With regards open banking, through APIs customers can only benefit as the services they desire, account aggregation, instant transfers, better choice will now be securely delivered by their bank albeit through a third party provider with the inherent assurances that they have come to expect.

The problem that Fintech has to face is changing the customer's acceptance or in this case reticence with sharing their login credentials to their bank account. Screen-scraping or direct-access whatever they wish to call it can only work by accessing the bank using the customer's credentials. Whether they identify themselves or not is irrelevant as they still need the customers security credentials. Currently, neither the banks nor their customers are keen on this approach for obvious security concerns.

Chapter 5 – Issues with Screen-Scraping

The PSD2 RTS specifies that banks must offer TPPs a dedicated interface which allows them to communicate using a secure common channel with the customer's accounts. It also provides a number of high level requirements for this interface but the EBA have decided against a prescriptive model for the design of the interface and instead left the technical details up to the bank. Leaving the dedicated communications interface definitions and specifications up to the banks however may lead to a more expansive type of communication interface arising across the market which will result in heterogeneous and perhaps incompatible solutions creating silos of functionality across the European digital market.

The RTS in a strenuous effort to remain technology neutral avoids discussing the nature of the dedicated interface that the bank must present to the TPPS in any detail but it does discuss some options.

In order to request information from and receive information about bank accounts and to initiate a payment transaction from the customer's account the TPP needs to access the accounts over a dedicated interface with the consent from the account holder. Furthermore, in Article 27(2) banks can offer this interface in following two ways:

a) Via a dedicated interface - In this model the bank develops a new interface specifically to support TPPs. Messages exchanged via this interface should be structured according to the ISO 20022 standard, which is already heavily used for electronic data interchange between financial institutions. Although not mandatory, the dedicated interface is generally expected to be based on RESTful APIs or similar technology. Many banks are expected to opt for this approach based on dedicated interfaces.

b) Via the customer interface - With this model the bank will reuse the existing online interface that it already offers to its customers. For example, the bank could reuse its existing web or mobile banking applications to fulfil this obligation. The only difference being that the TPP rather than the user needs to be authenticated with the bank. Also there is the additional obligation that the banks must provide TPPs with a test version of their communication interface, so that they can test the connectivity and functionality of the interface, as specified in Article 27(6).

Some accounts information services (AIS) and payment initiation services (PIS) already use a technique called 'screen-scraping' or as they prefer to call it direct-access to interact with a customer's account data. In this case, customers give the third party provider full access to the login details for their online bank account so that the provider can scrape transaction history data from their online account and use that as the raw data when providing analysis and aggregated financial information for their customer. Technically, banks may be able to continue this model of allowing screen-scraping as a way to meet PSD2 regulations.

Interfaces such as the dedicated API may be the solution of choice but on the other hand another bank may decide upon reusing their current online communication interface (the website) with the only adjustment being to allow the TPPs to identify themselves via a header to the bank. Which path the bank may decide to take is really up to their perspective and attitude to the PSD2 legislation. If for example they do not wish to get involved and spend any more money than they have too then the clever move would be to just let the Fintech firms carry on screen-scraping – if that remains an option. It will cost the bank nothing to reuse their online website as the dedicated channel and all the development work, time and effort falls on the Fintech firm. Conversely, should they go down the API route then it will be an onerous burden in costs and effort to implement, maintain, support but most problematic will be onboarding new AISPs and PISPs as that is likely to be ongoing and time consuming.

The techniques of screen-scraping have been used by TPPs for the past 15 years, and an out right ban could cause untold harm as they may be required if FinTech firms are to maintain the same level of service post PSD2 as they currently offer their customers. Mature FinTech firms have developed the user web interface and their screen-scraping technology to provide advanced banking services to their clients and they claim perfectly securely for a decade and a half. Screen-scraping or as the FinTechs prefer 'direct-access' is something of a emotive subject between the parties, as although there is little doubt it has enabled innovation and delivered advanced products and services it is still regarded as being a shadow form of banking based on a mechanism with a much longer yet maligned but ultimately a misunderstood history.

Strangely for such a simple concept the technology behind screen-scraping can be extremely complex using behaviour tracking and recording, software robots and orchestration to automate the service but that is nowhere near as dense as the arguments that rage around its use. Simply put, screen-scraping is the automated, programmatic interaction with a website, where the software is impersonating a web browser in order to extract data or perform actions or tasks that users would usually perform manually. However this is an internet era definition as screen-scraping has been used for decades even before the internet or websites were ever dreamt off as it was used to auto fill forms back in the days of the mainframe and dumb terminals. Today screen-scraping techniques are used throughout industry to enable legacy applications to interact with modern Service Orientated Application systems. Furthermore they have found a use in automating repetitive or predictable tasks that once a human might have performed. For example, screen-scraping would be used in automating common online banking tasks by software robots impersonating a bank employee manually entering data into forms when processing loan or mortgage applications.

However, what makes screen-scraping different in the Fintech scenario is twofold a) it is not the FinTech firms systems, these are the banks systems they are scraping and b) they log on to the banks systems albeit with the explicit consent of the customer but using what should be the customers secret security credentials.

In the latter case which is the most controversial Fintech firms have no option, for screen-scraping to work the FinTech firm needs the customer's bank login credentials. They can then use these details to log into the bank's customer-facing online banking system and then impersonate the user. Subsequently, in the more advanced systems the software robot can mimic the customer and hence defeat even behavioural analysis defences, which build a digital profile of a customer's actions, tempo and browsing behaviour. Nonetheless the purpose is to perform the same tasks or access the same services available to the customer. By automating this process through orchestration the TPP can use the screen-scraper to perform scheduled fund transfers, access the user's balance periodically on all their accounts and check the most recent transactions. To the bank the screen-scraping robot is to all intents and purposes, the customer, hence the TPP can access via this sleight of hand the same data with the same rights and permissions as the customer.

For FinTechs screen-scraping is by far the most prevalent technology used to access users' financial data, for example by Mint.com. However it is not exactly innovative or even ideal indeed its popularity come through it being the only practical and convenient way to access users' banking data. However it is hardly reliable and relies on the bank taking a blind-eye approach as screen-scrapers can be readily detected in most cases and sessions terminated. The fact that the banks can and could technically block this technique at any time – it is only their reluctance to upset their customers that prevents them - means that it is not an ideal model on which to build a business. Despite this screen-scraping has endured but this is more down to a lack of open Bank APIs, rather than a technological advantage or so we are told. Therefore, for FinTechs' making use of online banking services that are available to their customers are the only way possible in most cases to provide the advanced services their clients demand. For this reason it was erroneously believed that Fintech firms would rush to embrace the banks opening APIs as that would provide stability and future proof their businesses, but it appears this is actually far from their perspective of APIs.

Indeed it appears from the FinTech Alliance that this technique of screen-scraping, which is increasingly being referred to by them as "Direct Access", is the preferred method for mature firms. Furthermore they are most vociferous in their desire to keep screen-scraping as the de facto standard today for working with financial data. This is not to say they are against APIs per se it is just they would prefer to have the choice to use the API or the direct-access (screen-scraping) interface.

The major issue that springs to mind when contemplating screen-scraping is the sheer scale of the problem. It is easy to slip into the trap of minimising the problem only to forget the scale, for example there are around 4,000 banks in the EAA and approx 9,000 in the US and what is more as there is no standard website build, DOM, or directory structures then each website would requires a custom screen scraper to be built. Admittedly few FinTechs would ever aim to connect to them all as for example in the UK and Australia the top 7 and 5 banks hold over 80% of the nations account holders. Therefore, realistically FinTechs may only connect and scrape perhaps the top 10 national or regional banks determined by client/market demand, but it is still a significant challenge to growth. It is also something to bear in mind when we contemplate the issues and benefits discussed throughout this chapter and that applies not just too screen-scraping but also to any proposed alternatives.

Nonetheless, the over riding concern with screen-scraping in the financial services industry is not scalability but that it requires the third party providers to request and then store their users' security credentials for the bank or banks they use. This is, despite what many FinTech firms claim, a significant security issue and is the predominant difference between the screen-scraping that goes on elsewhere and what we see in the world of financial services. In some other common applications of screen-scraping the applications are trying to harvest public data, such as hotel availability and prices so there is no need to log in as the user with their personal credentials. This does not mean that screen-scraping is then somehow ethical or okay under these circumstances but it certainly is less contentious. As a rule of thumb it is considered to be ethical behaviour when screen-scraping to obey the robots.txt file which is a way that webmasters can indicate to robots on what pages or areas of the site they are not welcome. Of course these are not mandatory rules as such they are merely considered to be good behaviour on the web. Hence a TPP can on an individual basis decide whether to ignore the robots.txt file in much the same way they can unilaterally choose to ignore the bank's website Terms of Service.

However, when TPPs start screen-scraping consumers' bank accounts, there arise a few significant problems. The way the TTP handles the security credentials of the customer is paramount for as a service provider they must send the web-server when challenged the credentials in exactly the same format that a user would type in to log in to their online banking, for example a password and a piece of memorable data such as a PIN. In some cases it was possible to send a hashed password if the TPP knew the hash type supported by the bank but that method is dependent on the banks unique security policy and may well be different for other banks or likely to change without notice.

Regardless of whether the TPP s going to deliver the password as a hash or more likely in encrypted text over a secure HTTPS link there still remains the not inconsiderable burden of storing the customers username and password and these must be stored with due diligence to their security. This means they must be encrypted at rest in the database, and in flight but at the same time be in an unencrypted form when presented to the server doing the scraping simulated login.

Unfortunately storing sensitive data is a risky business and requires significant security knowledge as there's a real-world danger that these credentials could be compromised. The FinTech Alliance boast of hundreds of millions of transactions without a security compromise through loss or misuse of the customers' credentials but such talk is unwise and may indicate an unwillingness to realise the scale of the problem. For example many industries could make the same boasts but it only takes one of their members to be less than diligent to mess it all up for everyone. For example, in the case of mobile service providers, an industry with similar vast customer bases and under rigorous regulation but they would be confident of their security and their industry best practices when securing their customers personal details. However it only took 'Talk Talk' a UK national provider to be breached three times in one year to demonstrate clearly to the public that not only was the industry poorly regulated and their security paper thin for 'Talk Talk' were storing the client records in clear text or with weak encryption. While there haven't been any reported incidents in the FinTech industry so far it is unlikely to continue, for like 'Talk Talk' who had weakened their security to facilitate innovation i.e. making it easier to test prototype products, its likely FinTech firms might also favour such an agile DevOps ecosystem and unintentionally become lax with security. Consequently there will be the occasional startups eager to get to market and importantly mature firms that build and forget their defences and end up with weak security. Add to the mix developers with little knowledge of network protocols – just look at the shambles of the Internet of Things – and these firms in this imperfect world will be the weak links in the chain. Realistically it is only a matter of time before a Fintech breach does occur if it hasn't already happened and we may see a catastrophic data leak like those reported at companies such as Yahoo, LinkedIN or Equifax.

Given that customers' will often reuse their passwords across many websites that they visit, it might take only a breach from such a compromised site to defeat the FinTechs network and subsequently compromise the consumers' bank accounts.

From a more fundamental point though is that screen-scraping on websites that require a login actually is very poor practice as it legitimises and desensitises consumers to sharing their passwords with third-parties. The technology and security industries spend vast amounts educating ordinary consumers in good online security practices in recognising social engineering and become wary of 'phishing' attacks. Unfortunately the methods that FinTechs use to capture the customers credentials such as having them enter them into a third party frame embedded within the FinTechs website goes against all that effort.

Asking consumers to enter their banks credentials on third-party websites or on third party apps further compromises these efforts, going against and thus undermining what they have been taught about online security. Muddying the water by suggesting its safe because hundreds of thousands of transaction have gone through without a hiccup is irresponsible and you only have to look to a tech giant like Yahoo to see the terrible consequences of that misguided confidence.

Furthermore from a customer perspective, by handing over their security credentials to a third party to enable screen-scraping is, for most banks, a violation of their account's terms and conditions, or at the very least of the Terms of Service. What this distils down to is that if there is a hiccup and the customer is a victim of fraud then they could be liable for any mistake made by the TPP as the bank certainly will not entertain them.

From another customer perspective screen-scraping is also not ideal as not only do they have to share their login credentials but they forfeit or delegate all control. Screen-scraping does not allow users to have granular control over what permissions they delegate to the TPP such as what they have access to and for what duration. For example they cannot practically limit the TPP to only accessing an account balance for once they hand over their password they effectively forfeit all control and the TPP can do everything that the customer can do – even if that is well out with the purpose that the customer gave permission and access.

As a final point there are no regulations so there is no method for the customer to change TPP and to safely revoke or transfer permissions other than to change their bank password. The fact that this is so primitive should have alarm bells ringing for the customers but alas no, there still seems to be sufficient customers willing to take the risks. Indeed sufficient numbers to ensure that the FinTech industry is very keen to maintain screen-scraping as one of their methods of access.

For the FinTech TPP it is even harder to understand their desire to maintain screen-scraping as a tool as it is inherently unstable, costly and stifles any so-called innovations because the systems are out with their control. They are utterly at the mercy of circumstance or so it would appear.

Building a business based upon scraping the data from a banks' online customer interface that is not a partner and keen collaborator in a join venture, is a high-risk operation. As the design and development of the site is out with the TPP's control so it is highly likely to make any interface the TPP's develops at best fragile, unpredictable and inherently unreliable. This is simply due to the developer having no insight into how long the site will remain unchanged, for any change the bank makes to the DOM, directory structure, or URIs could potentially break the app necessitating a complete redesign of the TPP interface. This inherent fragility results in unpredictable levels of availability for consumers but also unpredictable levels of maintenance costs for development and support. Worse, as can be seen by the furore over the RTS what if the banks simply ban the use of the screen scraper – then what will these Fintech firms do if all their business is built upon such an unstable foundation? It is highly likely they could topple and fall.

Despite these concerns FinTech firms are doing very nicely and are accessing customer data successfully using screen-scraping, but it is doubtful that even they truly believe that it's the preferable solution. The problem though is more nuanced because perhaps the PSD2 is not as welcome to FinTech TPP as we might first imagine. It is only when we dig a bit deeper that we begin to see why that may be.

One complaint that has surfaced is that banks do not intend nor are they required by PSD2 or RTS to send a response to a payment transaction initiated by a TPP which in effect assures the payee they will receive the funds. This is interesting because it raises the question of how have Fintech worked around this using screen-scraping and how have the TPPs their customers and the retailers been handling payment transactions –out with the banks - to date? After all why is there such concern about the banks not freely providing their risk assessment tools to send a response to the retailer which in effect guarantees the payment, if the banks do not do so for screen scrapers today?

The issue that retailers and the TPPs predict and it is realistic and well founded is that without such a timely guarantee from the bank then the retailer will be reluctant to release the goods and thus unlikely to use the service in the future. Hence the financial instrument of direct payment from the payer's account to the retailers (payee) account will be unlikely to gain traction.

The concern may well be sound but FinTech TPPs having been doing such payment and remittances for more than a decade so how have they managed to mitigate this concern. Well it appears that not all FinTechs have the same type of access using their screen-scraping tools and in some cases do not just check balances but can collect other information as well as being able to initiate a payment automatically. Not all FinTechs work the same way as some still require their client to manually perform a payment where as others have automated this process as well but to do so also requires them to further manipulate the client's account.

For example if we consider a simple payment transaction being automated by a FinTech then they would, with the delegation from the client, access the account and perform the payment transfer to the payee (retailer). However payments are a little bit more complex that just performing a fund transfer, as there is still the issue of assurance or guarantee of payment that the retailer will demand before they release the goods. With a traditional payment process such as a debit or credit card this assurance is given by the bank. The retailer is then happy to release the goods in the knowledge that payment will be honoured. However, when a FinTech firm performs a payment exercise they will have to operate and work around the issue where the merchant requires some sort of assurance that the payment will be executed. In order to accomplish this fintech firms need to be satisfied prior to reserving or withdrawing the funds from the payer's bank that the transaction will be fulfilled. Therefore, the FinTech retrieves apart from the current balance some other data, e.g. overdraft allowance, outstanding commitments or orders, upcoming direct debits or previously declined transactions, and they do this to identify the risk of non-execution. Based on the information collected the FinTech makes their own risk assessment so that merchants may be given a sufficiently risk-mitigated, realtime "payment confirmation". The FinTech must accept the risk because the bank will not do this for free, presently this is a successful alternative, but will it be sustainable when the market deepens and the customer demographic becomes less affluent.

Regardless the question is rhetorical as none of this will be allowed post PSD2 unless the FinTech firm is both a PISP and an AISP. This is because PISP's can execute payment transactions but not query for information. Conversely an AISP can request account information but not execute a payment transaction. This well intentioned separation of duties will be strictly enforced if APIs are made available from the banks but does not exist in a screen-scraping environment so its little wonder the FinTech TPP do not wish to let the method slip away post PSD2.

If separation of duties between the defined roles of PISP and AISP limits the actions and scope for the TPP it is clear to see why they would not be overwhelmed by the PSD2. But if that is the case then what are the banks problems with FinTech firms screen-scraping their client's data over the internet via the standard customer web site as one or other of the defined post PSD2 roles? There are actually several issues from a PSD2 perspective that need to be addressed. The new directive is based upon strong customer authentication and securing the customer's interests during any electronic payment transactions. The first issue is down to the requirements for SCA and the way the customer delegates authority for managing their bank account to a third party. The fact that the customer is handing over their website login credentials to a third party is in most cases against the Terms of Service. This is likely to mean that they will forfeit any rights or protections they might normally been afforded by the bank in case of loss. The sharing of credentials is a serious issue that FinTech firms have to address as it not only inhibits customer onboarding as it is a big turn-off for most potential clients who are reluctant to share their passwords but also because it is inherently insecure.

FinTech firms will often maintain that they do not store usernames or passwords and that may be true in some cases but it others that is clearly not the case as the client signs into a pop-up frame on the TPP website. This frame is not associated with the client's bank but with the TPP or more often their third party screen-scraping vendor, which in the latter case is how many TPP can claim they are not in possession at any time of the clients credentials. This is true but a bit disingenuous as they knowingly have passed them to a third party screen-scraper vendor or in FinTech terms financial data aggregators that the client has in most cases no knowledge. This is inherently insecure and most certain poor practice as entering banking credentials into a third party site is never a good idea – yet the RTS appears to allow this. Indeed, strangely when challenged as to why the EBA appeared to be allowing TPP to collect, pass through or transmit customer credentials or have them enter their passwords directly into a TPP app. The EBA's response was that they had no realistic authority to prevent a customer choosing the same password for the TPP as they used for the bank.

Perhaps not, and this might just be feasible for a simple username/password but how will it work when SCA is implemented and there will be a choice of two out of three mechanisms, knowledge, possession or inherence. Today most banks use double knowledge for web based service such as a username and a password/pin combination so sharing that knowledge no longer makes it unique so the security has been seriously weakened and is no longer SCA. Furthermore should the banks post PSD2 wish to upgrade their SCA techniques then they will be limited to ways that a challenge or a one-time-password (OTP) can be passed back to the bank via a third party. The issue being is there would have to be a way which will allow the third party screen-scraper to have the capability to intercept and pass through these security prompts such as a one time password or pin. Sending readable text works via SMS or some other out-of -band channel but that will not be sufficient for something like a touch-screen response when identifying an image, using a fingerprint ala Apple Pay or clicking on a one time QR code.

In addition, allowing the client to perform the SCA through a third party whose internal mechanisms are a black-box to the customer and the bank actually defeats the SCA and puts the customer at great risk. FinTech firms will likely respond that there is practically little difference between the customers entering their credentials into a browser or into a TPP app however that is a false equivalence as there is no comparison between the security levels and scrutiny applied to modern browsers and those that are applied to third party apps, if any. Additionally, the browser initiates and sets up the SSL/TLS encryption between the customer and the bank well before the customer enter their credentials so they would never be seen by the local browser. On the other hand the third party app that the screen scraper uses requires that the credentials are unencrypted and in clear text as they are behaving as a proxy for the user, so have to send the credentials exactly as the user would enter them, hence the difficulty with handling OTP derived from touch screen actions and/or QR code images.

The previous section describes the issues of handling and passing the customers security credentials from the TPP to the bank from a single access payment perspective initiated by a PISP. However from an AISP perspective where the TPP may be connecting to multi-banks using a set of different credentials for each as will be the case the problems associated with collecting, handling, storing and retrieving these multi-sets of credentials securely becomes far more problematic. For this reason AISPs previously tended to stay away from retrieving consumer accounts and instead collected and collated the pricing for public data associated with the banks products and services. However as screen-scraping technology advanced they too started to venture into the consumer market, which brought them eventually into conflict with the large banks. This is evident in the US market where banks such as Wells Fargo and Bank of America were determine to put a stop to screen-scraping from aggregators such as Yodlee and Intuit.

Indeed the process of sharing or entering credentials into a TPP website or app is bad practice as it removes any possibility of non-repudiation as the bank cannot tell definitively who logged in and performed the transaction. The FinTech companies claim that they do often announce themselves through identification within the header and that PSD2 will require them to do so. That may well be so, but presently that is not standard procedure and indeed most of the effort appears to being spent developing increasingly advanced mechanisms that will defeat the banks defences. Post PSD2 none of this will be allowed as the TPP will need to identify itself through an e-IDAS certificate so this should remove much of the security concerns with regards identity but there is still the thorny issue regards granular authorisation.

Presently the customer has to provide the TPP with full permissions and it is left to the TPP to be responsible for their actions of only accessing the minimum data required to fulfill a task or perform a purpose. However as we can see with the typical FinTech TPP payment process we described earlier in the chapter the minimum permissions and data they require for a simple payment transaction isn't always clear to the customer. Furthermore, the customer may not even know who they are giving permission too. Not every FinTech TPP is in the position to build and maintain their own technology hence they outsource to a third party vendor which typically is a data aggregator. This raises the thorny issue of trust, for the customer gives permissions and delegates authority to FinTech 'A' based on some trust criteria but in some cases it may be that FinTech 'A' is passing the security credentials and delegating the authority to Aggregator 'B' without the customer's knowledge, which breaks informed and explicit permission – a cornerstone of the PSD2 and worryingly the GDPR.

The only secure method to manage this third party access between a Fintech, a customer and their bank is for the customer to be redirected to their bank to login and then be redirected back using a token for authentication and permissions for a session or limited lifetime. The customer must login using OAuth or similar which will provide a permission limiting token or code which will allow the bank to determine what access and permissions the TPP has been given by the customer. Of course this is not possible with screen-scraping or at least non-collaborative screen-scraping as the bank will not entertain this unless it is forced upon them by the EU over-ruling the EBA and legitimising the use of screen-scraping.

With regards the banks they are is a somewhat difficult position but mostly of their own making. The banks have produced a muddled response to screen-scraping in effect allowing it for customers doing it themselves via Excel Query while at the same time taking a hard-line approach on TPPs basically doing the same thing, before eventually turning a blind eye. However that doesn't mean there are not legitimate concerns emanating from the banks or from any other commercial website providers' perspective as they are supplying a service for their clients to access in person, manually via a web browser. They expect their clients to abide by the website's terms of service relating to fair usage and certainly not to place unnecessary load or stress the site by using automated tools, (Excel aside it would appear) which could aversely affect the experience for other customers. As a result banks would prefer to supply and control access to their systems in these perilous days of cyber security threats by providing controlled access over dedicated channels called APIs. Originally the EC and EBA were in agreement however vigorous lobbying by mature FinTech firms has brought about a change of heart by the European Committee. In a remarkable intervention the EC proposed that screen-scraping should not be banned per se but remain as a back-up for contingency purposes. The EBA strongly refute the reasoning.

The Need for Back-end Enablers

Ideally, banks would share a common open banking standard so that all banks use a common way to describe DOM, fields and functions, making queries, and returning results. This would go a long way to help TPP developers and partners to more easily create new applications and services for customers that can scale and be used consistently across all European banks. Unfortunately building a universal bank catalogue of web-site criteria using a common standard is extremely difficult. After all it would require collaboration and standardisation of the DOM as well as the base data sets and data\directory structures which is key to any standardisation of a screen-scraping app. Basically it would require practically every bank to redesign their website to a common architecture with a standard data structure and nomenclature and that is not likely to happen any time soon.

Of course tat issue is not just with screen-scrapping but also is true for APIs as they too will be non-standard and require the TPPs to rework their scripts to fit each banks service.

Unfortunately, FinTech TPPs also look upon APIs as a way that provides key advantages for the banks. This advantage materialises in their minds as initially PSD2 APIs will have a core set of functions that are required as part of the PSD2 regulation but for each API, there will be one specific purpose, for example:

```
\banks\bank_id\account_id
```

Consequently these APIs are deemed to be of sufficient benefit to the TPP but this also leaves the control of data flow up to the banks.

This philosophy does help ensure banks meet the mandatory requirements of the PSD2 regulations. Furthermore it will drive how a bank deploys and builds its PSD2 TPP interfaces which will require innovation and insight into the platform, business and technology, while minimising the information it releases. Also using an open source solution may provide economies of scale since multiple banks will test and contribute to their collaborative development. In addition, it is possibly beneficial to build a developer testing environment, such as the popular testing sandbox, where developers can experiment with the TPP interface on test data, or redacted live data, so as to entice them away from the open screen-scraping methods.

However scaling these solutions and moderating the efforts and expense will be hugely important and this is where there is a requirement for middleware or rather an aggregator that can mediate communication interfaces between TPPs and the banks. There are currently only a few established aggregators active providing the screen-scraping services for many of the FinTech firms. The service the aggregator provides is that it will present a standard or custom interface to the TPP and also to the bank thereby providing the interconnection hub required connecting the plethora of TPPs with the thousands of banks. In this idealised solution a TPP or a bank would only have to maintain one interface the aggregator will handle the interconnections and any protocol translations. Currently Yodlee and mint provide this service for screen-scraping but similar aggregation architectures will be needed for managing the same amount of API mesh connections between TPPs and the banks.

Chapter 6 – Service Orientated Architecture and the API Interface

APIs are not new. They've served as interfaces that enable applications to communicate with each other for decades especially in SOA architectures. But the role of APIs has changed dramatically in the last few years. Innovative companies have discovered that APIs can be used as an interface to the business, allowing them to provide all sorts of self-service inter-department services but it is the potential to safely offer these same services outside of the business which has caught the imagination. Tech Giants such as Google, Facebook, Amazon, and Microsoft amongst other have opened up services to the outside world in order to monetise their digital assets and bring added value to their partners and customers.

When you create an API, you are allowing others within or outside of your organization to make use of your service or product to create new applications, add value, attract customers, or expand their business. Internal APIs enhance the productivity of development teams by maximizing reusability and enforcing consistency in new applications. Public APIs can add value to the business by allowing 3rd party developers to enhance services or build open source style communities of innovation. As developers find new applications for the services and data, they expand the feature set and functionality, thereby increasing the utility of the service and its further suitability for other applications. This network effect occurs, delivering significant benefit to every node in the network which often is visible through bottom-line business impact – or rather that is how it typically works with PSD2 it is likely to be less harmonious with considerably more inertia and friction induced through politics.

The Value of a Successful API

As we covered in the previous passage a successful API is more than a technical feature or a product it can be an effective enabler of the business strategy. However the dilemma arises when parties do not share the same high level strategy and are not collaborative? Indeed as we have witnessed via the communications between all relevant parties over the screen-scraping debate, for some the issue is highly emotive and indicative of their hostility and lack of commitment to APIs as an alternative to their current practices. There is justification in their scepticism as allowing the banks to have the control over an API, as they must, it is only technically feasible way to develop one, renders the FinTech to be merely a consumer of the services that the banks deem fit to present. Hence the concern of FinTech is that they may well be deliberately starved of opportunities for innovation and may well wither and die.

Needless to say, this is a really bad place to start when designing an API as there is suspicion and lack of trust on both sides. Indeed it could in this instance be described as being a toxic environment where there is little likely to be gained by either side where it not for the fact that FinTech will have to use the APIs, at least when they are available.

FinTech for their part have placed a marker, perhaps cunningly by pre-empting the result and insinuating that the banks will restrict their access and provide low quality and highly restrictive APIs. As a result the banks now must respond by providing the highest quality and expansive APIs that they can possibly deliver.

Consequently the banks must look to delivering a great API that not only silences their critics but undeniably encourages developers of the FinTech community to use it. Only then can they create a virtuous cycle where each additional successful implementation leads to more engagement and more contributions from developers who add value to the service leading to the '*what have the Romans (banks) ever done for us?*' scenario. Importantly, it is only through delivering a Rolls-Royce level of service to the FinTech community that the banks can eventually win the argument.

For FinTech they alas have set up their stall mired in negativity and the suspicion must be that they long for the banks to fail in delivering a successful API so that they can revert back to screen-scraping. However that avenue has now been effectively closed. Although the FinTech community may get the green light to continue practicing the technique after PSD2 it will be under highly restrictive codes of practice dependent on their defined role as a PISP or an AISP the days of roaming free and loose are gone.

It therefore is in both the banks and the Fintech communities interests to make a success of the opportunities of API if not the industry will likely end up with banks presenting API services that no-one consumes and the FinTech's screen-scraping for crumbs of authorised data dependent on their role.

An alternative is for them to collaborate to build a great API that could help grow an ecosystem of banks, partners and customers that provides a platform that enables banking to evolve and produce advanced modern services in ways that are mutually beneficial. Unfortunately, the promise of the open banking APIs can only be realized when the FinTechs begin to use them and in the current climate that doesn't seem to be anytime soon.

FinTech developers will only – possibly reluctantly - use the banks API if they believe it's the best, most efficient way to achieve their goals. Hence the onus is on the banks to deliver well designed APIs that are easy to use and will deliver the services that Fintech developers require. Encouraging the adoption of the API by developers, thus paves the way to a better-defined, more consistent and maintainable approach to development and can mitigate political interference. However the huge opportunity for the bank is that they can reimagine all their development work in producing the PSD2 API and issue it as a public API to their own customers. Then the situation is ironically even more critical as opening APIs to the public allows the bank's customers if provided with a bank produced app to DIY and hence they would have no need for a shadow FinTech service.

As is to often the case some banks are going through the tedious motions and dragging their feet when it comes to building their APIs and thus building before thinking through the critical success factors, resulting in APIs that are sufficient for sandbox and experimental usage but ultimately fail to meet business objectives. On the other hand the new breed of challenger banks are focused on successful API delivery tightly aligned to business strategy. These progressive banks such as Atom Bank and Starling are strong proponents of the mobile and API driven architectures but they are not alone in this as other established banks are already experimenting or have released open APIs to partners and developers such as the AIB Group, Bank of Ireland, Barclays, Danske, HSBC Group, Lloyds Banking Group, Nationwide, RBS Group and Santander to name just a few.

Why Are APIs Important for the Banks?

1. Banks Create Controlled Access with APIs

API's are the way that the banks can retain control while complying with PSD2 legislation and allowing the TPPs to communicate in real-time with their customer's payment accounts but importantly only those accounts. APIs are the way banks can provide direct communications with their backend applications without the outside developers understanding the database schema or knowing how to write the specific queries or code. The bank developers create APIs that TPPs may use as templates to retrieve information or to process transactions by using a standard process and procedure.

2. Business People Use External API

API allows banks and businesses to interact and collaborate through social media and external applications such as Twitter, Facebook and Amazon. Google and other web-scale giants also make their API open and available for the public's use. The bank's open external APIs will be accessible and heavily use by marketing and the media for connections to Facebook or Twitter. But bank developers may also consume other companies services for example, a programmer can access and call Google Maps and Geo-locator API then use the service's functions within their own applications for example to produce a mobile app that displays the bank branches and ATM locations nearest to the user's current location.

3. Banks Rely on Open APIs

Open APIs are hugely important for providing access to third parties and trusted partners by giving them secure access to data and for project collaboration. Service orientated Architecture and enterprise scale applications make open APIs available to developers, partners and IT for system integration, innovation and development purposes. Open web based APIs are open to everyone.

API: A Technical Perspective

For an API to work it must be configured and detailed by the application programmer and typically the database designer. This is because normally you are reading or writing data from one application into another application hosted on another system and so it will need to be retrieved from or stored permanently in the database. Hence, the API must have very strict inputs and outputs that are precisely related to the operation being undertaken. This is why APIs are such a good fit for TPP interaction as it inherently limits the permissible actions available. An API for example, that requests or posts a payment transaction, doesn't require to retrieve mortgage account information, and vice versa. Therefore a good description of an API is being:

"API is a precise specification written by providers of a service that programmers must follow when using that service. The API describes what functionality is available, how it must be used and what formats it will accept as input or return as output."

As a result we can consider an API as being a specified template for initiating an authorised action or inputting or retrieving data into an application or its database.

API Analogy

In order to have a clearer understanding of how an API works, it is better to look upon it as basically a form (template) that is being used, let's look at an appropriate analogy. Let's consider for the sake of argument that every time you want to submit or access a set of data from an application, you have to call the API. However, there are certain rules that you must follow and the programmer determines these rules when they construct the format of the API template. After all when designing the API the programmer will have to determine that there is only certain types of data the application will let you access, similarly there is only specific data that he will allow you to input to the database, therefore you have to communicate in a very specific protocol and format— which is also a syntax appropriate to each programmable language.

To help understand this concept, imagine an API as the security guard between you (the user) and an application. The security guard accepts your requests and checks your authentication and who gave you your permissions. Subsequently, when happy that you are who you say you are, and you do have the required permission the security guard supplies you with a form with the correct format for the request and the data. When you complete the form with your request and the details of the request criteria, i.e. what data you wish to store or retrieve, the security guard will check the format is correct. If the presentation is correct, the security guard will forward the request to the application. The application subsequently performs further authentication and authorization control and if the request passes its security checks then the application will allow the request/input, and the application returns or stores the data too or on behalf of you.

Example of an API

A company may give their staff the ability to run reports on their own data, reports or social media from the company databases. However, in order to run those database queries requires a SQL query to be entered against the database.

It is not feasible for the user to send an email to the Database Administrators (DBA) whenever they need that information and for security and operational reasons, the

DBA cannot give users the access to run the query themselves.

This is where the API comes into play. The Database administrators have written unique SQL queries in scripts that trigger whenever a user makes an API call. The database can then return requests for data from the store to the user in real time. Consequently, whenever people execute an action or request any data analytics using the API, the results are returned without the users having to know any coding or SQL and more importantly they are not interacting directly with the database system.

What Is an API Call?

One common misunderstanding with regards an API is that it is envisaged as being something like a URL for a website such as;

/banks/BANK_ID/accounts/public

However these URLs are only the service calls that the service provider publishes to those that wish to use (consume) the service can access programmatically. Behind the scenes is most likely a vast an often in banking legacy system that has been laboriously divided into microservices where each distinct service or functional module has been segregated and then can be called from a unique URL. Whenever a user, developer or system requests information from an application or wishes to post information to another application, they need to make a request to that API, using the URL assigned to that preformatted template.

Of course having external users and systems make requests to the API requires strict security measures to be in place to limit bandwidth, usage, as well as illegal requests. Web based API are URLs, which are used to activate the call using common HTML commands, such as POST and GET. These URLs are not activated by clicking on them as they will typically return just a blank screen (unless they have been constructed to send data back to the web page) so they typically are used within programs and scripts. As a result, programmers can build APIs using a whole array of languages, PHP, Ruby, Python etc. The programmer can then construct the URL within their scripts, and call the API URL when the programming language script is executed.

RESTful API

REST was designed specifically for web and mobile applications using HTTP as its communications protocol. However, these days, when people refer to an API they are most likely referring to an open web-service HTTP API, which can be a way of accessing and sharing application data over the internet. For example, Twitter has an API that allows a request for tweets to be served up in a format that makes it easy to import into host applications. It is this ability of being able to "mash-up" multiple application API into a single application, is what makes web-based open HTTP APIs so powerful, flexible and so useful. Similarly, the ability to create an application, which enhances the experience of using someone else's application, is another major use for HTTP API.

For example, let's say we have an application that allows you to view, create, edit, and delete accounts from a bank sandbox web site which is hosted in the cloud on a third party web-site. We could create an HTTP API that allows you to perform these functions:

```
/banks/BANK_ID/accounts
/banks/BANK_ID/accounts/public
/banks/BANK_ID/accounts/private
/my/accounts
```

For the first three functions a typical response would look something like this:

```
{
  "accounts":[{
    "id":"8ca8a7e4-6d02-48e3-a029-0b2bf89de9f0",
    "label":"NoneLabel",
    "bank_id":"gh.29.uk",
    "views_available":[{
      "id":"1",
      "short_name":"HHH",
      "is_public":true
    }]
  }]
}
```

The URLs for the first three REST APIs, use the method 'GET' to return all accounts, only public accounts, and only private accounts, respectively. However the final API does something different as it lists all of the stated user's accounts at all connected banks. Therefore, the response from the API my/accounts will look something like this:

```
{
  "accounts":[{
    "id":"String",
    "label":"String",
    "bank_id":"String",
    "account_routing":{
      "scheme":"IBAN",
      "address":"DE89 3704 0044 0532 0130 00"
    }
```

```
}]

}
```

These URLs are how REST APIs are accessed or called
and they each have a specific function. However, you can
probably see that the first issue that will arise is the non-
standard use of URLs, which will come about when
everyone starts implementing their own APIs and URL
standards. For example, without a standard way of naming
URLs, there will always be a requirement for the user to
refer to the documentation to understand how the API
works. One API might have a URL
like /banks/BANK_ID/accounts whereas another API
might use /banks/BANK_ID/accounts/all. It might well
seem trivial but it is small details like that, which can make
editing scripts very frustrating.

REST API however has a technique built-in to overcome
this potential mess.

What is REST?

REST stands for **Re**presentational **S**tate **T**ransfer. This is a
term invented by Roy Fielding to describe a standard way
of creating HTTP APIs. He noticed that the four common
actions (view, create, edit, and delete) map directly to
HTTP verbs that are already implemented within the
protocol: GET, POST, PUT, DELETE.

HTTP methods

For those unfamiliar with HTTP there are technically 8 different HTTP methods:

GET
POST
PUT
DELETE
OPTIONS
HEAD
TRACE
CONNECT

Generally, when users are browsing the internet and navigating around in their browser, they are only ever using the GET HTTP method. GET is the method used, as its name suggests when you are "getting" a resource from the internet. However when you submit a form, you may be using several others methods such as POST, UPDATE and CREATE however as typically used it will be the POST method to "post the form" back to the website. As for the other methods, some browsers don't even implement them all, so all we are concerned with in addition to GET and POST are the DELETE and PUT methods. What really matters is that these basic HTTP methods are a collection of "verbs" to choose from which help to describe the actions being taken. Additionally, client libraries, which already know how to use the different HTTP methods, are used to assist with building and executing the REST API.

Examples of REST

The following examples show what makes an API "RESTful" by using an example of a typical banking API such as 'Base_URL/banks'. It should be noted that this is merely an illustration of a REST API and is not a tutorial.

To view all available bank services and products, the URL would look like this:

GET /banks/BANK_ID/products

To create a new set of products or services we have to upload the relevant data to the application or database the PUT method is used:

```
PUT /banks/BANK_ID/products
Data: { "bank_id":"bankid123", "code":"prod1",
"name":"product name", "category":"category",
"family":"family", "super_family":"super family",
"more_info_url":"www.example.com/prod1/more-
info.html", "details":"Details",
"description":"Description", "meta":{ "license":{
"id":"5", "name":"Test Product" } }}
```

In order to view a single service, we use the "GET" method by specifying the Product_Code which is the specific identifier for each individual product or service in the catalogue

```
GET /banks/BANK_ID/products/PRODUCT_CODE
```

Moreover, to update the customer comments record in the database the POST method of "posting" the new data into the application or database is used:

```
POST
/banks/BANK_ID/products/PRODUCT_CODE/CUSTOM
ER_ID/messages
 Data: product_code = 1243, customer_id = 1010203040,
"message":"String",
```

Finally, to delete that specific message from the database we use the DELETE method:

```
DELETE
banks/BANK_ID/products/PRODUCT_CODE/CUSTOM
ER_ID/messages
  Data: product_code = 1243, customer_id = 1010203040,
"message_id = 123,"message":"String",
```

Anatomy of a REST URL

In the previous example, it may be clear that the REST URLs use a consistent naming scheme. When the URLs are interacting with an API, they are almost always manipulating some sort of object. In our examples, this is a 'base_url\banks\' record in the database. In REST terminology, this is termed a resource. The first part of the URL is always the plural form of the resource:

```
/banks
```

The plural form is always used when referring to the collection of resources for example when you wish to "list all" action. When you are working with a specific resource, the specific ID or the resource is added to the URL as shown below.

This specific URL is used when with the action required is to "view", "edit", or "delete" that particular resource.

HTTP Status Codes

Another important part of REST is responding with the correct status code for the type of request made. For those new to HTTP status codes, here is a quick summary. When you make an HTTP request, the server will respond with a code, which corresponds to whether or not the request was successful and how the client should proceed. There are four different levels of codes:

- 2xx = Success
- 3xx = Redirect
- 4xx = User error
- 5xx = Server error

Here's a list of the most important status codes:

Success codes:

- 200 - OK (the default)
- 201 - Created
- 202 - Accepted (often used for delete requests)

User error codes:

- 400 - Bad Request (generic user error/bad data)
- 401 - Unauthorized (this area requires you to log in)
- 404 - Not Found (bad URL)
- 405 - Method Not Allowed (wrong HTTP method)
- 409 - Conflict (i.e. trying to create the same resource with a PUT request)

API response formats

When you make an HTTP request, you can request the format that you want to receive. For example, making a request for a webpage, you want the format to be in HTML, or if you are downloading an image, the format returned should be an image. Ultimately, it's the server's responsibility to respond in the format that was requested.

JSON has quickly become the format of choice for REST APIs. It has a lightweight, readable syntax that can be easily manipulated. So when a user of our banking API makes a request and specifies JSON as the format they would prefer data returned in:

```
GET /banks/BANK_ID/atms/ATM_ID
Accept: application/json
```

The API will return an array of all catalogued ATM services matching the request parameters formatted as JSON:

```json
{
  "id":"atm-id-123",
  "bank_id":"bank-id-123",
  "name":"Atm by the Lake",
  "address":{
  "line_1":"No 1 the Road",
  "line_2":"The Place",
  "line_3":"The Hill",
  "city":"Berlin",
  "county":"",
  "state":"Brandenburg",
  "postcode":"13359",
  "country_code":"DE"
  },
  "location":{
  "latitude":11.45,
  "longitude":11.45
  }
}
```

RESTful JSON web services

REpresentational State Transfer, or REST, is a design pattern for interacting with resources stored in a server. Each resource has an identity, a data type, and supports a set of actions.

The RESTful design pattern is normally used in combination with HTTP, the language of the internet. In this context the resource's identity is its URI, the data type is its Media Type, and the actions are made up of the standard HTTP methods (GET, PUT, POST, and DELETE).

This style of service differs from Request-Response style web services:

- Request-Response services start interaction with an Application, whereas RESTful services typically interact with data (referred to as 'resources').

- Request-Response services involve application defined 'operations', but RESTful services avoid application specific concepts.

- Request-Response services have different data formats for each message, but RESTful service typically share a data format across different HTTP methods

The four major HTTP methods define the four operations that are commonly implemented by RESTful Services. The HTTP POST method is used for creating a resource, GET is used to query it, PUT is used to change it, and DELETE is used to destroy it. The most common RESTful architecture involves a shared data model that is used across these four operations. This data model defines the input to the POST method (create), the output for the GET method (inquire) and the input to the PUT method (replace). This simple design pattern is popular within the RESTful community, but it's not the only RESTful design pattern. The HTTP status code is used to indicate success or failure of the operation. Some RESTful APIs are designed in other ways.

A fifth HTTP method called 'HEAD' is sometimes supported by RESTful web services. This method is equivalent to GET, except that it returns only HTTP Headers, and no Body data. It's sometimes used to test the Existence of a resource. Not all RESTful APIs support use of the HEAD method.

.The URI

The identity of a RESTful service is indicated by its URI. A URI can be made up of several components, including the host name, port number, the path, and an optional query string. The domain name and port number together target a TCPIPSERVICE resource. The URI path is a qualifier, and might be sufficient to uniquely identify the service. However, many RESTful web services use an additional query string to identify the precise resource. Consider the following examples:

- http://www.example.org:10000/JSONServices/AccountService

- https://www.example.org:10000/JSONServices?Service=Account

In the first example the URI path is JSONServices/AccountService. In the second example the path is JSONServices and there is an additional query string of Service=Account. Both styles of URI are considered to be acceptable for JSON. This is an important difference compared to SOAP. Under SOAP the first style of URI is preferred.

API affordance

When designing an API we have to consider for what purpose it will be used. If one of the objectives is to create an open API where opening the internal application to the Internet is the goal then one of the objectives of an API design strategy should be to make the API as useful and useable to as many developers as possible. It is therefore critical that the API be well documented and, intuitive and as simple as possible to use. This is necessary so that developers will know intuitively the purpose and requirements of the API without the need to refer to the documentation.

The term associated with this type of design is *affordance*: the API suggests its own usage and is self-descriptive. Therefore, to achieve affordance in API design the following principles should be adhered to:

- The API semantics must be intuitive, self-descriptive whereby the URI, payload, request or response should be easy for the developer to understand and they should be able to use them without referring to the API documentation.
- The terms used should be intuitive, common and concrete, rather than be derived from a functional or technical phrase not in common parlance - *Customers, accounts, branches, products* are all good examples
- There should be one and only one way to achieve the same desired action.

Names or Verbs

To describe resources, programmers now consider it to be best practice to recommend the use of common and concrete names and not action verbs.

This may seem odd as for decades programmers have used action verbs in order to expose services in RPC API, for instance:

- getClient
- createClient
- deleteClient

By contrast, the modern RESTful approach is to use:

- GET /
- POST /
- PATCH /
- PUT /
- DELETE /

The use of HTTP verbs falls into line with the core design goals of a REST API in so much as REST uses HTTP as its protocol and that provides for consistency and this also provides for interaction over a ubiquitous and well understood protocol between applications and systems.

Furthermore in theory, because of the common use of the HTTP verbs (GET, PUT, POST & DELETE) - as these are used to describe what actions are performed on the resources, - this makes an API more intuitive, self-descriptive and helps developers understand how to manipulate the resources, therefore enhancing the API's affordance. In practice, it is the developers' tools and language IDE's, which help them generate HTTP requests with the appropriate HTTP verbs and the associated and appropriate payloads based on an up-to-date object model.

Plural or Singular

When considering the open APIs from the web-scale companies, such as Google and Yahoo it is interesting to note how they have a consistent behavior with regard to resource names being singular or plural. Indeed, it is okay to use either plural or singular, the main concern and therefore the design objective is not to use both in the same API: having resource names vary between singular and plural reduces the "browsability" and "Editability" of the API.

Programmers' generally consider it to be a best practice to use plural, as it is believed that resource names seem more natural to us when they are set to plural. Moreover, the use of plural to describe resources allows the programmer to address both *collections* and *instances* of resources with consistency. For example:

- Resource collections: /banks
- Resource instances: /banks/bank_id

Case consistency

URI case

When it comes to naming resources in a program, there are 3 main types of case conventions: CamelCase, snake_case, and spinal-case. They are just three conventions that programmer typically use when naming their resources in order for them to retain meaning and be readable, while avoiding spaces, apostrophes and other strange characters. This convention is universal in programming languages where only a finite set of characters are allowed for names.

- CamelCase is common and is particularly prevalent in the Java language. It intends to emphasize the beginning of each word by making the first letter uppercase. E.g. CamelCase, CurrentUser, AddAttributeToGroup, etc. Its main issue and a cause for debate is not just its readability but that not all contexts are case sensitive. Two variants coexist:
  - **lowerCamelCase:** where lowercase is used for the first letter.
  - **UpperCamelCase:** where the first letter is capital.

- snake_case is widely used by C programmers, and more recently in Ruby. Words are joined by underscores "_", thus letting a compiler or an interpreter understand it as a single symbol, but also allowing readers to separate words. Unlike camel case, it is not case sensitive so snake case can be used in just about every context. Examples: snake_case, current_user, add_attribute_to_group, etc.

- spinal-case is a variant of snake case which uses hyphens "-" to join words rather than the "_" . Spinal-case is also not case sensitive but is not as ubiquitous as snake-case due to some contexts where variables, etc are not allowed to use hyphens. It may look very familiar as it's also the traditional way of naming folders and files in Linux systems. Examples: spinal-case, current-user, add-attribute-to-group, etc.

According to RFC3986, URLs are "case sensitive" (except for the *scheme* and the *host*). In practice, though, a sensitive case may create dysfunctions with APIs hosted on a Windows system.

As a summary, the table below illustrates what the web-scale companies use as their best practices:

	Facebook	Google	Twitter	Paypal	Amazon
snake_case	x	x	X		x
spinal-case		x		x	
camelCase		x			x

As illustrated in the table above the most commonly adopted formats and therefore the recommend ones for choosing a consistent case convention are in order of preference:

- **snake_case**
- spinal-case
- camelCase

Examples

1 POST /v1/specific-orders

1 POST /v1/specific_orders

Body case

There are two main formats regarding the data body.

Snake_case is used noticeably more often by the web-scale companies, in particular it has been adopted by OAuth2 specifications so that makes it a good choice. On the other hand, the prevalence and growing popularity of the JavaScript language makes a case for using the camelCase adoption. However, be aware that the REST purists maintain that REST should remain language independent, therefore whether the script is in Python, Ruby or PHP it should not influence the choice of body case.

Again choose a consistent case for the body case, the choices are:

- snake_case (frequently used by Ruby programmers and web-scale companies)
- lowerCamelCase (frequently used by the Java and JavaScript communities)

Versioning

Versioning is very important as developers of other apps using your API must be able to track changes made to the API over time. This is an important consideration because most API will have to evolve over time. The problem is though how do we go about detailing the version, so that others will know about it. Some considerations to be taken into account regards versioning are that new version numbers should refer to full major releases of the API, not to just incremental minor bug fixes or trivial updates that are backward compatible and do not affect the operation of the API. For example, adding attributes to an existing resource does not imply incrementing the API version number. REST and JSON, in comparison to SOAP/XML, provide a lot of flexibility when developing the API without impacting all the clients, and changing the version number.

There are several conventions used when displaying the versioning of an API:

- With a *timestamp*, and/or a *release number*
- In the *path*, at the beginning or at the end of the *URI*
- As a parameter of the *request*
- In a *HTTP Header*
- With an *optional* or *mandatory* versioning.

In general the API version number is a key piece of information regarding the API. Therefore, it should be considered as essential information in accordance with the goals of affordance. The version should therefore relate to a major release number, so that it is readily understood and not a timestamp which is ambiguous and unlikely to be understood by other developers. Therefore it is better to have the version number displayed as a major release to appear in the URL than in the HTTP header or as a parameter in a request.

Additionally, by placing the version in the URL, it will be part of the path and this prevents uncontrolled changes to versioning as it is effectively prevented because in the case of code changes being made in the API, the developers are unlikely to have the control over renaming the path directories.

If we look at how the web-scale companies version their APIs we will get a good idea of common best practice:

API	Versioning
Google	https://www.googleapis.com/youtube/v3/
Facebook	URI (optional) https://graph.facebook.com/v2.0/{achievement-id} https://graph.facebook.com/v2.0/{comment-id}
Twitter	https://api.twitter.com/1.1/statuses/show.json https://stream.twitter.com/1.1/statuses/sample.json

The most common way appears to be including a compulsory one digit version at the highest level of the *URI's path*.

Example

```
1 GET /v1/Customers
```

As opposed to a URL/Optional Parameter

CRUD

As stated earlier, one of the key objectives of the REST approach is using HTTP as an application protocol therefore; we should use HTTP verbs to describe what actions are performed on the resources. The following table illustrates the best practices:

HTTP Verb	CRUD action	Collection : /orders	Instance : /orders/{id}
GET	READ	Read a list of orders. 200 OK.	Read the detail of a single order. 200 OK.
POST	CREATE	Create a new order.	–

			201 Created.
			Full Update. 200 OK.
			Create a specific order. 201 Created.
PUT	UPDATE/CREATE	–	
PATCH	UPDATE	–	Partial Update. 200 OK.
DELETE	DELETE	–	Delete order. 200 OK.

The HTTP verb POST is used to create an instance within a collection. The id of the resource to be created does not need to be provided as it will be auto-incremented and generate and returned within the location URL as shown below:

Example; creating a new order for customer id: 123 with the status: running

```
1 CURL –X POST \
2 -H "Accept: application/json" \
```

```
3  -H "Content-Type: application/json" \
4  -d '{"state":"running","id_client":"123"}' \
5  https://178.16.1.10/api/clients/123/orders
6  &lt;201 Created
7  &lt; Location: https://178.16.1.10/api/orders/1234
```

Note:

1) The return code is 201 (created) rather than 200 (ok).

2) The resource URI and newly created order id are returned in the *header* "Location" of the response.

However if we state the resource id in the request and it is specified by the client, the HTTP verb PUT is used for the creation of an instance within the collection. However, in practice this use case is rarely used.

Example; the PUT command is to specifically create a new order whilst stating the new order_id for client:123 with an order state: running

```
1  CURL –X PUT \
2  -H "Content-Type: application/json" \
3  -d '{"state":"running","id_client":"123"}' \
4  https://178.16.1.10/api/clients/123/orders/1234
5  &lt;201 Created
```

Another use of the HTTP verb PUT method is to do a full update of an instance in the collection where all attributes are replaced with those supplied and those which do not exist are deleted.

In the example below, we update the attributes state and id_client. All the other fields will be deleted.

```
1  CURL –X PUT \
2  -H "Content-Type: application/json" \
3  -d '{"state":"paid","id_client":"123"}' \
4  https: //178.16.1.10/api/clients/123/orders/1234
5  &lt;200 OK
```

When doing partial updates the HTTP verb PATCH is used instead of PUT

In the following example, we update the state attribute from state: running to state:paid (line 3) but the other attributes of the instance within the collection are left untouched.

```
1  CURL –X PATCH \
2  -H "Content-Type: application/json" \
3  -d '{"state":"paid"}' \
4  https: //178.16.1.10/api/clients/123/orders/1234
5  &lt;200 OK
```

The HTTP verb GET is used to read a collection. In practice, the API generally does not return all the collection items, as we may have bandwidth concerns, in the example below we use GET to retrieve the status of orders.

```
1  CURL –X GET \
2  -H "Accept: application/json" \
3  https: //178.16.1.10/api/clients/123/orders
4  &lt;200 OK
5  &lt;[{"id":"1234","state":"paid"},{"id":"5678","state":"running"}]
```

The HTTP verb GET is also used to read an instance in a collection when we state the specific ID

In the example below the state for order ID: 1234 is retrieved

```
1  CURL –X GET \
2  -H "Accept: application/json" \
3  https://api.fakecompany.com/v1/clients/007/orders/1234
4  &lt;200 OK
5  &lt;{"id":"1234","state":"paid"}
```

Partial answers

Partial answers allow clients to retrieve only the information they need. This feature is vital in preserving bandwidth and increasing performance times and efficiencies it is particularly useful in mobile applications where bandwidth usage must be optimized.

The web-scale companies use the following techniques:

API	Partial responses
Google	?fields=url,object(content,attachments/url)
Facebook	&fields=likes,checkins,products
LinkedIn	https://api.linkedin.com/v1/people/~:(id,first-name,last-name,industry)

It is recommend to select only the attributes to be retrieved, over 1 level of resource,

```
1 GET /clients/001?fields=firstname,name
2 200 OK
3 {
4 "id":"001",
5 "firstname":"James",
6 "name":"Mcarthur"
7 }
```

In contexts where performance is a strong concern, use the Google notation fields=objects(attribute1,attributeN). As an example, if we want to retrieve only the first name, last name, and the street of a client's address:

```
1 GET /clients/001?fields=firstname,name,address(street)
2 200 OK
```

```
3 {
4 "id":"001",
5 "firstname":"James",
6 "name":"Mcarthur",
7 "address":{"street":"Queens Chapel Road"}
8 }
```

Errors

Error Structure

A good error structure to stipulate in the REST API is
shown below in the following *JSON* structure:

```
1 {
2 "error":"short_description",
3 "error_description":"longer description, human-readable,
4 "error_uri": "URI to a detailed error description on the A
5 PI developer website "
  }
```

Status Codes

When considering error codes it makes a lot of sense to use the existing HTTP return codes, as a code exists for common cases, which are commonly understood or readily referenced.

SUCCESS

200 OK is the usual success code for most cases. It is especially used when the first GET request on a resource is successful.

HTTP Status	Description
201 Created	Indicates that a resource has been created. Typical answer to PUT and POST requests, including a HTTP Header "Location" which points toward the new resource URL.
202 Accepted	The request has been accepted and will be processed later. It is a classic answer to asynchronous calls (for better UX or performances).

	The request has been successfully processed, but there is nothing to return. It is often returned to a DELETE request.
204 No Content	
206 Partial Content	The content returned is incomplete. Mostly returned by paginated answers.

Client Errors

HTTP Status	Description
400 Bad Request	Commonly used for calling errors if no other status matches. We can distinguish between two error types:Request behaviour error Application condition error
401 Unauthorized	Unidentifed/unathorized
403 Forbidden	You are identified, but you do not have the necessary authorizations.
404 Not Found	The resource you asked for does not exist.
405 Method not allowed	Either calling a method on this resource has no meaning, or the user is not authorized to make this call.
406 Not	Nothing matches the Accept-* Header of

| Acceptable | the request. As an example, you ask for an XML formatted resource but it is only available as JSON. |

Server Error

HTTP StatusDescription

| 500 Server error | This request is correct, but an execution problem has been encountered. The client cannot really do much about this. return a Status 500. |

Open Source Resources

There are many open source projects available when it comes to finding API tools and example code. In this section we will briefly introduce some of the projects that have open source APIs, API explorers and sandboxes that you can play around with.

Open Bank Project API

The Open Bank Project is an open source API and App store for banks that empowers financial institutions to securely and rapidly enhance their digital offerings using an ecosystem of 3rd party applications and services.

Like online banking today, every financial institution will offer an API in the near future even if they are restricted to read only information services. According to Gartner, by 2016, 75% of the top 50 global banks will have launched an API platform and 25% will have launched a customer-facing app store.

The Open Bank Project produces a gallery of APIs that abstracts away the differences in banking systems and provides a uniform technical interface so that software developers can easily build secure services on top of the bank. It is very secure because the customers, the account holders, always log into the bank. Neither the applications nor the API see their username and password. And since it is open source technology, there is no vendor lock-in. The ideal method of development is to use the APIs in their sandbox laboratory using the OBP SDK and then "fork" the code and use commercial or open source licenses.

So that the Banking APIs can be consumed by mobile apps, web apps, and by other APIs the OBP build them in a RESTful architectural style with data represented in JSON. Therefore, these APIs are platform agnostic when it comes to app development.

Security is paramount for banking APIs hence a trusted relationship must be built between the API provider and the developer. Therefore, developers for third-party app providers will need to go through the following registration steps to use the OBP APIs:

1. Register as a developer on the OBP portal (registration will be complete after verification)

2. Create an app to consume the banking APIs

3. Subscribe to one or more digital products, each of which is a set of APIs grouped based on the consumption need of the third-party developer

4. Obtain app credentials that include a client ID and secret for each app

5. Use the app credentials to authenticate

6. Try the APIs using the sandbox

7. Make API calls from the app

Before developers begin integrating the APIs into their app, they should have a good understanding of the use case(s) and which APIs to use. They will also have to present necessary information and documents as part of their app creation process.

With the Open Bank Project you can:

- Integrate bank account information via example REST API

- Use secure authentication via the OAuth implementation

- Write once - run it everywhere.

- Leverage a consistent and bank-agnostic interface

Open Banking Sandbox

(https://open-banking-sandbox.developer.eu.apiconnect.ibmcloud.com)
The aims of the Open Banking Sandbox are to build a sandbox that will enable developers to prototype and test solutions using the read/write open banking interfaces (APIs) defined by the UK Open Banking implementation entity.

The Open Banking Sandbox contains APIs to enable developers to prototype solutions using the read/write open banking interfaces defined by the UK Open Banking implementation entity. The APIs available are Payment Initiation and Account Information.

Before you can use an API you have to register your application – there is nothing to this other than a project name a description and an email address. When you register an application, the application is assigned a unique client ID and client secret. You will need to keep hold of these as they will be required later as you must use the client ID when you call an API that requires you to identify your application by using a client ID, or a client ID and client secret.

There is also a comprehensive and extremely useful test guide that will step you through building APIs that you can embed into your applications.

Building API Requests in Applications

In the Open Banking API sandbox (https://open-banking sandbox.developer.eu.apiconnect.ibmcloud.com/node/1 13) there are many examples of building API requests such as get /accounts in several programming languages. For example the API request to retrieve all the accounts from the bank specified is show in both curl and python in the following tables.

The required parameters that require to be entered to suit the API being exposed by the bank are:

- x-fapi-financial-id (required, string)

  The unique id of the ASPSP to which the request is issued the unique id will be issued by OBP

- x-fapi-customer-last-logged-time (Optional in header, string)

  The time when the customer (PSU) last logged in with the TPP

- x-fapi-customer-ip-address (Optional in header, string)

The PSU's IP address if the PSU is currently logged in with the TPP.

- x-fapi-interaction-id (Optional in header, string)

An RFC4122 UID used as a correlation id.

- Authorization (Required in header, string)

An Authorisation Token as per https://tools.ietf.org/html/rfc6750

- Accept (Optional in header, string)

application/json

The request will look like this in Curl

```
curl --request GET \

 --url

https://api.eu.apiconnect.ibmcloud.com/cmarcoliukibmcom-
open-banking-aggregator/rw-sandbox-production/open-
banking/accounts \

 --header 'accept: application/json' \

 --header 'authorization: REPLACE_THIS_VALUE' \

 --header 'x-fapi-customer-ip-address:
REPLACE_THIS_VALUE' \

 --header 'x-fapi-customer-last-logged-time:
```

```
REPLACE_THIS_VALUE' \

--header 'x-fapi-financial-id: REPLACE_THIS_VALUE' \

--header 'x-fapi-interaction-id: REPLACE_THIS_VALUE'
```

In Python it will look similar to this:

```
require 'uri'

require 'openssl'

require 'net/http'

url =
URI("https://api.eu.apiconnect.ibmcloud.com/cmarcoliukibmcom-
open-banking-aggregator/rw-sandbox-production/open-
banking/accounts")

http = Net::HTTP.new(url.host, url.port)

http.use_ssl = true

http.verify_mode = OpenSSL::SSL::VERIFY_PEER

request = Net::HTTP::Get.new(url)

request["accept"] = 'application/json'

request["x-fapi-financial-id"] = 'REPLACE_THIS_VALUE'

request["x-fapi-customer-last-logged-time"] =
'REPLACE_THIS_VALUE'

request["x-fapi-customer-ip-address"] =
'REPLACE_THIS_VALUE'

request["x-fapi-interaction-id"] = 'REPLACE_THIS_VALUE'

request["authorization"] = 'REPLACE_THIS_VALUE'

response = http.request(request)
```

```
puts response.read_body
```

The expected responses are shown below:

```
{
  "Data": [
    {
      "AccountId": "3528171105352583",
      "Currency": "BSD",
      "Nickname": "Esther Kelly",
      "Account": {
        "SchemeName": "IBAN",
        "Identification": "4761796275601408",
        "Name": "Sam Riley",
        "SecondaryIdentification": "110330384482304"
      },
      "Servicer": {
        "SchemeName": "UKSortCode",
        "Identification": "2297526474506240"
      }
    }
  ],
  "Links": {
    "self": "ziadac",
    "first": "Hilda",
    "prev": "kadel",
    "next": "rutbo",
    "last": "Mann"
  },
  "Meta": {
    "total-pages": 49980701
```

```
    }
}
```

Apigee OpenBank

(https://openbank.apigee.com/create-app)

Apigee have also set up a sandbox for prototyping and testing APIs for banking applications. There is a registration process required that unlike Open Banking or the Open Bank Project does need an FCA or regulators ID. However even without getting access to the sandbox there is still a wealth of information and sample APIs available to study.

Some examples of their open public resources that do not need authorisation an that you can run directly from their site are;

```
https://apis-bank-test.apigee.net/apis/v2/locations/atms
```

Returns a list of ATMs with Address, Latitude and Longitude with some optional parameters, which include search filters, wheelchair access, latitude, longitude and radius of search

```
GET /apis/v2/locations/atms?wheelchair=true HTTP/1.1

Host: apis-bank-test.apigee.net

Cache-Control: no-cache
```

Postman-Token: e795a3b4-1902-1c40-5cc0-
aa8545492734

Response

```
{
  "AtmId": "90244201",
  "AtmServices": [
  "CashWithdrawal",
  "Balance",
  "PINChange",
  "PINActivation",
  "BillPayments"
  ],
  "Address": {
  "StreetName": "Anderstown Road",
  "BuildingNumberOrName": "202",
  "TownName": "Anderstown",
  "Country": "GB",
  "PostCode": "BT119EB"
  },
  "Currency": [
  "GBP"
  ],
```

Another public an open API that they have as an example
is Get \products which returns a list of products and
services from the banks catalogue.

https://apis-bank-test.apigee.net/apis/v2/products

Response

```
[
  {
    "name": "PL1",
    "Category": "Loans",
    "Landing-page": "http://bank.com/loans",
    "More-info": {
      "Rate-of-interest": 16,
      "Maximum-tenure": 96
    },
    "Sub-category": "Loans",
    "Text": "Personal Loan",
    "Id": "PL1",
    "Name": "Personal Loan"
  },
  {
    "name": "AL1",
    "Category": "Loans",
    "Landing-page": "http://bank.com/loans",
    "More-info": {
      "Rate-of-interest": 16,
      "Maximum-tenure": 60
    },
    "Sub-category": "Loans",
    "Text": "Auto Loan",
    "Id": "AL1",
    "Name": "Auto Loan"
  },
  {
```

```
"name": "HL1",
"Category": "Loans",
"Landing-page": "http://bank.com/loans",
"More-info": {
  "Rate-of-interest": 10,
  "Maximum-tenure": 240
},
"Sub-category": "Mortgages",
"Text": "Home Loan",
"Id": "HL1",
"Name": "Home Loan"
},
```

We can make good use of these public data APIs to make a bank App mashup as described at the beginning of our discussion on APIs. For example all we require is three open APIs such Google maps, a geo locator for perhaps an IP locator and an API for the banks branch and/or ATM locations. With them doing all the heavy lifting our mashup app will only require some glue code to hang it all together.

Ironically, the banks now despite their early tenacious resistance find themselves in a position where the API has become the interface of choice for the PSD2 required dedicated-interface with the TPPs. This is so because despite the additional costs and burden associated with building and supporting this dedicated interface it is still seen as being less intrusive than screen-scraping. Importantly it is also highly restrictive for the TPPs activities. Well designed APIs will in effect restrict and police TPPs to only activities compatible with their roles as either AISP or PISP under the PSD2 and they will no longer have the freedom to do as they please. In the last chapter we contemplated screen-saving technology in some detail so now we will consider API technology and why it appears to be the choice of industry – other than understandably the mature Fintech firms.

From a business and a business leadership perspective, some bank's will most likely start as implementing PSD2 APIs as an internal resource as it is an industry standard with or without a compliancy burden. The development project will use the PSD2 APIs that they produce for their own needs i.e. SoA infrastructure but by using them internally first they may enable and improve operational efficiency. Furthermore, by improving operational efficiency through faster credit decisions more efficient account onboarding processes, and quicker more efficient fraud detection, as well as gaining insights into customers' digital needs this will lead to improved up and cross-selling and ultimately to provide significant competitive advantage.

What we may see is if the best-in-breed interfaces and APIs perform and get noticed in the market and if these prove to be robust, banks will begin to open up specific API resources to external partners. Also if proved successful and third party providers can monetise the interfaces which will be a welcome contribution to the return on investment (ROI) for all concerned.

Opening up the interfaces need not be a burden or a security risk as robust authentication, authorization and identity management techniques can be used to ensure that only the API resources suited to external partners are accessible. With a collaborative mindset banks will forge new partnerships with leading fintech operators via the bank's PSD2 APIs which will allow cooperative prototyping and market-testing of new data products at rapid pace.

At a minimum PSD2 will require:

• Third party authentication (e.g. OAuth)

• Third party access to Payments (Transaction Requests)

• Third party access to Account information (Balances and Transaction history)

• Fees Transparency (Static Financial Product and fees information)

• Fees Transparency (Real time charges transparency during Transaction Requests)

• Fine grained entitlements (Customer selected Views on accounts). Under PSD2, open banking APIs will become mission critical systems. Banks will have to consider:

• API versioning (how does a bank release a new version without breaking existing applications and services)

• Software Development Kits (SDKs) to aid developers and provide patterns for best practices

• OAuth or other delegated authentication schemes

• Step up authentication strategies

• Sandboxes so developers can test their applications without accessing real resources such as payments. Sandboxes will be used by both internal and external teams and also in testing scenarios

• Fraud and penetration attempt monitoring (e.g. Spark) and strategies for containment

• Supporting tooling for developers and DevOps (e.g. Docker)

• Performance strategies to keep load from core banking (e.g. Caching with Redis)

• API Explorers so developer and business teams can discover and interact with the APIs in sandbox, test and production scenarios

• Documentation that can be used in API Explorers, REST clients and SDKs in a common format (e.g. Swagger)

• Unique IDs (e.g. Bank ID, Account ID, Transaction ID)

• Flexible entitlements (different views on accounts) to support increased data sharing and transparency requirements (e.g. for granting access to accountants or regulators)

The pitfalls of a half-hearted API

It will be almost certainly counter-productive to decide to build an API without fully considering key success factors or without first engaging the FinTech stakeholders. In either case, the risk is that the API does not fit the needs of the prospective consumers and as APIs that don't fit the needs of users are technically – though maybe not politically – worthless, yet will still have a high cost in development. Subsequently if there is limited adoption by developers and ultimately a failure to meet business objectives then they can be hard to justify. The issue is further compounded that adjusting a political stance may require a rethink but once an API is designed and built, undoing these mistakes is hugely expensive, difficult and time-consuming. In most cases, it is best practice to just start over again, redesigning a new API, implementing it by connecting to backend services, then rolling it out again to the less that enthused developer community.

Another common technique of API developers is to design their API by the constraints of internal systems or processes and when the backend functionality lives in legacy systems whose data schemas are overly complex using hard-coded workarounds and convoluted logic it is typically a recipe for failure. APIs modelled after internal systems are difficult for partners to comprehend and to utilise and developers simply won't invest the time it takes to become familiar with them. What the banks developers need to do is focus on designing an API that is simple for others to understand and hence easy to integrate into their apps. Third party developers should be able to assess the functionality of your API and start using it in just a few minutes but the only way to deliver that kind of ease of use is to design it into the mix.

Design for great user experience

For banks to design and deliver APIs that will prove to be fit for purpose even under the most stringent FinTech scrutiny, the design must be paramount. Optimizing the APX (API User Experience) should be a primary concern in API development. An optimal API design enables applications developers to easily understand the purpose and functionality of the API so that they can quickly understand and appreciate how to integrate the service. APX also focuses organizations on precise API design and getting it right before investing in major back-end implementation, which can be time consuming and expensive especially on legacy systems.

Optimize for use case

There is no such thing as a one-size-fits-all API indeed quite the reverse an API should have a single function.

Even for the same underlying service or set of services, multiple APIs might be required to support different types of users and use cases and this is one of the reasons that FinTech may be against APIs as they can be highly focused and prescriptive. An API should be optimized to fulfill a specific business request in a specific context and importantly no other.

API Summary

In addition, there is great benefit in having an established communication channel with your developer community. Your API is not a static entity – as new use cases are identified and use of your API expands, enhancements and fixes are inevitable. When you release a new version of your API, you can easily communicate the enhancements in the new version through your developer portal. You can also quickly assess who's using each version of your API and communicate an upgrade path to them as you deprecate older versions. Finally, understanding your developer community and having accurate insight into use cases and patterns provide invaluable knowledge that you can use to enhance your API over time.

APIs are becoming ubiquitous as their potential to transform business is becoming widely recognized. But delivering a successful API program that achieves defined business objectives requires a systematic approach to designing and managing APIs. Great APIs aren't difficult to develop if you design for your users and the business processes the API will support, if you make it easy for developers to find and consume your API, and you actively manage your API developer community as an extension of your business.

We closed this chapter with a few very simple APIs that we can use to gain access to publicly open material. However to do anything useful we will need to be able to authenticate ourselves to the bank in order for them to provide us with the necessary authorisation to access secure content.

Chapter 7 – Delegating permissions through Open Authentication Protocol

Security is paramount when accessing any enterprise through an API especially should it be a bank. Therefore there has to be a means to prove our identity to the bank and receive secure access with sufficient authorisation to perform our tasks. OAuth is the security protocol for authentication and delegation when using APIs as we will see in the next section.

There are many phases to building an API strategy—from establishing assets and a use case to monetizing the API and turning it into its own viable line of business. When planning an API's architecture, however, one of the very first things that need to be established is the security of that API.

There are three main security measures in an API security stack: identification, authentication, and authorization. Other types of standards-based security measures can tackle delegation, which gives authorized users limited access and rights to an API and lets an app function on a user's behalf, and federation, which is a next-level security measure that separates key resources from users, often with encryption measures.

Identification

Identification is the first line of defense and answers the question: "Who are you?" This is typically done through API keys, unique codes that developers are given and can use to access your API. API keys are randomized, unique identifiers so there's no need to mess with passwords. Think of them just like a key: they unlock a lock and let you in. In the same vein, SCIM (simple cloud identity management) allows you to create and manage users. Your entry-level approach to API security probably includes API keys, but these shouldn't be treated as the end-all-be-all of your API security plan. There are inherent issues with API keys, mainly surrounding the fact that keys are like passwords—they can be compromised, duplicated, and stolen. Also, the API key provider has little to no oversight into who is using those keys.

An API key can give you the ability to monitor use and metrics. API keys make it simple to shut off access to your API if someone is breaching terms of use or a glitch is causing too many calls into your API. API keys aren't encrypted, so don't think of them as the last and final word in security. API keys can grant someone access to an API, but they can't prove who that someone is. That's what authentication is for.

Authentication

Authentication answers the question, "How can I determine that you are who you say you are?" By implementing things like usernames and passwords, you get the next level of security. Authentication can also affect throttling, allowing an application to make more or fewer calls to the API based on authentication method. Examples include HTTP Basic Authentication and third-party authentication services like Google.

Tokens & Authorisation

Just because you're authenticated to use an API doesn't mean you can do just anything with it. While authentication lets an API know who someone is, authorization answers the question "What can you do with the API?" It does this with tokens, 2-factor authentications, and one-time use codes. It also authorizes an app to do things like collect data in the background, use your profile information from one app in another app, or allow an app to post things on your behalf.

Delegation & Token Handling with OAuth2

OAuth2 is a standardized protocol for managing the exchange of tokens that makes secure API connections possible. OAuth is designed to bypass the need for a user to enter their username and password, using tokens instead of passwords makes APIs less susceptible to security issues.

OAuth deals with four points along the API flow of information: clients (the mobile or web apps using them), the authorization server, the API (and the resources it shares), and the API owner who's authorizing and delegates users. OAuth is really just a framework that resides on the authorization server, granting user permission via tokens that are generated for one-time use between the client and end user. It does this by collecting a credential, like a 2-factor SMS question sent to a mobile device. OAuth tokens are more secure than API keys alone because access is delegated to a specific user. That access can also be taken away—something you can't easily do with keys. For encrypted HTTPS web connections, JSON web tokens (JWTs) are a more lightweight option for user identity that are ideal for mobile API security. They're also widely used in APIs in microservices environments.

OpenID Connect

OpenID Connect is all about making things easier on your users, allowing them to use their same credentials so they don't have to register and sign in at multiple domains. It's an example of a federation protocol that's specifically designed for mobile use.

Encrypting API Traffic

Encryption should go hand in hand with any API design that's granting access to sensitive information. Using an SSL (Secure Sockets Layer) or TLS connection is another level of security that keeps API keys secure. It can be more complicated to set up, but is very important given most of this data is being transferred over wireless networks, which can be more vulnerable.

This is a just quick intro to API security measures, which is only one part of the bigger mobile security field as a whole. Consult an OAuth security professional when building your own API or building an app that's based on an API to make sure you've covered rights management, authorization, authentication, and data security from all angles

API authentication

Typically, in web applications, authentication is handled by the application initially challenging the user for a valid username and password. However as HTTP is stateless, this would require the user's login credentials to be sent with every request to the application. The way around this is that the application saves the user ID in the session itself. Therefore so long as a session is valid a user can access and browse the site without having to continually enter his password and user id. The way this works is that the user's browser creates or updates an existing cookie with the session ID. When the user make subsequent visits to a page on the site, they may browse away to other sites and return to a page that requires authentication, the browser sends the web application its cookie. The app looks up the session by the ID (to check if it hasn't expired), and since the user ID was saved in the session ID, the user is allowed to view the page without being prompted for their login credentials.

With an API, using sessions to keep track of users is not usually the best approach. Sometimes, your users may want to access the API directly, other times the user may want to authorize another application to access the API on their behalf. Furthermore, the client requiring authentication may have limited input functionality such as a network printer or a POS (point of sales) terminal.

The solution to this dilemma is to use token-based authentication. How this works is that the user logs in with their username and password as normal but this time the application responds with a unique token that the user can use for future requests. This token can be passed onto other applications that the user may use to access the website. This has the added benefit of the user being able to revoke that token later if they choose to deny a particular application further access.

Token-based authentication has been standardized and the method that has become very popular especially with API authentication and authorization is called OAuth (pronounced Oh – Auth). There are two versions of OAuth, version 1 and version 2. However, when considering support for token-based authentication for API, version 2 is the one best suited and supported. However, authentication with API is not just about token-based OAuth there are other methods being used.

Basic Authentication w/ TLS

Basic authentication, a username and password, is the easiest form of authentication to implement, because it can be implemented easily without any crypto libraries. Therefore it is ideal in application development scenarios. Everything needed to implement basic authentication is included in your standard framework or language library. However, it does also offer the lowest security options of the commonly adopted authentication security protocols. As you are just sending a username and password that is simply Base64 encoded it should never be used without SSL/TLS encryption because the username and password combination can be easily decoded in seconds.

OAuth v1.0a

OAuth 1.0a is the most secure of the three common protocols but by far the most complex to deploy. Despite this OAuth1 is still widely-used, as it is a proven, tested, secure, signature-based protocol. The OAuth protocol uses a cryptographic signature, typically it uses a HMAC-SHA1 value that encrypts the token secret, nonce, and other request based information. However here is its weakness, configuring OAuthv1 is not trivial and requires extensive crypto libraries to be installed, so gone are the days when developers could quickly and easily write useful APIs using just a username and password. However the advantage of OAuthv1 is the protocol never directly passes the token secret across the wire, which eliminates the possibility of a MiTM (Man in the middle) or network snooping attack. Also, this is the only of the other authentication and authorization protocols that does not require SSL as it has its own inbuilt cryptography. However, supporting inherent crypto-libraries and internal functional encryption/decryption comes at a price, which is that the generation and validation of signatures can be a complex process. However, nowadays this complexity isn't often an issue as OAuth's popularity and widespread use resulted in every major programming language creating a library to mitigate the complexity and its inherent overheads. However, OAuth does have some severe drawbacks, not least its complexity and system performance toll, consequently the industry moved towards finding a more developer friendly solution, the result was OAuth v2.

OAuth v2

Surprisingly OAuth2 is not an evolution of OAuth1, but is really a complete rewrite with a significantly different approach to authentication. With OAuth v2 the protocol designer's goal was to attempt to simplify the OAuth v1 process and architecture. OAuth2's design subsequently no longer uses signatures and dispenses altogether with its own crypto security responsibilities, so you no longer need to use cryptographic algorithms to create, generate, and validate signatures. All the security burden of encryption is now passed to the HTTP protocol and it in turn relies on

TLS, which is theoretically a required external component. There is though in practice nothing to prevent OAuth v2 working without TLS but it would be highly insecure and very inadvisable.

The other significant changes in OAuth v2 are that there are now more OAuth Flows to allow better support for non-browser based applications. One of the main criticisms against OAuth was that that there was little or no support for client applications that were not browser based. For example, in OAuth 1.0, a mobile phone app that was not browser based still was required to direct the user to open their browser to authenticate with the required service. This is not a good user experience, because it only interrupted the user from using the mobile application, it also required that the user open the browser and connect to the service that way. Furthermore the user then had to copy the token from the service back to the application. With OAuth 2.0, there are now new ways for an application to get authorization for a user and support non-browser clients.

The major change is that OAuth 2.0 no longer requires client applications to have cryptography and this greatly reduces the time to develop and deploy APIs. With OAuth 2.0, security is delegated to the HTTP protocol to manage via SSL/TLS. Therefore developers no longer have to be concerned with complex cryptography instead the application can make a request using only the issued token over HTTPS. Secondly, OAuth 2.0 signatures are much less complicated, which greatly reduces the burden of special parsing, sorting, or encoding. Thirdly, OAuth 2.0 Access tokens are "short-lived" but authentication has "long life". Typically, OAuth 1.0 Access tokens could be stored for a year or more which is insecure and cumbersome to manage. Instead, OAuth 2.0 has the notion of a refresh token which facilitates having shorter life-time tokens without the complications of re-authenticating the client application. Instead the refresh token is used by the client to request a new short-life token without requiring the user's intervention.

Although we have discussed previously how OAuth is used in securely authenticating APIs by using a token-based system and why that is preferable to other types of authentication we haven't really described how an API gets authentication and authorization. We know it comes about through OAuth v2, so in this section we will discuss authorization and authentication.

For example if the client application is to use a Google API to access a user's Google drive it requires user authorization, so for example, there has to be some process where the client application gains that authorization prior to the issue of a token.

To understand how this comes about we need to look at some of the additional authorization flows that OAuth v2 introduced through the concept of 4 key roles:

- Resource Owner - The resource owner is the *user* who authorizes an *application* to access their account. The application's access to the user's account is limited to the "scope" of the authorization granted (e.g. read or write access).
- Client - The client is the *application* that wants to access the *user*'s account. Before it may do so, it must be authorized by the user, and the authorization must be validated by the API.
- Resource Server - The resource server hosts the protected user accounts,
- Authorization Server - the authorization server verifies the identity of the *user* then issues access tokens to the *application*.

The roles interact with each other through authorization request flows, below is an example of how they interact as roles during an authorization flow.

Abstract Protocol Flow

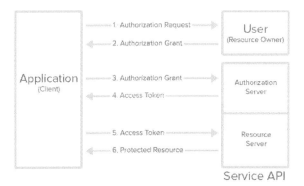

With reference to the diagram above:

1. The *application* requests authorization to access service resources from the *user (access to their Google drive)*

2. If the *user* authorized the request, the *application* receives an authorization grant

3. The *application* requests an access token from the *authorization server* (API) by presenting authentication of its own identity, and the authorization grant

4. If the application identity is authenticated and the authorization grant is valid, the *authorization server* (API) issues an access token to the application. Authorization is complete.

5. The *application* requests the resource from the *resource server* (API) and presents the access token for authentication

6. If the access token is valid, the *resource server* (API) serves the resource to the *application (access to the user's Google drive)*

From what we have already seen, OAuth authorization and authentication includes two main parts: obtaining a token by asking the user to grant access (authorization), and using that grant access to gain tokens to access protected resources (authentication). The methods for obtaining an access token are called **flows.** We have already stepped through how OAuth handles the flow for user authorization and how the application client obtains a grant access. However we still have not seen how that grant access is used to obtain a token, and then access to the resource (the user's Google drive).

If we look at how Google handles a token request flow for a typical web application you can see each of the stages required to acquire a token and complete the authentication process using OAuth v2.

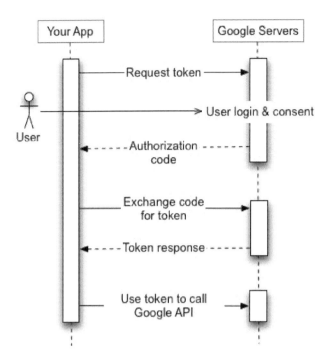

In the diagram above the Google OAuth 2.0 endpoint supports web server applications that use languages and frameworks such as PHP, Java, Python, Ruby, and ASP.NET. The authorization sequence begins when the client application redirects a browser to a Google URL; such as:

https://www.googleapis.com/auth/drive.metadata.readonly

The URL, which is a read only access to a user's Google drive, includes query parameters that indicate the type of access being requested.

The first step is that the client application sends its user login credentials and the grant access it has obtained earlier from the user as an initial token request. The Google authorization server handles the request checks the validity of the login and the grant access and if it is satisfied returns an authorization code to the client application.

The second stage is that now that the client application has possession of an authorization code it must swap this for an access token, which it will obtain from a Google resource server. The Google resource server upon receiving the authorization code from the client application returns an access token plus a refresh token to the client application.

The client application should store the refresh token for future use and use the access token to access a Google API. Once the access token expires, the application uses the refresh token to obtain a new one.

Handling Non-browser and Limited Input Devices

In order to address some of the issues with using OAuth on non-browser clients OAuth v2 introduced 6 new flow types:

- User-AgentFlow – for clients running inside a user-agent (typically a web browser).

- Web Server Flow – for clients that are part of a web server application, accessible via HTTP requests. This is a simpler version of the flow provided by OAuth 1.0.

- Device Flow – suitable for clients executing on limited devices, but where the end-user has separate access to a browser on another computer or device.

- Username and Password Flow – used in cases where the user trusts the client to handle its credentials but it is still undesirable for the client to store the user's username and password. This flow is only suitable when there is a high degree of trust between the user and the client.

- Client Credentials Flow – the client uses its credentials to obtain an access token. This flow supports what is known as the 2-legged scenario.

- Assertion Flow – the client presents an assertion such as a SAML assertion to the authorization server in exchange for an access token.

The rationale behind the introduction of new flows was to address outstanding issues with non-browser based clients. Now in OAuth v2 there is a flow model for just about every scenario.

An example is where there is a requirement for a non-browser and limited input device to gain authentication, such as a network printer. In this use case flow a second device is temporarily required to obtain the token as shown below:

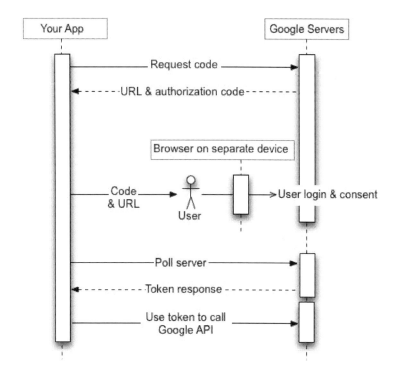

The Google OAuth 2.0 endpoint supports applications that run on limited-input devices such as game consoles, video cameras, and printers that are unsuited to the standard authorization and authentication flow for web services. To address this issue of devices that do not support browsers or have very limited input capability Google has a flow designed especially for them.

The authorization sequence begins with the client application making a web service request to a Google URL for an authorization code. The response from the Google authorization server contains several parameters, including a URL and an authorization code that the application shows to the user.

The user obtains the URL and authorization code from the device and then the user will switch to a separate device or computer with richer input capabilities. The user launches a browser, navigates to the specified URL, logs in, and enters the authorization code.

Meanwhile, the client application polls a Google URL at a specified interval. When the user receives and enters the URL and authorization code they are prompted for their user login and consent. When the user approves access, the response from the Google authorization server contains an access token and refresh token. The application should store the refresh token for future use and use the access token to access a Google API. Once the access token expires, the application uses the refresh token to obtain a new one.

Open Banking APIs for Oauth

Now that we know how OAuth works and the type of flows that we will have to address we can turn the focus of the rest of the chapter towards OAuth for open banking APIs.

OAuth 1.0a

A very good example of how to build an API for OAuth 1.0 server is shown on the Open Bank Project's github.com site (https://github.com/OpenBankProject/OBP-API/wiki/OAuth-1.0-Server#step-1--obtaining-a-request-token-)

To start a sign in flow, the application must obtain a request token by sending a signed message to:

POST **BASE-URL**/OAUTH/INITIATE with the following parameters :

- **oauth_callback**: an absolute URI back to which the server will redirect the resource owner (user) when Authorization step is completed. If the application is unable to receive callbacks the parameter value MUST be set to "oob" (case sensitive), to indicate an out-of-band configuration.

- **oauth_consumer_key** : The identifier portion of the client credentials (consumer key) which is obtained after application registration.

- **oauth_nonce** : A nonce is a random string, uniquely generated by the client to allow the server to verify that a request has never been made before. The nonce value MUST be unique across all requests with the same timestamp, application credentials, and token combinations.

- **oauth_signature** : the result of signing the request.

- **oauth_signature_method** : The name of the signature method that will be used by the application to sign the request, as defined in OAuth protocol. The Open Bank Project OAuth server support "SHA1" and "SHA256" so the parameter MUST be set to "HMAC-SHA1" or "HMAC-SHA256"

- **oauth_timestamp** : The timestamp value MUST be a positive integer and is expressed in the number of seconds since January 1, 1970 00:00:00 GMT.

- **oauth_version** : OPTIONAL. If present, MUST be set to "1.0". Provides the version of the authentication process as defined in the OAuth 1.0 protocol specification.

Example :

```
POST /oauth/initiate HTTP/1.1
Host: api.openbankproject.com
```

```
Authorization: OAuth
oauth_callback="http%3A%2F%2Fprinter.example.com%2Fready",
oauth_consumer_key="cChZNFj6T5R0TigYB9yd1w",
oauth_nonce="ea9ec8429b68d6b77cd5600adbbb0456",
oauth_signature="F1Li3tvehgcraF8DMJ7OyxO4w9Y%3D",
oauth_signature_method="HMAC-SHA256",
oauth_timestamp="1318467427",
oauth_version="1.0"
```

important: We will explain below in the "signature" section how to calculate the value of the "oauth_signature" field.

According to the OAuth 1.0 protocol specification the signature computation is done following theses steps :

a) Signature Base String :
The signature base string is a consistent, reproducible concatenation of several of the HTTP request elements into a single string. The string is used as an input to the signature methods.

The signature base string includes the following components of the HTTP request:

- The HTTP request method (e.g., "GET", "POST", etc.).

- The authority as declared by the HTTP "Host" request **header** field.

- The path and query components of the request resource URI.

- The protocol parameters excluding the "oauth_signature".

The signature base string does not cover the entire HTTP request. Most notably, it does not include the entity-body in most requests, nor does it include most HTTP **entity-headers**.

The signature base string is constructed by concatenating together, in order, the following HTTP request elements:

1. The HTTP request method in uppercase. For example: "HEAD", "GET", "POST", etc. If the request uses a custom HTTP method, it MUST be encoded.

2. An "&" character (ASCII code 38).

3. The base string URI from, after being encoded.

4. An "&" character (ASCII code 38).

5. The request parameters as normalized in Section 3.4.1.3.2, after being encoded.

Example:

```
POST /oauth/token HTTP/1.1
Host: api.openbankproject.com
Content-Type: application/x-www-form-urlencoded
Authorization: OAuth
```

```
oauth_consumer_key="91919",

oauth_token="OGESD9MrWQ…7BPelWJjnomibV6bePU",

oauth_signature_method="HMAC-SHA256",

oauth_timestamp="1340878170",

oauth_nonce="DFXOQFZVK8K46KDR11",

oauth_signature="bYT5CMsGcbgUdFHObYMEfcx6bsw%3D
"
```

Is represented by the following signature base string (line breaks are for display purposes only):

```
POST&https.openbankproject.com&

oauth_consumer_key%3D91919%26

oauth_nonce%3DDFXOQFZVK8K46KDR11%26

oauth_signature_method%3Dhmac-
sha256%26oauth_timestamp

%3D1340878170%26oauth_token%3DO……U%

26oauth_verifier%3DT0dXUD

U9NSlhIUUc%26oauth_version%3D1
```

The request parameters normalization:

1. The name and value of each parameter
   are **encoded**

2. The parameters are sorted by name, using
   ascending byte value ordering.

3. The name of each parameter is concatenated to its corresponding value using an "=" character (ASCII code 61) as a separator, even if the value is empty.

4. The sorted name/value pairs are concatenated together into a single string by using an "&" character (ASCII code 38) as separator.

B) Signing the request:
The Open Bank Project OAuth 1.0 implementation uses the "HMAC-SHA1" and "HMAC-SHA256" as signing methods. The key to sign the base string is the concatenation of the consumer secret and the token secret with the "&" character in the middle like this: oauth_consumer_secret&oauth_token_secret, in the first step the application does not have yet a token so it will be an empty string.

The signature that results from the signature process MUST be encoded in base 64 also since the protocol requires encoding all the OAuth parameters.

Note : line breaks are for display purposes only, the application MUST send the parameters on one line and the only separator between the parameters is a coma ",".

The server validates the request and replies with a set of temporary credentials in the body of the HTTP response.

Example (line breaks are for display purposes only):

HTTP/1.1 200 OK

```
Content-Type: application/x-www-form-urlencoded
oauth_token=hh5s93j4hdidpola&

oauth_token_secret=hdhd0244k9j7ao03&

oauth_callback_confirmed=true
```

The application should examine the HTTP status of the
response. Any value other than 200 indicates a failure. The
body of the response will contain
the oauth_token, oauth_token_secret, and
oauth_callback_confirmed parameters.

The application should verify
that oauth_callback_confirmed is true and store the other
two values for the next steps.

Step 2 : Redirecting the user:

The next step is to direct the user to Open Bank Project so
that he may complete the authentication. Direct the user to
: GET OAUTH/AUTHORIZE and the request token
obtained in step 1 should be passed as the oauth_token
parameter.

The most seamless way for a website to implement this
would be to issue a HTTP 302 redirect as the response to
the original request. Mobile and desktop applications
should open a new browser window or direct to the URL
via an embedded web view.

Example :

```
BASE-URL/oauth/authorize?

oauth_token=NPcudxy0yU5T3tBzho7iCotZ3cnetKwcTIRlX0iwRl0
```

Upon a successful authentication, the callback URL would receive a request containing the oauth_token and oauth_verifier parameters.

The application should verify that the token matches the request token received in step 1.

If the callback URL was not specified (oob) than the verifier will be shown in the page and the user has to enter it into the application manually.

Step 3: Converting the request token to an access token

To convert the request token into a usable access token, the application must make a:

```
POST BASE-URL/OAUTH/TOKEN
```

This request contains the oauth_verifier value obtained in step 2. The request token is also passed as oauth_token parameter of the **header**.

Note : The oauth_callback_url parameter is not necessary any more.

Example :

```
POST /oauth/token HTTP/1.1
Host: api.openbankproject.com
Authorization: OAuth
```

```
oauth_verifier="9312832",
oauth_token="aze2342352aze",
oauth_consumer_key="cChZNFj6T5R0TigYB9yd1w",
oauth_nonce="ea9ec8429b68d6b77cd5600adbbb0456",
oauth_signature="F1Li3tvehgcraF8DMJ7OyxO4w9Y%3D"
,
oauth_signature_method="HMAC-SHA256",
oauth_timestamp="1318467427",
oauth_version="1.0"
```

As in step 1, a successful response contains the oauth_token & oauth_token_secret and they should be stored and used for future authenticated requests to the OBP API.

The application can now use the access token to access protected resources.

Step 4 : Accessing protected resources :

Once the application has received an a access token and a secret token, it can access protected resources. The request is the same as in step 3 except the oauth_verifer which **MUST NOT** be included in the **header**.

Example:

```
POST /oauth/token HTTP/1.1
Host: api.openbankproject.com
Authorization: OAuth
oauth_token="aze2342352aze",
```

```
oauth_consumer_key="cChZNFj6T5R0TigYB9yd1w",

oauth_nonce="ea9ec8429b68d6b77cd5600adbbb0456",

oauth_signature="F1Li3tvehgcraF8DMJ7OyxO4w9Y%3D"
,

oauth_signature_method="HMAC-SHA256",

oauth_timestamp="1318467427",

oauth_version="1.0"
```

Having to use a digital signature method makes OAuth
1.0a extremely complex for those starting out using the
protocol. However if you are new to OAuth and would like
to use version 1.0 due to its reputed superior security then
there is a wonderful walk through the digital signing
process at his site:

http://obp.sckhoo.com/obpwalkthrough/Page2_obtainrequesttoken.as
px

Authentication using OAuth v0.2

There are several distinct stages when generating the
OAuth tokens that we require to secure access and delegate
permissions.

1. Obtain an access token to invoke the Payments API,

```
POST /cmarcoliukibmcom-open-banking-aggregator/rw-
sandbox-production/tppoauth2security/oauth2/token
HTTP/1.1

Host: api.eu.apiconnect.ibmcloud.com
```

Accept: application/json

Content-Type: application/x-www-form-urlencoded

Cache-Control: no-cache

Postman-Token: 01352922-b391-7066-49bb-3f7be0ec48bb

grant_type=client_credentials&client_id=3c11b520-8b3b-428e-bb4d-b9df146765cc&

client_secret=oH0gI1eL1jS0vM7lE4vA0fG0uM2jF4sJ1fJ1e

F6hO6fO7aS7bB&scope=tpp_client_credential

2) The next stage is to invoke the Payments API to obtain a payment ID,

POST /cmarcoliukibmcom-open-banking-aggregator

/rw-sandbox-production/open-banking/v1.0.5/payments HTTP/1.1

Host: api.eu.apiconnect.ibmcloud.com

authorization: Bearer

AAEkYzFkTkzSk -...

Accept: application/json

Content-Type: application/json

Cache-Control: no-cache

Postman-Token: e2fa9935-3c2e-667d-2312-14741665db3d

{"Data":{"Initiation":{"InstructionIdentification":

"5791997839278080",

"EndToEndIdentification":"8125371765489664",

"InstructedAmount":{"Amount":"700.00","Currency":"GBP"}
,

"DebtorAgent":{"SchemeName":"BICFI","Identification":"

1313908532969472"},

"DebtorAccount":{"SchemeName":"IBAN",

"Identification":"6689126562660352","Name":"John Smith",

"SecondaryIdentification":"6686302651023360"},

"CreditorAgent":{"SchemeName":"UKSortCode",

"Identification":"3846889942286336"},

"CreditorAccount":{"SchemeName":"IBAN",

"Identification":"2773743013199872",

"Name":"Lucy Blue","SecondaryIdentification":

"8380390651723776"},"RemittanceInformation":

{"Unstructured":"emeherpakkaodafeofiu","Reference":

"ehoorepre"}}},"Risk":

{"PaymentContextCode":

"PersonToPerson","MerchantCategoryCode":"nis",

"MerchantCustomerIdentification":"1130294929260544",

"DeliveryAddress":{"AddressLine":["totbelsanagrusa"],

"StreetName":

"Morning Road","BuildingNumber":"62","PostCode":

"G3 5HY","TownName":"Glasgow","CountrySubDivision":

["Scotland"],"Country":"UK"}}}

3) Get consent

GET /cmarcoliukibmcom-open-banking-aggregator

/rw-sandbox-
production/psuoauth2security/v1.0.5/oauth2/authorize?

response_type=code&client_id=c1d81a9a-609a-47be-
9363-

8fa038b987da&state=123456&scope=payment
openid&redirect_uri=https:

//example.com/redirect&nonce=4987594875485-
j&request=eyJ0eXAiOiJ...OiJIUzI1NiJ9....HTTP/1.1

Host: api.eu.apiconnect.ibmcloud.com

Cache-Control: no-cache

Postman-Token: 181cc684-e6f1-7913-2c7f-e8cfce56539f

4) Get the access token required

POST /cmarcoliukibmcom-open-banking-

aggregator/rw-sandbox-production

/psuoauth2security/v1.0.5/oauth2/token HTTP/1.1

Host: api.eu.apiconnect.ibmcloud.com

Cache-Control: no-cache

Postman-Token: a2ea375c-...-ffc237127e47

Content-Type: application/x-www-form-urlencoded

grant_type=authorization_code&redirect_uri=https%3A%2F%2F

example.com%2Fredirect&code=" "

Typical Response

{

  "token_type": "bearer",

  "access_token": "5610361538099356",

  "expires_in": 38372337,

  "scope": "pehlud",

  "refresh_token": "d7405f904e83917...1b55462e47fed8"

```
}
```

5) Introspect the token (optional step)

```
POST /cmarcoliukibmcom-open-banking-aggregator/rw-
sandbox-
production/psuoauth2security/v1.0.5/oauth2/introspect
HTTP/1.1

Host: api.eu.apiconnect.ibmcloud.com

Accept: application/json

Content-Type: application/x-www-form-urlencoded

x-ibm-client-id: c1d81a9a-609a-47be-9363-8fa038b987da

x-ibm-client-secret:
qJ4dE5yO6xK2oM0fQ5w....dB7dJ4iU7qI0yB

Cache-Control: no-cache

Postman-Token: 1f709df4-eac9-25cd-2726-49ec26174aba

token="fgfgFEFEWQWC"
&token_type_hint=access_token
```

Chapter 8 – Open Banking Initiatives

As the EBA has taken the option to develop the Regulatory Technical Standards for Strong Customer Authentication and Secure Communications as a high-level, principle-based and technology-neutral set of requirements rather than to develop detailed requirements prescribing the concrete authentication procedures it leaves the field open to others to provide the technical guidance.

Taking the non prescriptive route may well have been the wise choice for the EBA with time being of the essence. Nevertheless as the market races to meet the prescribed milestones for implementation the chosen route not only risks fragmenting the payments segment but leaves the market if left to the Third Party Players to the whims of innovation, trends and fashions. Fortunately the banks and system integrators are likely to take a much more stoic approach and look for tried and tested technology on which to build these dedicated communication channels and for that they are turning to a serendipitous and parallel initiative running through the financial services industry – Open Banking.

The concept of Open Banking has been quietly blossoming in the financial services sector with its provenance in financial technology startups, governments, regulators and the bank's customers asking the pertinent question, 'who's data is it anyway?'. This conundrum has been something the incumbents in the financial sector have been keen to avoid and their reluctance to address the issue have encouraged a groundswell of interest in the concept of a more open but regulated industry. Hence, the Open Banking premise means that banks provide communication interfaces to Third Party Providers (TPPs), so that these companies can have access to data about the bank's customers, initiate financial transactions, and consult the transaction history of the customer – albeit with the customer's explicit consent. The initiative promises to unlock innovation that will profoundly transform and improve the banking experience of consumers. Furthermore, by providing direct access to customer's accounts it will bring new financial services to consumers and provide a society benefit for all. For instance, TPPs will provide applications allowing consumers to aggregate and interact with multiple bank accounts from several sources within a single application and even look for an alternative loan or mortgage, it will also allow banks to find customers that are well matched to a new product, and allow businesses to share data more easily with their shareholders and partners. Furthermore, Open Banking will provide a massive boost to the nascent FinTech industry in fact it sounds so familiar it could be PSD2. One key difference is that banks can decide for themselves whether they want to participate in the Open Banking paradigm and not surprisingly many banks have been proactive in this field.

The basic idea of open APIs in banking is not new. Over the last few years a growing list of banks – including Crédit Agricole, Standard Chartered, Citi, Capital One,

Saxo Bank, HSBC as well as the new breed of digital banks such as Monzo and Starling – have launched open APIs. These banks aim to attract FinTechs and other front-end service providers to write apps that take advantage of the bank's customer data, which is made available via an API. This should not be taken to mean that there has been a rapprochement between the warring parties – the banks and Fintech. Instead it reflects an alternative culture and approach that was initiated by some banks and FinTech firms long prior to the RTS delivery.

So far, each bank has created its own proprietary API without any reference to open standards or in collaboration with any other bank. Therefore, a provider of an aggregated accounts display would thus have to use a different interface for each bank where an account was held. This led some to hope that regulators would provide or enable a move towards industry-wide standard APIs. However, the regulatory technical standards (RTS) for the much anticipated EU PSD2 regulation, do not in themselves include any overarching requirement for standardisation of the API (or "dedicated interface" to use its language), indeed the RTS goes out of its way to avoid mentioning API in its determination to be non-prescriptive and technology-neutral. Therefore the banks are free – or rather on their own - to design this PSD2-compliant, dedicated interface, provided only that they meet the various security requirements, and provide free technical documentation to any service provider which wants to use it.

Fortunately, there has been movement on other fronts as the banks working on Open Banking projects now see the strategic error of non collaboration and the lack of standard interfaces. This has resulted in the emergence of several Open Banking projects and one of these is the UK initiative launched in 2015 by the Open Banking Working Group (OBWG). The UK initiative is to explore ways that financial data access can help consumers understand their finances and make smart choices. The concept of the Open Banking Standard relies principally on data being securely shared or openly published through open APIs that would facilitate third party access such as to fintech companies to access customers' data through their bank accounts.

An open API can provide both easy access to openly available data (such as a bank's product catalogue, ATM or branch locations) but also to secure shared access to private data such as a customer's payment account and their transaction history. These APIs would be built and provisioned by banks and could be integrated with third-party technologies to carry out specific functions related to the banking data. For instance, apps could allow customers to compare banking services and prices to choose what products best suits their needs; in the UK, consumers could potentially save up to £70 a year by switching to a bank account that's a better fit for their lifestyle.

The OBWG suggests that an Open Banking Standard would supply the impetus to launch a wave of banking innovation bringing benefit to customers, technology partners, and payment service providers; it would also ultimately benefit the banks. Customers would be the beneficiaries of an array of options of financial products and services from which they could make informed choices. It would benefit technology firms and PSP developers because easy access to data would let them streamline existing banking or payment apps, making them faster and easier to use, and develop new apps to fulfill customers' ever-evolving needs. Finally, the Open Banking Standard would benefit banks by improving their interactions with customers by letting them cross-sell and up-sell their products from a portfolio of new enhanced financial services.

By encouraging the banks and third-party developers to work together, there are six main categories in which customers' financial lives can be improved:

- Current account comparison services, which would eliminate the friction involved with manually comparing prices and bank offerings on the Internet or uploading and downloading documents to do so.
- Personal financial management to help consumers budget better and easily see snapshots of their financial history.
- Access to credit, which would allow third-party lenders to offer users and businesses the best possible loan rates instead of relying simply on loans from their banks.
- Affordability check, which would speed up loan processes by allowing lenders one-time access to a user's bank data. Currently, many loan product

applications require a user to manually upload bank statements.

- Online accounting, which would allow businesses to connect accounting software directly to bank accounts, eliminating many manual processes
- Fraud detection by third parties, which can provide specialized attention to threats across accounts.

While the UK's Open Banking Standard is currently in the works, with implementation rollout occurring in phases through 2019, other countries have also begun to explore the idea. In 2010, Germany implemented the Open Bank Project, and many American startups are working with banks to develop mutually beneficial APIs.

While similar regulations do not yet exist in the United States, there is growing pressure from FinTech lobbying groups and the Consumer Financial Protection Bureau to make financial data more accessible. In Asia, the Monetary Authority of Singapore (MAS) supports APIs as part of its Smart Financial Centre initiative. Finally the Economics Committee of Australia and the Financial Services Commission in South Korea also promote the idea of APIs.

In the UK for its part the Open Banking Working Group (OBWG) was assembled in 2015 to deliver a framework for open banking and data sharing via APIs for the UK's banking industry. The joint industry/government initiative recently released its report on establishing the framework for an Open Banking Standard for the UK alongside a timetable for implementation.

At first glance its objectives look quite familiar and run parallel with the EU's PSD2 initiative. The aims of the Open Banking initiative though are to allow data sharing via an open standard (API) in order to facilitate innovation in the financial services industry where as the aims of the PSD2 are more payment focused. Despite that small difference in focus they are indeed very similar in their objectives and the initiative was set up with one eye on pre-empting PSD2. Nonetheless, it goes a few steps further in its intentions, namely to put the UK at the vanguard of setting and implementing open banking standards globally, to establish a competitive advantage for the UK's banking industry in this new environment, and ultimately to influence how the final drafts of the PSD2 technical standards will look.

The OBWG has explicitly stated in its framework that it will define the API technical standards and architecture necessary to deliver its Open Banking Standard. This goes a lot further than the EBA, which has no appetite for introducing similar prescriptive measures within the PSD2 regulation.

There are however as we can see some subtle differences between the Open Banking Standard proposals and that of PSD2, one of which is in timings. It is intended that the framework for the Open Banking Framework will continually evolve and be rolled out over the next 5 years.

Within that timeline there are milestones to be met for defining and releasing the necessary API standards. These milestones don't align with those proposed for PSD2, especially if we take January 2018 as the date at which the directive comes into effect at a national level.

But the dates for the RTS on Authentication and Secure Communication are not set in stone, as arguments rage over the banning of screen-scraping its likely many of the RTS specifications and guidelines will not be delivered until late 2018 in which case the PDS2 may only come into force sometime in the mid-to-late 2019. This would loosely correlate with the Open Banking Standard dates, especially those for write access (i.e. payment initiation).

However the UK is not alone in pursuing parallel initiatives and another forum investigating a standard API that is suitable for PSD2 is The Berlin Group, which is a working group of EU wide industry experts that are developing their NextGenPSD2 Initiative. It is envisaged that this EU based project will help overcome the emergence of multiple competing mechanisms in the market by providing a harmonised API standard for accessing bank accounts but unlike the OBWG the NextGenPSD2 Initiative is focused solely on and tightly coupled with the PSD2 legislation and thus the RTS for strong customer authentication.

The Berlin Group is highly influential within the European market, with membership comprising ACHs and financial industry bodies across the length and breadth of Europe. The NextGenPSD2 initiative is built as an 'Access to Account Framework', and the Berlin Group says the standard will offer operational rules and implementation guidelines with detailed data definitions, message modelling and information flows based on RESTful API methodology. It will be published for consultation in Q4 2017.

Ironically despite all the focus on APIs neither the PSD2 legislation nor the RTS mandates banks to use APIs as a way to meet their obligations to TPP interconnectivity and operability. This is because the EBA chose the line of least resistance and the non-prescriptive path and left defining the interface specifications up to the individual banks. Despite this many industry observers believe that APIs are the best, if not the only, way forward when opening up customer accounts to third party providers, as it is an accepted technology that works effectively. Furthermore, API technology is well understood and is used by developers around the world, so implementation could be quicker and more uniform.

The problem being with not setting a standard specification is that each individual bank could create its own API to manage payments authorization and customer transaction data in line with PSD2 responsibilities. This would create market fragmentation and destroy the vision of an EU wide open digital market. It would also mean a lot of duplicative effort, unnecessary cost as third party providers would need to integrate each bank's API separately and possibly writes different code to manage how the API works for each of their customers that have different bank accounts. Even small differences mean third party providers would need to manage how they integrate each individual bank's API.

To avoid this fragmented and silo scenario there needs to be an open banking API standard that sets up a schema for how bank's data and functionalities (like authorizing payments) should be organized so that all banks are using the same basic API structure, and naming conventions when making payments functionalities available. This does not mean that everyone must do every thing the same way but that everyone must at least understand what one another are doing so that they can interoperate.

The UK, for example, is moving towards an open banking API framework that will establish standards that banks should use when creating an API that shares customer banking information and payment transaction data. It has aims to allow customers to share their information giving the control of their own personal data back to the customer. PSD2 on the other hand is payment orientated, and it requires that banks open up only payment accounts to third party payment providers that have the prerequisite customer consent. Hence both initiatives have differed aims but are highly compatible and so the UK Open Banking Initiative aims to make standard interfaces, APIs, which are also compatible and compliant with PSD2. This is the type of proactive designs that open banking and the nascent FinTech industry requires if we hope to develop an open pan-European digital market.

Chapter 9 – PSD2 Security Concerns, Controls & Guidelines

The fundamental premise of the PSD2 Regulatory Technical Standards requires *"that banks and TPPs perform Strong Customer Authentication (SCA) when a user accesses a payment account, initiates a financial transaction, or performs any other action via a remote channel that might imply payment fraud."*

(EBA - RTS)

Security requirements for the dedicated communication interface

To establish secure communications at the fundamental level of the communication link between two or more parties we must first establish and agree a strong link protocol. In line with best security practices, one could expect that the RTS requires banks and TPPs to communicate over a secure channel, providing mutual authentication of both the bank and TPP(s), thereby protecting the confidentiality and integrity of data exchanged over this channel.

In addition, the bank should be capable of verifying whether a certain TPP is indeed authorized to perform a certain function i.e. it must be able to authorise actions as well as to authenticate. For instance, Account Information Service Providers (AISPs) may have the right to obtain information regards a customer's account from a bank, but should not have the right to initiate a payment. Conversely, a PISP should be able to initiate and execute a payment but should not be allowed access to account information above perhaps a binary response (Yes/No).

In practice the draft RTS contains the following high-level security requirements for the communication between a bank and TPP:

1) Mutual authentication. The draft RTS contains very limited provisions about the authentication of the bank and TPP towards each other. Banks have always had to authenticate themselves in online communications to clients through SSL/TLS (X509) digital certificates however the client rarely if ever had to authenticate themselves as the bank was static but the clients (the customers) could well be mobile. Article 27(1) of the RTC does now require clients such as TPPs to identify themselves to the banks through client digital certificates. More specifically TPPs need to identify themselves towards banks using certificates issued by a Qualified Trust Service Provider (QTSP) in accordance with the European e-IDAS regulation. Furthermore these identities are issued with a license and authorisation so limiting TPPs to a regulated body and defined role thus restricted capabilities.

2) Confidentiality and integrity. Article 27(3c) as well as Article 30 require banks and TPPs to protect the confidentiality and integrity of the data they exchange using encryption. Unfortunately the earlier draft

recommendation for compliance with industry standards for security, specifically ISO 270001 was removed from the final draft, due to technology-neutrality, leaving it unclear as to what security standards should be used as a benchmark.

4) Other security requirements, Article 30 also requires TPPs to terminate the session with the bank's communication interface as soon as the requested action is completed. Finally, the communication sessions between the user and TPP on the one hand, and between the TPP and bank on the other hand, need to be linked to each other. The trouble is though that this dogleg session structure does not permit the use of end-to-end encryption between the customer and the bank. As such many details of the security requirements are not present in the draft RTS and are left to the European organizations developing API standards. This approach may be administratively and politically correct but technically absurd as standard bodies work to very long timelines a typically measure would be 3-5 years.

Security Guidance for the Customer Authentication

Hence, an important topic of the RTS is therefore how the SCA methodologies and techniques can be integrated with the bank. According to Article 27(3) of the RTS, the online communication interface of the bank – whether it's a dedicated or existing customer interface – "*it must allow*

TPPs to rely on the mechanisms used by banks to authenticate its customers ".

Furthermore and perhaps of much more concern is that Article 27(3c) states that it must be possible to submit personal security credentials and authentication codes to the bank via the TPP. In other words, the user may be able to enter his bank-provided credentials into a webpage or mobile app provided by the TPP, and the TPP would then forward these by pass through or retransmit to the bank for authentication.

This sets a very poor example to the customer of the need for password confidentiality. Indeed it is more akin to an example of irresponsible security practice with unacceptable level of risk. As such a scenario would be likely to place the customer's security credentials at very high risk of compromise. In addition, if that was not enough the procedure would also give rise unnecessarily to a number of significant security vulnerabilities and threats when there already are strong alternatives on offer.

There are some well establish approaches for the authentication flow between a customer, their bank and a TPP, which would not require the TPP to ever handle or view the customer's bank login credentials. The following models could meet the requirements but not jeopardise the customer's security or lead them into bad practice:

a) Redirection: The common solution for this three legged scenario is for the user to be redirected from the TPP's application to the bank's application for the sole purpose of authentication, and is then redirected back to the TPP's application. The user enters his authentication credentials (e.g. user ID, one-time password) into the bank's secure HTTPS login page that fronts their authentication application. This model is used, for instance, by the OAuth authorization protocol and 3-D Secure protocol for card payments as is ideal for the PISP use-case.

b) The 'Push-Method' whereby initially the customer logs on to their banks or the institution that holds their accounts this provides just as in a) the authentication and require authorization that bank requires to issue a token to the TPP. The TPP can then request a selection of preconfigured services which the server at scheduled times runs and pushes the data out to the client thereby avoiding an exchange of passwords whereby the proxy requires to holds, store or exchange the customers password. This model is suitable for the AISP use-case.

c) Decoupled: this is similar to the approach based on redirection, but now the user is directed to a neutral highly-trusted third party – also called Identity Provider (IdP) – of authentication services instead of the bank. In this scenario the customer and TPP will be required to onboard with the IdP rather than the bank so will be exchanging the IdP provided account credentials which are linked to the customer banks accounts. This model is more complex an expensive but is well suited to both AISP and PISP use cases.

These are the standard ways to address the issues of third party authentication while protecting the privacy and security of the customer. Unfortunately the EBA seems to consider that another model is acceptable and that is the;

Embedded Model: In this model the user enters his authentication credentials into the TPP's application, and the TPP captures and passes them on to the bank for verification. This approach is the one allowed under Article 27(3c) described above and is extremely poor practice. Presumably this nonsense has found its way into the RTS to provide a back-door for TPP screen-scraping but even using undeclared screen scraping techniques would still be far better served by the redirect model standardised throughout finance, commerce, and industry.

As we say in the previous section there is still some ambiguity regards who, where and when authentication will occur specifically with regards the Payment Service User, i.e. 'the customer'. The RTS makes clear that the ultimate onus for authentication of the customer, the 'PSU', remains with the bank. However from the text in Article 27(3c) of the RTS it appears for whatever reason that the EBA are overlooking the fundamental requirement that the bank must be responsible for authentication of its customers and to be able to authenticate their customers requires that the bank must have confidence in the integrity as well as the confidentiality of the credentials being passed to it. The necessity, the requirement for CIA, Confidentiality, Integrity and Availability are the fundamental tenets and key pillars of information security.

The EBA through the RTS are instead contemplating that TPP must have the right to pass through or transmit customer security credentials for authentication purposes to the bank. By allowing such a thing actually legitimises users to enter their banking passwords or security credentials into third party apps i.e. screen-scraping. This must not be allowed – this does not forbid screen-scraping if it uses a redirect authentication mechanism - as the TPP are in effect acting as proxies and are relaying the customer's security credentials through some mechanism that passes or retransmit them and as such will effectively absolve the bank of any responsibility.

For example if we consider the option being discussed by the EBA:

The embedded security/credential authentication model requires the user to enter his authentication credentials into a webpage or mobile app provided by the TPP rather than the bank's website. This scenario is about as high risk and cavalier as you can get. Not only would the bank have to have high assurance in the TPP security capabilities, and remember its not just one TPP there could be thousands, they would also have to audit every TPP network, systems and application, as well as any subsequent changes to make sure the security controls meet the bank' owns security standards. What must be kept in mind is that many of these TPPs build and deploy their software every night – that doesn't leave a lot of time for the developers to diligently safety check the code but it makes it impossible for the banks to vet the changes - to the developers it doesn't matter if there is a problem it will be fixed in tomorrow's release.

Furthermore, the fact that the customer is required to input the banks security credentials into a third party web site or a mobile phone app that caches or stores the passwords within the product should nonetheless mandate it fails any security or SCA authorisation as the product has not got a viable secure authentication mechanism. In addition to it being a horrible security example to set for customers it also prevents the end-to-end encryption for the communication channel between the customer and the bank.

Resistant to and Alternatives for Strong Customer Authentication

As we have discussed at length there are issues an ambiguities with SCA and the way it is to be implemented not least is the concern over the extra security steps it will introduce thereby increasing friction. Merchants with experience of 3D-Secure and other such strong authentication techniques often complain of a downturn in conversions – this is the successful payment processing of a prospective shopping-cart sale. Consequently, there is considerable resistance from merchants to implement any payment authentication mechanism which may introduce friction into the payment process and thus the popularity for one-click payments. However on the other hand we must consider that the Banks should adopt a number of technical and organizational security measures to protect their customers through the application of SCA. Indeed what we see in practice is that banks and retailers will actually use a technique called transaction risk analysis (TRA) to detect fraudulent transactions and set their own borders for acceptable risk. In the context of Open Banking, banks can use transaction risk analysis in several ways in order to detect:

1) API implementation vulnerabilities that consist of weaknesses in the implementation of APIs which might give rise to fraudulent transactions and unusual user behaviour, and these can be detected using advanced fraud monitoring techniques.

2) Fraudulent transactions and anomalous user behaviour. The draft RTS mandates PSPs, including banks, to perform risk analysis of all financial transactions that they process. It is therefore mandatory in this case the PSPs have in place measures to detect payment fraud, such as Card-Not-Present (CNP) fraud.

3) Security incidents at TPPs. The use of in-house Transaction Risk Analysis is often used to detect abnormal sales transaction behaviour originating from TPPs, identify suspicious transactions

from TPPs, detect anomalies, and
highlight typical fraudulent transactions.

Retailer Transaction Risk Analysis

When we contemplate Transaction risk analysis it is
common to think that it consists of a comprehensive and
intelligent assessment or a platform that accurately detects
and prevents fraud, which through sophisticated, real-time
risk analysis. In truth, Transaction Risk Analysis can
deliver depending on the goals some dynamic protection
against fraudulent activities across multiple channels,
including web, mobile, API and others. However, a TRA
system can work in several formats sometimes at its
simplest form as gut instinct otherwise as a mechanism
working in the background collecting and scoring activities
and transactions based on intelligent analysis of
behavioural, contextual, qualitative and quantitative data,
and by doing so thereby challenging unusual patterns.

The basics of TRA is that the retailer takes onboard the
burden of any risk assessment and hence any losses. The
way it works is quite simple TRA is a method for
identifying fraud by observing the behaviour in the
transaction by the counterparties involved over time. For
example it tries to work out a risk factor by considering
what it knows about previous customers that you resemble
in conjunction with the type and value of the transaction. It
is not a new method of fraud detection but PSD2
strengthens the use case for TRA, particularly when it can

be deployed in real time. TRA happens in real time but is invisible to the customer; therefore it does not add friction to the customer journey. To keep customers content and retain them, PSPs must reduce friction to a minimum, and TRA is very effective at achieving this.

SSL/TLS providing authentication, confidentiality and integrity

In order to assist retailers the banks and credit card companies are certainly aware that they should ensure they reduce the friction at the check-out and also protect the communication channel to secure the customer's data during the transaction. In order to do this requires a secure communication channel between the bank via their API and the TPPs using mutual authentication and secure encryption in order to minimize the risk of man-in-the-middle attacks. The industry standard for internet or web based communication is to use security protocols like SSL/TLS. However, SSL/TLS is still often complex to deploy for the SMB and can be subject to misuse. For example, it can be easy to miss-configure certificates or let them expire at the server-side and many developers do not properly validate certificates, despite this SSL/TLS is by far the most prevalent form of web-based secure communications.

Security Best Practices

Throughout industry developers and security practitioners rely upon the Open Web Application Security Project (OWASP) to keep them updated with the latest threats. The OWASP produces and maintains a detailed list or the best known and prevalent threats as well as recommending mitigating techniques and security best practices. However as it is still unclear as to which approach the banks will take with regards constructing a dedicated communication interface or if they will repurpose the existing customer facing websites or will do both, hence security practitioners will need to familiarise themselves with both technologies and their corresponding threats and vulnerabilities.

At a minimum the security practitioners will need to understand application, web and API security ecosystems and their most common vulnerabilities. However as this book focuses on PSD2 an Open Banking from a DevOps(Sec) perspective we will consider some of the more pertinent points regarding API.

API implementation vulnerabilities

It is the consensus of opinion throughout the industry that banks will likely go down the route of providing a dedicated communication channel rather than continue allowing screen-scraping to continue – albeit they may not have that decision to make. However despite what has been widely propagated throughout the industry APIs are not in themselves any more secure or free from the foibles of the much denigrated technology of screen-scraping. Indeed some weaknesses in the implementation of APIs might give rise to heightened vulnerability to fraudulent transactions. Therefore security practitioners must be wary of approaching APIs as being secure channels they can connect and forget. APIs require security monitoring for anomaly detection as any unusual user behaviour especially within the context of a bank will require advanced fraud monitoring.

Security and privacy threats against the APIs of banks

In this section we discuss the most important security and privacy threats that the security practitioners of banks and their TPP will need to consider when evaluating the security of communication interfaces.

The table below provides a summary overview of the most important potential security and privacy threats against the APIs provided by banks to TPPs.

Risk	Examples of Threats	Business Liability
Leakage of financial information of users	• API vulnerabilities, resulting in injection attack causing dump of personal	• Legal liability (e.g. GDPR fines)

	information of bank's users • Compromised or malicious TPP leaking financial information obtained from bank	• Reputational damage
Fraudulent financial transactions via API	• API vulnerability leading to man-in-the middle attack manipulating transaction data • Compromised or malicious TPP issuing fraudulent transaction request	• Financial loss • Reputational damage
Unavailability of API	• Flooding of API affecting quality of service for users • Compromised or malicious TPP locking out users with invalid authentication requests	• Contractual liability • Reputational damage • Negative impact on users

The introduction of APIs, if that is the path that the banks ultimately decide upon will mean that their security and privacy becomes more dependent on the security of each and every TPP that uses these APIs. Examples of threats resulting from this dependency are:

1) Leakage of personal data about bank's payment account holders from compromised TPP is a high risk. The issue is that TPPs may store financial as well as personal data from the bank's account holders and as there is still some ambiguity as to what is *sensitive financial data* banks will have to be vigilant as to what they share with TPPs. On the other hand if banks hold back or are overzealous in their redaction of customer account data the TPP might feel aggrieved enough to complain to the regulator or if in practice revert back to screen-scraping. Hence, security practices and data management strategies at the banks as well as security measures at the TPPs might impact the reputation of the bank. This has become a significant threat due to the imminent arrival of the dreaded European General Data Protection Regulation (GDPR), which demands that banks – if they are deemed to be the controller - make sure that their TPPs – deemed to be another Controller or Processor - implement appropriate technical and organizational measures to protect the data they share. The catch22 situation for the banks however is that the PSD2 does not put the onus on the banks to regulate the TPPs access to what is deemed an appropriate and minimum levels of information to perform a task instead it is the responsibility of the TPP to ensure they only access the minimum data necessary. Hence the bank should not in effect police the actions of the TPP while at the same time somehow ensure they remain compliant

with the stringent demands of the GDPR in robustly
protecting customer privacy.

2) Fraudulent requests from a rogue or compromised TPP.
It is entirely plausible that a security breach at a TPP might
result in the secure API being compromised and hence
there being access for fraudulent payment initiation
requests from the TPP to the bank. The threat of such an
incident might arise due to malware or similar
vulnerabilities in the TPP's mobile app or web application.
This does not absolve the banks of their responsibility
since they are liable for unauthorized financial transactions
from a payment account holder's bank account, therefore a
security breach at the TPP may also have consequences for
the bank.

3) Fraudulent requests from malicious TPPs. A small but
possible threat exists of course from the disgruntled
employee at a TPP who might initiate fraudulent payments
or request inappropriate information regards account
holders at the bank.

4) Fraudulent repudiation from a bank/TPP customer. A
more likely threat is that of fraudulent transactions arising
from the banks own customer's who may erroneously or
not repudiate and contest a payment transaction. As the
PSD2 is insistent that all such direct debits from the client
account must be refunded immediately and without
question the bank must comply before they start an internal
investigation. The opportunity to take advantage of this

rule is considerable as pre-pay day expenditure could be offset for a few days.

5) Account lock-out by compromised or malicious TPP. A security breach that leads to an operational compromise at a TPP might enables an attacker to send invalid authentication requests to accounts of users of the bank. Such a scenario would require the bank to temporarily or permanently block the bank accounts of those users, which is in line with Article 4(3b) of the draft RTS resulting in a loss of service to the respective account holders of the banks.

6) Denial of Service. Probably the most common yet effective threat to any shared resource is that of a denial of service. A DoS as they are termed need not be malicious indeed most DoS attacks arise as the results of technical glitches or application loops. Regardless of the potential root causes there is a requirement to monitor API availability from both the bank and the TPP perspective. From a banks viewpoint this is easy enough to check the API's availability but from the TPP stance it can be problematic as its not a case of testing the condition of a link, i.e. traditional network monitoring, instead they will need to check the status of each and every functional API to every bank – remember a feature of RESTful APIs is they should be limited to a single function such as 'check balance'. Hence a TPP will have to ensure that there is a satisfactory level of service for their customers so must regularly check the functionality of each API presented by each bank. This will soon become a full-time job for

someone in the TPP to monitor, support and maintain availability of the APIs by collaborating with the banks technical teams.

The Traditional Banking SoA Model

Modern banking applications are built upon the SOA (Service Orientated Architecture) which comprises rich clients (PC browser, mobile,) that connect to back-end RESTful APIs (e.g. microservices or web services) over HTTPS to gain access to a modular service. If not implemented properly, APIs can be vulnerable to many security threats as application developers appear to struggle with clean an secure implementations of SSL/TLS. Weaknesses in the implementation of the SSL/TLS modules might result in vulnerabilities that an attacker could exploit for theft, destruction of sensitive financial data, leakage of sensitive financial transactions, unauthorized financial transactions, or even remote control of the banking application through backdoors. The most relevant security threats against APIs are the following:

1) Injection attacks are a threat which can occur when developers do not properly sanitizing input to the APIs.

The term comes about due to the way the attacker crafts their API function call to contain rogue commands as data into the payload of a seemingly innocuous function call which is then sent to an interpreter. The interpreter will execute these commands if the input is not sanitised – checked for correctness and boundaries – resulting in the backend server fulfilling the attackers commands. Injection flaws are usually the result of an attack on the back-end database. An example of such an attack is SQL injection, whereby an attacker places malicious SQL statements into an entry field within a form for execution. In this way the adversary could obtain sensitive financial or personal information from the database. Another example is HTTP Parameter Pollution (HPP) attacks, whereby an attacker this time will craft an HTTP request in such a way that the attack payload is split across multiple parameters of the HTTP request. The attacker splits the attack vector payload (e.g. the URI, the request body, the request header) and fragments the IP packet in order to deceive any security mechanisms such as IDS (Intrusion Detection Systems). Upon arrive a neat feature of IP is that the recipient HTTP server upon receipt of the API function call will recombine all the fragments and reconstruct the original crafted request, resulting in the execution of the attack vector. In this way the attacker could initiate a fraudulent transaction by sending money to a bank account controlled by the attacker.

2) Authentication and session attacks. Developers often misunderstand the necessity for HTTPS beng applied on every page and maintained across the session. Often the

application is designed to only enforce HTTPS (SSL/TLS) on the pages related to authentication and session management and revert back to clear HTTP for the rest of the site. This dual-mode is not good practice and is often not implemented correctly, allowing attackers to capture session tokens, and assume other users' identities or obtain excessive privileges through basic WiFi eavesdropping. For example, an adversary could hijack the session of a customer if a session token is exposed in the URL on a non-secure HTTP page and the attacker can then replay the token to simulate the session. Another example of poor SSL/TLS implementation is where a developer does not properly validate the X.509 certificate of a TPP using its API, particularly to check if the certificate has been revoked. Consequently the result may be a rogue TPP connecting to the bank's API and as it is fully authenticated obtaining financial information about account holders of the bank or even initiating fraudulent financial transactions.

3) Man-in-the-middle attacks can be very common within insecure WiFi environments where an attacker can eavesdrop on airborne traffic and then tamper with legitimate API requests/responses and then replay their own crafted versions. These attacks usually occur because the banks customers are surprisingly obtuse when it comes to browser warnings and if the returned but suspicious URL from the bank\TPP triggers such a warning based upon a mismatch or non-existent certificate they often choose to ignore the warning allowing the bank or TPP to be spoofed.

4) Denial-of-Service (DoS) attacks can affect the availability of the API. APIs are potentially open to flooding and other types of DoS attacks that can bring back-end systems to a halt. However most DoS are self inflicted and are a result of poor report management. This is often a highly contentious field but developers should always try and provide the least amount of information per API. The common problem is a TPP or customer requesting transaction reports that go back to the start of time which places huge load on the database and on the capacity of bandwidth and hence the availability of the API for others. This example as with most other vulnerabilities is mitigated through placing simple boundaries on requests such as only the last two years of transactions, which is the PSD2 required timeframe. Another way to mitigate system overload is to restrict the number of automated transactions that can be run per day by the TPP and the PSD2 addresses this by restricting TPP to 4 self auto-generated requests per day, customer initiated requests are unlimited.

Top Tips for Avoiding Financial Fraud

Possibly one of the most effective techniques that is friction free but can be effectively utilised to help in authenticating a banks customer is to examine and compare the device that they use to logon. Device identification has become one of the pillars of the practice of establishing a digital identity for each customer. The advantages of device identity is that every time a customer accesses the bank's web-site they leave a digital footprint, which consists of valuable information regards the device, browser and connections used. This information can be leveraged to build a customer profile that matches their credentials to a range of devices, such as a desktop, mobile or tablet which provides an additional form of authentication such as 'something they have' and what is more this is invisible to the customer and hence avoids adding any friction to the customer journey.

Commonly, bank's will try to identify devices by using cookies, and these are a valued tool but they should not be the only technique used as they can easily be wiped. Instead banks need to look to performing full profiling of the device's characteristics such as browser type, operating system, language, location, and time zone settings.

The banks can use this easily captured data for User Behavioural Profiling and perform basic analytics to monitor for suspicious patterns of login requests or high-value transactions, based on device type, location, IP address, and persona identifiers. By collecting and analysing the data the bank can protect against downstream fraud by assessing:

• Device history: is this device known and associated with the behaviour, transactions and account activity from these login credentials?

• Device reputation: has this device ever been involved with fraud?

• Anomaly detection: are there any suspicious computer configurations such as declared browser location and IP address mismatch?

Although this is only the rudiments of Digital Identities it at least provides some valuable insights into customer behaviour and enables basic digital profiling. As customers continue to use the system and their online transactional data grows the customer's profiles matures and becomes more specific if not unique. The customer's digital profile then becomes a valuable tool for as each user leaves a digital footprint during their online activity this data can be compared and used in a risk assessment to determine whether a transaction is legitimate or fraudulent:

• Behaviour variables: Over a period of time, it is possible to track how quickly or often transactions normally occur to create an expected pattern of behaviour. This behavioural data can then be used to quickly distinguish a returning customer from a cybercriminal displaying known fraudulent behaviours.

• Age variables: Customers have unique traits such as how quickly they navigate menus, type or move the mouse. These measures can be observed and features such as the time since the first event, time since the last event and average time between events can create a profile of a consumer's activity patterns and enable software to spot anomalies and detect fraudulent or scripting attacks.

• Location and distance: In today's world customers are mobile and work from several devices but the customers' location and travel behaviours still provide valuable insights that establish normal usage vs fraud. As the customer is still curtailed by the laws of physics analysing their known trusted location, distance from the trusted location and also the distance between events in distance and time can highlight major anomalies.

A prerequisite though to establishing digital identities through profiling is to first establish that the bank's systems are equipped to detect evidence of malware on a legitimate customer's login session. For example the system must be able to detect the presence of keyloggers, Trojans, Man-in-the-Browser and Man-in-the-Middle malware. This is because an attacker may have a wide range of malware at their disposal, which they may use to collect critical personal data or payment information in order to better control any remote web sessions using an end user's device. Man-in-the-Browser malware despite being a well-understood technology is still one of the most successful Trojans attack vectors and often the user is unaware they have been compromised. Therefore any identity and access management strategy should have the competence to:

• Detect if malware is present on devices accessing the network through malware analysis

• Understand and recognise known attack patterns and identify contextual patterns which typify malware attacks

• Employ malware detection techniques that work transparently in the background without the need for any user interaction, downloads or update indeed it is best if the process is invisible to the customer

Unfortunately, we cannot rely on basic device anti-virus as malware developers have become skilled in avoiding signature-based malware detection. Anti-virus software is certainly helpful in reducing device resident malware, but it often produces a false sense of security where customers and the bank network are concerned. Consequently the bank's security practitioners must have the capabilities to recognise non-signature-based threats so that it can protect against zero-day attacks where there is no known attack-signature.

Rather than relying on signature-based malware detection there are alternatives such as advanced page fingerprinting, which can detect Web page elements that have been altered and these techniques can mitigate zero-day MiTB attacks. Banks are being actively targeted by fraudulent transactions made by criminals using these type of Remote Access Trojans as they are difficult for regular anti-fraud techniques to spot as the customer's security credentials, location and device will all appear completely normal. This is where behavioural analysis is becoming a vital technique in the banks armoury to detect this anomalous activity. These attacks are often deployed specifically to target high-value transactions, which can have severe financial and reputational repercussions for the bank if they fail to be spotted in real time.

Digital identity profiling is a wonderful thing as it not only profiles and attempts to establish the authentication of genuine customers but it also importantly profiles risky entities. Therefore a digital identity system will attempt to collate information of risky devices and IP addresses which have been involved in attacking other websites, or which are accessing multiple accounts from the same device. By leveraging such global threat information, including known fraudsters and botnet behaviour, security practitioners can be prepared and proactively block their attacks. Gathering market intelligence is important as cybercriminals in the aftermath of a security breach will often have to employ botnets to carry out large-scale testing and verification of the stolen data - in order to resell - or to use fraudulently. The trend attacker favour presently is a patient "low-and-slow" bot attack as they stay below the detection threshold of existing defence systems. However, these botnet attacks do leave an identifiable digital footprint therefore it is important to access intelligence from outside the banks own perimeter in order to get insight into global-scale active attacks.

By leveraging shared global intelligence to establish a digital identity and help authenticate customers will assist banks to detect when personal information and devices are being used illegitimately based on historical norms. After all every time a major network s breached every online business becomes vulnerable to the digital fallout, which includes valuable pieces of a user's digital identity such as their email addresses, phone numbers, Social Security numbers, bank accounts, credit cards and more. This information can be used repeatedly by fraudsters in online payment transactions and even fraudulent loan applications. Therefore the banks will need to look beyond their own firewalls to share actionable threat intelligence about compromised identities and devices.

Identifying devices that are infected by malware is important when authenticating on the customer device but so are anomalies in the basic configuration. These oddities may include settings which are at odds such as when disguising their actual geo-location using hidden proxies or which are on the Thor network – that in itself is not a reason for concern – but oddly-configured devices can be. Malware developers will use increasingly sophisticated methods to hide their true location and IP addresses because that can be a real giveaway – for example if the customer's browser claims it is located in the US but the geo-location and IP indicates a locale in Asia. This is a concern as legitimate users may for privacy reasons wish to hide their location but they rarely go to such lengths so this should a red flag when monitoring for fraud. There are ways to beat attackers using configuration to mask their location such as proxy-piercing techniques which will expose the true IP address of a device in order to unmask fraudulent activity but its still good practice to be alert for spoofed devices and device manipulation and if suspicious challenge for strong authentication.

However, challenging for strong customer authentication (SCA) is a real dilemma as merchants who are customers of the bank and whom SCA is designed to protect against fraud, will strongly suggest its deployment should be kept to a minimum if used at all. This anomaly has arisen because merchants have noticed the sharp increase in shopping-cart abandonment whenever SCA is enforced. They prefer to use their own Transaction Risk Analysis methodologies and only use SCA reluctantly where PSD2 demands.

This places the bank's security practitioners in an awkward situation as they are inclined to enforce SCA in order to protect the customer, merchant and not least the bank from fraudulent payments. On the other hand if they do take to strong a position an enforce SCA on every transaction then the merchants may well take their business else where. Unfortunately the enforcement of SCA is not a theoretical argument of principle it comes down to the hard real-world fact that merchants will lose business if SCA is enforced. Hence the banks dilemma, for not only must they do their best keep their customers happy an not introduce unnecessary friction into the payment process they must also work diligently to reduce and protect against fraud. They do this effectively using strong authentication in order to maintain compliance with the EU PSD2 which is underpinned by very principle of strong customer authentication but that is the polar position that their customers and the online merchants wish them to take.

Consequently, there is pressure on the banks to limit 2FA techniques wherever possible an allow the merchants to do their own TRA, whether the banks will agree will be base upon each banks risk appetite. However as the PSD2 states that the responsibility and liability of a fraudulent transaction will be with the payee (the merchant) if they do not accept SCA this does provide the bank some room for manoeuvre as they will be not liable for financial loss but may still incur reputational damage with their customers.

Presently the situation is that the PSD2 allows sales under €50 online to be exempt from SCA but the authentication process occurs on a mobile for example before the transaction details are even passed to the bank. Therefore the process of when and where SCA is applied during an online payment becomes nuanced and so the bank is likely to insist on SCA at login regardless of whether the purpose of the customers visit is to obtain a balance or make an online payment.

An alternative approach that the banks may employ is to use a risk scoring approach when analyzing transactions in real time, using step-up authentication as a last resort when the risk is deemed to be elevated beyond an acceptable risk ceiling. This approach would:

• Provide a frictionless online experience for the customer

• Drive up conversion rates and online revenues for the merchants

• Decrease the operational costs of employing costly two-factor authentication methods across the board

However regardless of whether the bank must apply SCA in a particular instance or whether the transaction is exempt is rather a moot point as the mechanism will be required for some suspicious transactions, such as many already discussed. Therefore security practitioners would be best to try and avoid lots of technologies working in silos to authenticate customers; instead a more complete view of the customers' identities would be a better approach to protect against fraud. By employing an approach that integrates identity analytics, device identification, behavioural analytics to produce a single unified view of the risk associated with that event will increased the accuracy, efficiency of customer authentication and thus confidence in the integrity of the transaction.

Finally, it is not just about detecting fraud and bad players it is also very important to ensure that there are mechanisms in place to recognize returning trusted customers as every day online businesses turn away payment transactions from genuine customers. This may be that their bank's fraud systems lack the intelligence to identify that they are genuine, or more often because customers are annoyed by being made to jump through hoops by some burdensome authentication mechanism.

The EBA's Guidelines on Security

The EBA were aware prior to drafting the Guidelines on Security that they were dealing with an environment that was fast changing, and where threats evolved and emerged at a rapid rate. An extensive risk assessment was therefore carried out to try and establish the threats and vulnerabilities to which PSPs are exposed. The results confirmed the EBA's suspicions that such was the volatility of the threat landscape that the draft Guidelines would require to be flexible and adaptable to address currently unknown threats and vulnerabilities.

Despite this however the EBA risk analysis did identify a range of threats and vulnerabilities:

(i) inadequate protection of communication channels used for payments;

(ii) inadequately secured systems and devices including but not limited to applications, servers, user's payment devices;

(iii) unsafe behaviour of users or PSPs' staff;

(iv) increased complexity of the payments environment; and

(v) technological advancements and tools that are available to potential fraudsters or malicious attackers.

However these are just the categories of currently identified threats and vulnerabilities, and as the threat landscape is constantly evolving the EBA took the view that PSPs would be required to take a dynamic and agile approach to risk management with appropriate mitigation measures and control mechanisms to address current and future threats and vulnerabilities.

In terms of the key objectives, the EBA considered that, *"for the purpose of managing operational and security risks in the provision of payment services, PSPs should establish and implement security measures to prevent, react to and correct the unauthorized use, disclosure, access, modification, and accidental or malicious damage or loss of their logical and physical assets, including in particular the payment service user's data, his sensitive payment data and the personalized security credentials delivered by a PSP to the payment service user for the use of a payment instrument."*

Furthermore, the EBA considered that PSPs should mitigate risks resulting from inadequate or failed internal processes and systems, inappropriate people's behaviour or from external events. In particular, PSPs should pay special attention to the risks stemming from inadequate physical security, cyber-attacks and inadequate design or implementation of security policies. Finally, the EBA considered that security measures should be fully integrated into the PSP's overall risk management processes and constantly monitored. Therefore, PSPs should conduct periodic reviews of their security measures and should ensure effective reporting mechanisms to the management body and to the senior management responsible for the provision of payment services.

The Guidelines has categories on governance, risk assessment, protection, detection and business continuity. Further categories were required to address, testing, situational awareness and continuous learning and these have been added, to ensure that the PSP is continually monitoring internal and external developments, internalising these to adapt its framework and to mitigate emerging risks, threats and vulnerabilities. The final category regards the role of the payment service user (PSU) relationship management, which has been included and PSPs will be required to ensure that their measures are well communicated to their user base, to reduce risks to and from them.

Therefore the EBA proposed a framework that should consist of the above eight components, and within each of these, the requirements should prescribe the establishment of the appropriate roles and responsibilities, structures, systems, policies and procedures with regard to the necessary security measures.

1: Governance Operational and security risk management framework

Guideline 1 *"proposes that effective governance should start with defining a clear and comprehensive operational and security risk management framework. The framework should be guided by security objectives and proportional to the underlying risks. It is essential that the framework is supported by clearly defined roles and responsibilities, and it is incumbent upon the senior management to create a culture which recognises that staff at all levels has important responsibilities in ensuring the PSP's security."*

The EBA Guidelines are that the PSPs should establish an effective operational and security risk management framework and should be fully integrated into the PSP's overall risk management processes. The framework should have the approval of management responsible for payments an where required by senior management.

The risk management framework should focus on security and operations and include:

a) the security policy, which sets the risk appetite of the PSP, its security objectives and measures;

b) definitions and assigned key roles and responsibilities as well as the relevant reporting lines required to enforce the security measures and to manage security and operational risks related to the provision of payment services;

c) establish the necessary procedures and systems to identify, measure, monitor and manage the range of risks stemming from the provision of payment service and to which the PSP is exposed to.

In essence the PSPs should ensure that the risk management framework is properly documented and reviewed on an ongoing basis, by the management body and where relevant, by the senior management, and updated with 'lessons learned' during its implementation and monitoring. In this context, Article 95 PSD2 requires PSPs to conduct an assessment of operational and security risks and the adequacy of the mitigation measures at least on a yearly basis by qualified personnel.

PSPs should also ensure that before a major change and after each major incident affecting the security of provision of payment services, they review whether changes or improvements to the risk management framework are needed.

Risk management and control models

PSPs should ensure that they have three effective lines of defence, or an equivalent internal risk management and control model, to identify and manage operational and security risks. However in the case of an internal control model it has to have sufficient authority, independence, resources and direct reporting lines to the management body and where relevant to the senior management.

The security measures should be audited by internal or external independent and qualified auditors in accordance with the applicable audit framework of the PSPs..

Outsourcing

When outsourcing services the PSPs should ensure that appropriate and proportionate security objectives, measures and performance targets are built into contracts and service level agreements with their outsourcing providers for the provision of payment services. PSPs should monitor and seek assurance on the outsourcing providers' level of compliance with the security objectives, measures and performance targets.

2: Risk assessment Identification of functions, processes and assets

PSPs should identify, establish and regularly update an inventory of their business functions, critical human resources (especially those with privileged system access or performing sensitive business functions), and supporting processes in order to map the importance of each function and supporting processes, and their interdependencies related to operational and security risks in the provision of payment services

PSPs should identify, establish and regularly update an inventory of the information assets used for the provision of payment services, such as systems, their configurations, other infrastructures and also the interconnections with other internal and external systems, in order to know the critical assets that support their business functions and processes for the provision of payment services.

Classification of functions, processes and assets

PSPs should classify the identified business functions, supporting processes and information assets in terms of criticality. PSPs should manage access rights to information assets and their supporting systems on a 'need-to-know' basis. Access rights should be periodically reviewed. PSPs should maintain access logs and use this information to facilitate identification and investigation of anomalous activities which have been detected in the provision of payment services.

Risk assessments of functions, processes and assets

PSPs should ensure that they continuously monitor threats and vulnerabilities and regularly review the risk scenarios impacting their assets, critical processes and business functions. PSPs should carry out and document risk assessments of the functions, processes and assets they have identified and classified in order to identify and assess key operational and security risks for the provision of payment services.

3: Protection

The Guideline on Protection recognises that a PSP's security depends on effective security controls that protect the confidentiality, integrity and availability of its assets, including the provision of its services.

PSPs are required to take a defence-in-depth approach by instituting multilayered protection controls, with each layer serving as a safety net for preceding layers.

3.1 PSPs should establish and implement preventive security measures against identified operational and security risks. These measures should ensure an adequate level of security according to the risks identified.

3.2 PSPs should establish and implement a 'defence-in-depth' approach by instituting multi-layered controls covering people, processes and technology related to the provision of payment services, with each layer serving as a safety net for preceding layers. Defence-in-depth should be understood as having defined more than one control covering the same risk.

3.3 PSPs should protect the confidentiality, integrity and availability of their critical logical and physical assets, resources related to the provision of payment services and sensitive payment data of their payment service users against abuse, attacks and inappropriate access and theft.

3.4 On an ongoing basis, PSPs should determine whether changes in the existing operational environment influence the existing security measures or require the adoption of further measures to mitigate for the risk involved. *These changes should be part of the PSP's formal change management process ensuring that changes are properly planned, tested, documented and authorised.* On the basis of the security threats observed and the changes made, testing should be performed to incorporate scenarios of relevant and known potential attacks.

3.5 PSPs should implement measures to protect sensitive data, including sensitive payment data, user data, personalised security credentials and certificates from unauthorized disclosure or modification, whether at rest or in transit. PSPs should protect their critical resources from unauthorised access or modification. Integrity checking mechanisms should be deployed by PSPs in order to verify the authenticity and integrity of software, firmware, and information.

3.6 In designing, developing and maintaining payment services, PSPs should ensure that segregation of duties and "least privilege" principles are applied. PSPs should pay special attention to the segregation of information technology environments, in particular to the development, testing and production environments.

3.7 In designing, developing and maintaining payment services, PSPs should ensure that data minimisation is an essential component of the core functionality: the gathering, routing, processing, storing and/or archiving, and visualisation of sensitive data should be kept at the absolute minimum level.

3.8 Upon access to the payment service, PSPs should check that the software used for the provision of payment services is up to date.

3.9 PSPs should have appropriate physical security measures in place, in particular to protect the personal and sensitive data of the PSU as well as its information systems used to provide payment services. Physical access to corresponding systems should be limited to authorised personnel only and regularly reviewed. Access control

3.10 Physical and logical access to systems should be permitted only for individuals who are authorised by the management body or, where relevant, by senior management; authorisation should be assigned according to the staff's tasks and responsibilities, limited to individuals who are appropriately trained and monitored. PSPs should institute controls that reliably restrict such access to systems to those with a legitimate business requirement. Electronic access by applications to data and systems should be limited to the minimum possible.

3.11 PSPs should institute strong controls over privileged system access by strictly limiting and closely supervising staff with elevated system access entitlements. Controls such as roles-based access, logging and reviewing of the systems activities of privileged users, strong authentication, and monitoring for anomalies should be implemented.

3.12 In order to ensure secure communication and reduce risk, remote administrative access to critical IT components should only be granted on a need to know basis and when strong authentication solutions are used.

3.13 The operation of products and tools related to access control processes should protect the access control processes from being compromised or circumvented. This includes enrolment, delivery, revocation and withdrawal of corresponding products, tools and procedures.

4: Detection Continuous monitoring and detection

The Guideline on Detection requires a PSP to have the competence to detect the occurrence of anomalies and events indicating a potential security incident as this is essential for achieving strong security. Early detection provides a PSP with useful lead time to mount appropriate countermeasures against a potential incident, and allows proactive containment of actual incidents. Given the stealthy and sophisticated nature of certain threats where multiple entry points exist through which a compromise could take place, Guideline 4 requires proportionate monitoring tools and organisational processes and structures to be used by a PSP for the detection of security incidents. With regard to reporting procedures, these are taken into account from the PSP point of view, focusing on internal classification and reporting to senior management.

4.1 PSPs should establish and implement processes and capabilities to continuously monitor and detect anomalous activities and events in the provision of payment services. As part of this continuous monitoring, PSPs should have appropriate and effective intrusion detection capabilities in place.

4.2 The continuous monitoring and detection processes should cover relevant internal and external factors, including business line and IT administrative functions and transactions in order to detect misuse of access by service providers or other entities, potential insider threats and other advanced threat activities.

4.3 PSPs should implement detective measures to identify possible information leakages, malicious code and other security threats, publicly known vulnerabilities for soft- and hardware, and check for corresponding new security updates.

4.4 PSPs should determine appropriate definitions, thresholds and early warning indicators for classifying an event as a security incident in the provision of payment services.

4.5 PSPs should establish appropriate processes and organizational structures to ensure the consistent and integrated monitoring, handling and follow-up of security incidents.

4.6 PSPs should establish a procedure for reporting such security incidents as well as security-related customer complaints to its senior management.

Guideline 5 therefore requires PSPs to have capabilities to respond to, and recover from, a broad range of scenarios, and the need for strong crisis communications and incident management processes.

5: Business continuity Business continuity management

Guideline 5 on Business continuity recognises that it is critical that a PSP's arrangements are designed such that it is able to resume critical operations rapidly, safely and with accurate data, in order to guarantee the continuity of the provision of payment services and limit negative impact on PSPs and PSUs in the event of severe business disruption.

5.1 PSPs should establish a sound Business Continuity Management to ensure their ability to provide payment services on an on-going basis and to limit losses in the event of severe business disruption.

5.2 In order to establish a sound business continuity management, PSPs should carefully analyse their exposure to severe business disruptions and assess (quantitatively and qualitatively) their potential impact, using internal and/or external data and scenario analysis. The PSP should identify its critical functions, processes, systems, transactions and interdependencies to prioritise business continuity actions using a risk based approach, which may, depending on the design of the PSP, facilitate the processing of critical transactions, for example, while remediation efforts continue.

5.3 On the basis of the above analysis, a PSP should put in place: a) contingency and business continuity plans to ensure a PSP reacts appropriately to emergencies and is able to maintain its most important business activities if there is a disruption of its ordinary business procedures; and b) mitigation measures to be adopted by the PSP in case of termination of its payment services, to avoid adverse effects on payment systems and on payments services users ensuring execution of pending payment transactions and termination of existing contracts. Scenario based business continuity planning

5.4 The PSP should consider a range of different extreme but plausible scenarios to which it might be exposed, and assess the potential impact such scenarios might have on the PSP.

5.5 Based on the analysis carried out and plausible scenarios identified, the PSP should, where appropriate for the size, business model and complexity of their activities, develop a set of response and recovery plans, which should: a) focus on the impact on the operation of critical functions, processes, systems, transactions and interdependencies; and b) be clearly documented. The documentation should be available within the business and support units and stored on systems that are physically separated and readily accessible in case of emergency. c) be updated in line with lesson learned from the tests, new risks identified and threats and changed recovery objectives and priorities.

5.6 The PSP should test its business continuity plans, and ensure that the operation of its critical functions, processes, systems, transactions and interdependencies are tested at least annually. The plans should support objectives to protect and, if necessary, re-establish integrity and availability of its operations, and the confidentiality of its information assets according to the PSP's size, business model and complexity of the activities;

5.7 Plans should be regularly updated based on testing results, current threat intelligence, information-sharing and lessons learned from previous events, changing recovery objectives, as well as analysis of operationally and technically plausible scenarios that have not yet occurred. The PSP should consult and coordinate with relevant internal and external stakeholders during the establishment of its business continuity plans.

5.8 The PSP's testing of its business continuity plans should: a) include a broad range of scenarios, including simulation of extreme but plausible ones; b) be designed to challenge the assumptions of business continuity practices, including governance arrangements and crisis communication plans; and c) include procedures to verify the ability of its staff and processes to respond to unfamiliar scenarios.

5.9 The PSP should periodically monitor the effectiveness of its business continuity plans, and document and analyse any challenges or failures resulting from the tests. Incident management and crisis communication

5.10 In the event of a disruption or emergency, and during the implementation of the business continuity plans, the PSPs should ensure it has effective incident management and crisis communication measures in place so that all relevant internal and external stakeholders, including external service providers, are informed in a timely and appropriate manner.

6: Testing of security measures

Guideline 6 on Testing of security measures requires that the elements of its operational and security risk management framework should be rigorously tested before and after implementation to determine their overall effectiveness. Sound testing regimes produce findings that should be used to identify gaps against stated security objectives and provide credible and meaningful inputs to the PSP's management of operational and security risks. Guideline 6 therefore sets out the areas that should be included in a PSP's testing programme and how results from testing should be used to improve its operational and security risk management framework.

6.1 The PSP should establish and implement a testing framework that validates the robustness and effectiveness of the security measures and should ensure that the testing framework is adapted to consider new threats and vulnerabilities, identified through risk monitoring activities.

6.2 The PSP should ensure that tests are conducted to assess the robustness and effectiveness of the security measures in cases of changes to the infrastructure and procedures and changes resulting from major incidents.

6.3 The testing framework should also encompass the security measures relevant to: (i) payment terminals and devices used for the provision of payment services, (ii) payment terminals and devices used for authenticating the PSU and (iii) devices and software provided by the PSP to the PSU to generate/receive an authentication code

6.4 The testing framework should ensure that tests: a) are performed as part of the PSP's formal change management process to ensure their robustness and effectiveness; b) are carried out by independent testers that are not involved in the development of the security measures for the corresponding payment services or systems that are to be tested, at least for final tests before putting security measures into operation, and c) include vulnerability scans and penetration tests adequate to the level of risk identified with the payment services.

6.5 PSPs should perform ongoing and repeated tests of the security measures for its payment services. For critical systems these tests shall be performed at least on an annual basis.

6.6 PSPs should monitor and evaluate the results from the tests conducted, and update its security measures accordingly.

7: Situational awareness and continuous learning

Guideline 7 on Situational awareness and continuous learning covers requirements to ensure strong situational awareness that can significantly enhance a PSP's ability to understand and preempt security events, and to effectively detect, respond to and recover from scenarios that are not prevented. Specifically, a solid understanding of the threat landscape can help a PSP better identify and understand the vulnerabilities in its critical business functions, and facilitate the adoption of appropriate risk mitigation strategies. Therefore the Guideline on situational awareness of the threat landscape requires PSPs to proactively monitor the threat landscape and to acquire and make effective use of actionable threat intelligence to validate its risk assessments, processes, procedures and controls, with a view to building strong security measures.

In fostering strong situational awareness, the PSP should also implement an adaptive operational and security risk management framework that evolves with the dynamic nature of risks to enable effective management of those risks. Achieving this will require PSPs to instil a culture of continuous learning and security awareness and demonstrate ongoing re-evaluation and improvement of their security posture at every level within the organisation.

7.1 PSPs should establish and implement processes and structures to identify and constantly monitor security and operational threats that could materially affect their ability to provide payment services. This should include, but is not limited to: a) sharing information with third parties and

PSPs to achieve broader awareness of payment fraud and cybersecurity issues; b) participating in information sharing arrangements with external stakeholders within and outside the payment industry; c) distilling key lessons from security incidents that have been identified or have occurred within and/or outside the organisation, and updating the security measures accordingly.

7.2 PSPs should actively monitor technological developments to ensure that they are aware of security risks. Training and security awareness programs

7.3 PSPs should ensure that all their personnel are trained to perform their duties related to the provision of payment services and responsibilities consistent with the relevant security policies and procedures in order to reduce human error, theft, fraud, misuse or loss.

7.4 PSPs should ensure that critical personnel receive targeted information security training.

7.5 PSPs should establish and implement security awareness programmes in order to educate their personnel and to address information security related risks to the provision of payment services. These programs should require their personnel to report any unusual activity and incidents.

8: PSU relationship management PSU awareness on security risks

Guideline 8 on PSU relationship management stipulates that, in implementing the security measures, the PSP also has a responsibility to its PSUs (customers), who are the most critical stakeholders in the overall process. Strengthening the PSUs' understanding of the security measures, enhancing their understanding of the threats and vulnerabilities, and establishing effective channels of communication with the PSP, will improve the overall security of the ecosystem and potentially reduce risks to and from the PSPs. The section on external relationship management sets out the steps a PSP must take to improve the situational awareness of its user base, and the reporting mechanisms that should be in place to facilitate this overall process.

8.1 PSPs should establish and implement processes to enhance the awareness of PSUs to security risks linked to the payment services through assistance and guidance to the PSUs.

8.2 The assistance and guidance to PSUs should be constantly updated in the light of new threats and vulnerabilities and changes should be communicated to the PSU.

8.3 PSPs should also ensure that PSUs are provided, on an ongoing or, where applicable, ad hoc basis, and via appropriate means, with clear and straightforward instructions explaining their responsibilities regarding the secure use of the service.

8.4 PSPs should allow PSUs to disable specific payment functionalities.

8.5 Where, in accordance with PSD2 article 68 (1), PSP has agreed with the payer on spending limits for payment transactions executed through payment instruments or where a PSP has defined spending limits for specific payment services, the PSP should provide the payer with options to reduce these limits.

8.6 PSPs should provide the possibility for PSUs to set alerts related to the initiation, the execution and failed attempt to initiate a payment transaction, in the context of the PSU profile management services platform provided to the PSU, where relevant.

PSU secure communication and reporting procedures

8.7 The PSP should inform PSUs on the reporting procedure for suspected security breaches, in particular: a) the procedure for PSUs to report to the PSP suspicious incidents or anomalies during the payment services session; b) how the PSP will respond to the PSU; and c) how the PSP will notify the PSU about (potential) security breaches or the non-initiation of payment transactions, or warn the PSU about the occurrence of attacks.

8.8 The PSP should keep PSUs informed about updates in security procedures regarding payment services. Any alerts about significant emerging risks should also be provided via a secured channel.

8.9 The PSP should provide the PSU with assistance on all questions, complaints, requests for support and notifications of anomalies or incidents regarding internet payments and related services. PSUs should be appropriately informed about how such assistance can be obtained.

8.10 PSPs should set out the method and terms of the PSU notification, in case PSP has blocked a specific transaction or payment instrument, and define how the PSU can contact the PSP to have the payment transaction or payment instrument 'unblocked'.

Finally, EBA is of the view that, in the context of the provision of acquiring services, aspects related to the storing, processing or transmitting of sensitive payment data by payees could be addressed taking into account the security measures specified in these guidelines, however being applicable as requirements only to PSPs as such.

Printed in Great Britain
by Amazon

42979546R00248